My Father's Voice

A Tale of Undying Love

Alan Cohen

My Father's Voice: A Tale of Undying Love
Copyright © 2000 by Alan Cohen

Published and distributed in the United States by:

Alan Cohen Publications
455A Kukuna Road, Haiku, HI 96708
(800) 568-3079 • (808) 572-0001
www.alancohen.com

Library of Congress Cataloging-in-Publication Data Pending

ISBN 0-910367-01-9

00 01 02 03   4 3 2 1
First Printing, June 2000

Printed in Canada

To our fathers,
who loved us more than we knew

Chapter 1

With the exception of his wedding, he hadn't set foot in a church since he was thirteen, when the priest assured Angelo he would burn in hell for masturbating. Now, thirty years later, only the aching of his heart outcried his bent knees as the words rolled off his lips. "Please, God, don't let me turn into my father."

Clumsily Angelo raised himself from the thin faded green cushion behind the dark wooden pew. The heady aroma of melting candles found his nostrils. As a child he liked the smell when his mother lit candles at home; now it reminded him of the guilt he had absorbed, his anger at the church for its greed and hypocrisy, his revulsion at the dogma and politics. But now he needed help, and humbled, he was willing to set aside his judgments if he could get it.

His thoughts were interrupted by the sound of footsteps creaking on the hardwood floor behind him. Angelo turned toward the low arched door, where a heavy-set woman in a gray coat and white kerchief was lumbering down the aisle. She held a clump of crumpled tissues in her left hand, a pink rosary in her right. As she approached, Angelo recognized her. It was Sylvia, the Mexican woman who cleaned his lab after hours. Angelo turned into the next pew and made his exit through another aisle.

It had not been a good morning. He had blown up at Jesse again. This time it was over some toys the boy had left in the hallway outside the upstairs bathroom. In the dim morning light Angelo had tripped on a plastic yellow dump truck and nearly fell down the stairs. Furious, he stormed into Jesse's room, grabbed him by the shoulders, shook the child from his sleep, and screamed, "You stupid little shit!" Jesse, taken utterly by surprise, awoke with a start, his eyes opened from slits to saucers, his body went into convulsions, and he screamed in terror. Angelo shook Jesse so hard that boy began to scream at the top of his lungs and cough in horrible retching heaves.

Claudia, instantly aware of the commotion, ran into the room. Startled out of bed, her blue and white flannel pajamas were disheveled and her sandy hair hung unkempt over her thin face. She covered her heart with her left hand to quell the shock of the disturbance, then lunged at Angelo to get him off of their son. She wasn't strong enough to dislodge Angelo, but eventually he stopped and let go. "Damn kid ought to learn to keep his stuff out of my way," Angelo ranted.

"That doesn't give you the right to barge in here and nearly kill him!" Claudia protested. "Touch him again, and Jesse and I are out of here, you immature asshole!"

Angelo didn't even bother to return Claudia's glare; he just left her comforting the child. Angelo stomped back to the bedroom and began to get dressed.

It always ended like that. Angelo felt sentenced to his private hell, powerless to restrain himself when his anger surged from the pit of his gut without warning. As he stood before the mirror over the antique dresser, brushing his thick black hair, his mind drifted to the well in the back yard of his childhood home near the Berkshires. He saw himself leaning over the stonework edge of the well, trying to fish out a hammer he had dropped into the water. At the worst possible moment his father approached, peered into the well, saw his prized tool submerged in the pool, and began to thrash Angelo vehemently.

"How many times have I told you to leave my tools alone?" the leathery-skinned elder screamed, his murky veins bulging against the sagging skin of his neck. A wave of scarlet gushed over Lorenzo's face, marking a contrast to the white stubble on his chin. "I ought to throw you down there to go get it!"

Oh, God, no, please don't do that, Angelo pleaded silently. He did not dare answer his father out loud; then there was no telling what the old man's wrath would exact. Just keep your mouth shut and the beating will be over soon, he knew.

Before he could take another breath, the boy was leaning against the rock well, his britches down. Viciously the old man laid the switch into his son's bottom. Again and again Angelo winced as he absorbed his father's rage. The child wanted to cry at the top of his lungs, but he wouldn't give his father the satisfaction. Even at six he had learned to be stoic about pain.

By the time he arrived at his lab in the college research park, Angelo had calmed down. He liked seeing the students bustling about, riding bikes, eating lunch on the mall, doing their assignments under trees, making out by the lake. They were young and vital and full of hopes and dreams; no one had yet shot them down or squashed their creative impulses. He was glad that he had hung onto one teaching course; just being in his students' presence bestowed Angelo with a sense of the innocence he had all but lost.

He pulled the Lexus LX470 into his assigned parking space, marked by the small black-on-white wooden plaque inscribed "Dr. Angelo Mann." He remembered the day when he entered college and decided to shorten the name from "Mandolucci." As far back as grade school the other kids couldn't pronounce his name and made fun of him every time the teacher called it. When he entered Stanford on a science scholarship, he filled out all of his forms as "Angelo Mann." Though he had never legally changed the name, no one had ever questioned him about it. Somewhere in the recesses of his mind, though, Angelo felt guilty as he wondered if he had sold out on his ancestors.

"Claudia rope you in for a morning quickie?" Angelo's research assistant Lin queried over her shoulder as she drew latté from the office's new machine.

He wished that was his reason for being late. "Not today," he answered in a serious voice that effectively cancelled his feeble attempt to be cordial. Although Lin was young, she was quite perceptive and could read Angelo like a book; besides, he was bad at hiding, and usually didn't try. "I had some errands to do."

Again his gut churned. Angelo hated lying, but he was not about to try to explain why he had stopped off at church on his way to work. God was not a verifiable authority at Stanford, and until someone there proved His existence, the Supreme Being was as imaginary as Roger Rabbit.

"Anything going on I should know about?" he asked, to change the subject.

"Just this letter from Israel," Lin answered matter-of-factly as she placed the odd-sized piece of European stationary in front of her boss along with his coffee. Black, two sugars, filled-not-too-close-to-the-brim. "You don't mind teaching in a war zone, do you?"

Angelo leaned back in his overstuffed leather chair and, loath to admit his reading vision was becoming fuzzy, held the letter at arm's length, up to the light:

Dear Dr. Mann,

You may remember meeting me at the Western Region Fiber Optics Expo. I am Research Director in the Department of Applied Physics at the University of Tel Aviv.

Beginning November 14th we are hosting a four-day conference on Science for the New Millenium. I am honored to invite you to speak to our group about your latest research.

I do apologize for the short notice. Our conference chairman originally insisted that we invite Dr. Luchow of Dresden to be our keynoter. When he canceled unexpectedly, I convinced the chairman that your work would be of the highest interest to our assembly.

We are in a position to offer you an honorarium of $1000 plus expenses. Please fax or phone me as soon as possible with your response.

Sincerely,

Dr. Avi Goldman

Angelo sipped slowly on his coffee, scratching the side of his neck. "What do you think?"

"You're not really considering going, are you?" Lin turned around from the file cabinet, startled. "The middle east is a powder keg. The Jews and Muslims have been at each others' throats like rabid wolves. Just yesterday you were muttering about the *Chronicle* article on terrorism; I'd hate to see you come back packaged in pine. I sort of like you better behind mahogany."

Angelo sensed a fire in Lin that he had not seen before. She was angry. "Why is this such a sensitive issue for you?" he asked.

Lin became very quiet, as if she was deciding whether or not to speak. Then she said, "My brother was killed in Tienaman square."

Angelo was stopped short in his tracks. "I'm sorry. I didn't know."

"My parents and I moved here right after that. My father was in the government and he knew people." Lin took a deep breath and tried to compose herself. "I don't want to put a damper on your idea, Angelo. I just have strong feelings about war."

Angelo nodded. "I can understand, Lin. . .but there's something about this that intrigues me. I remember meeting Goldman; he was this wild and crazy character you'd never expect to see at a scientific conference; not your typical academic geek. He had a twinkle in his eye, as if he knew some secret that he was just waiting for everyone else to get. We went out for a couple of drinks, talked quantum theory, and made up science fiction stories about the people in the bar. This guy is a *genius*, like some eccentric character out of Kurt Vonnegut. I wanted to spend more time with him, but he left early. Maybe here's my chance to—"

"Okay, Angelo, I know how you are when you get your mind onto something. But please think about this. Israel is not a safe place to be. The whole zone could ignite into World War III with one spark."

Alan Cohen

Claudia cleared the cheesecake from the dinner table and walked into the kitchen, leaving Angelo alone with his son. Jesse just stared into his dessert plate, picking at the few remaining crumbs.

"So how was school today, Jesse?" Angelo asked.

"Okay," the boy answered shortly.

"What did you do?"

"Nothin'."

"Say, how about if you and I take a ride this weekend to the go-cart place?"

"I don't really feel like it."

"Then how about some Nintendo?"

"Dad, I have to go do my homework." Jesse got up without even looking at his father and ran into his bedroom.

Angelo's heart sank.

When Claudia came back for the dessert dishes, she sat in the seat Jesse had just vacated and breathed a sigh of relief. "It's so good to sit down. I've been going all day. . . .How was your day?"

"You remember that physicist from Tel Aviv I met last spring?" Angelo asked.

"Sort of. What about him?"

"I got a letter from him today. He wants me to come and talk at a conference in Israel in November."

"So what?"

"I'm thinking about going."

Claudia sat up straight and glared at her husband. "I need you here, Angelo," she stated with authority. "This has been a hard time for all of us. Jesse has been wetting the bed again. I'm up for a review in February, and I can't take any more time off from school. I can't afford you going now, let alone lose you to some holy war."

"I'm not going to get killed. I'd really like to just get away for a while. I haven't traveled anywhere in a year, and this conference could make a big difference in my career."

"Is your career all you ever think about, Mr. Big Shot Scientist?

Did you ever stop to consider that I could use some help around here? It's not easy raising a child, in case you hadn't noticed."

"Of course I notice. I notice every time I go to make love with you and you tell me you're too tired. Do you even remember when was the last time we made love?"

"Look, Angelo, it's not easy for me . . ." Claudia began to sniffle. "You know about my childhood . . . I can't just change overnight."

"I'm not asking you to change overnight. But I would like you to make even a small effort. How many therapists have you been to? Three?"

"Four."

"Four. And how long have you stayed with any one of them? Three months?"

"I didn't like any of them. They were all men, and none of them understood me."

"Okay, then see a woman. But, Jesus Christ, do *something.* I want a wife, not just a roommate."

"And I want a father for my son," Claudia burst out. She abruptly picked up the dishes and marched into the kitchen, sobbing as she went.

Angelo rose, walked to the dining room window, and stared into the back yard. His fights with Claudia always ended with her bursting into tears and storming out of the room. He remembered the long bitter arguments his own parents had, arguments that ended in the same way, but never really ended at all. Angelo looked out onto Jesse's swing set and remembered the one he had as a child. As soon as his father set it up, Angelo climbed on it to play and Lorenzo chastised him. He remembered Lorenzo coming home drunk and telling him that he loved him, while the odor of whisky fumed from his father's throat like a foul waft from a half-covered garbage can. The only time his father expressed his affection was when he was drunk; but then again he said many things during his stupors that he later denied and never repeated when he was sober. His mother hated her husband when he was wasted, and she told Angelo never to take him seriously with liquor in his blood. Angelo remembered the Christmas party when his father called him to come close, and then pulled down the child's pajama bottoms in public. Angelo had never forgiven Lorenzo for these atrocities, and a thousand others. Now he was becoming a clone to what he hated.

Too many things had stayed the same for too long. Yes, this conference and Goldman were interesting to him, but there was more at stake. This might be my chance to break the cycle, he reasoned; to be with myself; to hear my own thoughts; to feel my own pulse; to find some sanity away from this family. If I can get away for even a little while, I might have a chance to find some way out of hell for myself and my son.

Chapter 2

As the *El Al* DC-10 lowered its landing gear approaching the Tel Aviv runway, Angelo was struck by the stark whiteness of the buildings in contrast to the azure sea. Just offshore he could make out hundreds of bathers wading far out on the shallow reef. It was hard to believe that just sixty kilometers away tension was so unbearable that the notion of play seemed as remote as the moon.

The smell of war grew pungent when Angelo spied armed soldiers at the gates; the Uzi's frightened him. These were the kind of weapons that crazed criminals turn loose on subway cars. Just because a government produces them *en masse* for a war it calls "holy," does that make them any more sane?

"Angelo!" a friendly voice shouted, breaking Angelo's speculation. There, in a short-sleeved white shirt and navy blue slacks, stood the pleasantly rotund Goldman, like a Jewish Pillsbury Dough Boy. He looked tanner than when Angelo had seen him two seasons earlier, and his bald pate did not shine as brightly as it had under the meeting room lights at the Airport Hilton. Goldman was slightly more portly than Angelo remembered, still amiable and inviting, with a mischievous gleam in his eye.

"*Shalom*, my friend. Welcome to the Holy Land." Goldman shook Angelo's hand vigorously and the two began to walk together amid an onslaught of weary tourists and unruly natives.

"I trust your flight was uneventful?"

"Just fine—I even survived the kosher food," Angelo laughed. "I might even request it next time."—

"Yes, I wonder if Moses had a premonition about airline food when he prescribed the dietary laws!"

Angelo remembered how easy it was to be with Goldman. The middle-aged professor, speaking nearly perfect English with just a hint of an Israeli accent, sported a certain lightness conspicuously absent among his peers. Angelo had the impression that Goldman was willing to enjoy life even before he figured it all out.

"How has the conference been going?" Angelo asked.

"Pretty well, considering the political situation. We had a number of cancellations, which put a damper on morale, but the sessions have been well received, and we are looking forward to hearing from you."

"I'm afraid I won't be as lively as the news," Angelo reported as the two approached baggage claim.

Half-blinded by the stage lights, Angelo could barely make out faces, yet he was aware of many nationalities. At Stanford he worked with many Asians and Germans; this audience was brimming with brilliant minds from nearly every major nation on the globe.

"My esteemed colleagues," Goldman began his introduction, "it is my distinct pleasure to call to the stage an individual who is changing the course of the future. Through his work on parallel processing algorithms, Dr. Angelo Mann is revolutionizing imaging science. The moment I met this man I knew he had the kind of mind that could break into new dimensions. Today he will focus on future capabilities in virtual reality with his quantum leaps in data rates. Ladies and gentleman, Dr. Angelo Mann."

Amidst a wave of applause, Angelo stepped up to the podium. Egotistical as he was, he hated talking to groups. He liked admiration, but shunned large-group attention. If he could have taped or phoned in his lecture, he would rather have done that. Behind Angelo's confident facade, there still lived within him a little boy who feared being exposed in public with his pajama pants down. Nevertheless, he stood before the group and delivered his message with style and vigor.

"And so," Angelo began his conclusion, "we are on the threshold of previously unimaginable breakthroughs in combining parallel processing with holography in enhancing mental imagery as well as commercially viable virtual reality. With our current technology I predict that within a decade virtual reality will become more popular than television and revolutionize the way we think and live—a hundred times more than television has. You and I are at the helm of this staggering shift, and the power to shape the future of the planet is in our hands. Let us use it wisely."

As his last word trailed into the far reaches of the lecture hall, the audience rose to its feet and honored Angelo enthusiastically. The applause ricocheted off the glossy yellow cinder-block walls and made its way back to Angelo. Yet in spite of the thundering response, he walked offstage briskly. When anyone told Angelo he was brilliant, he squirmed. He wondered what they really wanted from him, or silently projected that if they discovered who he really was, they would never be uttering such praise. He flashed on the last time he came down heavy on Jesse, the way the child's eyes welled with tears and his head quivered and his frail body contorted. Angelo swallowed his guilt and kept walking.

As he stepped backstage Angelo found Avi Goldman waiting with a huge smile and energetic handshake. "Splendid!" Goldman blurted out, glowing. "Just splendid! Exactly what this conference needed!"

Angelo offered a polite half-smile and started to make his way toward the door. He did not want to offend Goldman, but if there was one thing that Angelo found even more uncomfortable than group applause, it was face-to-face acknowledgment. When presented with genuine affection, Angelo's mind went tilt.

To Goldman's left stood the next speaker, Jean-Claude Michaud, a virtual reality wizard from the leading-edge Parisian *Institut de la Decouverte Technoligique*. The previous evening Angelo had gone out to dinner with a group including Michaud, a strikingly handsome Frenchman sporting thick wavy black hair and a neatly-trimmed thin moustache. Michaud seemed out of place at a scientific conference; Angelo could more easily picture the fellow sitting at an outdoor café on the Champs-Elysée, sipping espresso and smoking *Gitannes* while discussing Camus' relevance to the twenty-first century. For a scientist he was remarkably slick, the antithesis of the stereotypical pallid computer nerd. If he wasn't a scientist, Angelo surmised, Michaud would have made a dashing actor.

To Michaud's left stood an unusually attractive woman Angelo had not noticed at the conference. She looked Swedish, with fine blonde hair pulled back into a French braid. Quite tall, she wore a gray suit tastefully trimmed with elegant silver artisan jewelry. Her makeup was conservative, yet behind her professional appearance she bore a tender air.

Even though he was to deliver his address momentarily, Michaud was on his cell phone speaking German, his free hand animating his conversation. Seeing Angelo approach, he put the phone down and reached out to shake Angelo's hand. "Excellent!" Michaud offered.

"Yes, your speech was brilliant," the woman added. Angelo liked her voice. "I especially liked your analysis of the robust dense wavelength division multiplexing market. I think the Qtera platform will provide us with a good scalable IP backbone."

Who is this woman? Angelo wondered. He started to respond, but she had already turned her attention to Avi Goldman, who was at the podium introducing Michaud. Angelo tried to read her name tag, but the darkness of the stage wing obscured the letters. Must be Michaud's girlfriend, Angelo deduced. He headed briskly for the door, hoping to avoid any question hounds before they cornered him.

Back in room 712 of the Sheraton Tel Aviv Angelo kicked off his shoes, fell back into the softness of his bed, and allowed himself to drift. Suddenly the phone rang in the trademark European double ring. "*Laila tov,*" the voice on the other end bounded, "Good evening."

"Hello, Avi."

"Angelo, some of us are going to Jerusalem tomorrow. Would you like to join us? I'll give you the insider's tour."

Angelo felt uneasy; he wasn't a tourist at heart. But before he had a chance to say, "No thank you," Goldman went on as if he had been reading Angelo's hesitation. "I can offer you a rare opportunity to see one of the most significant places on earth. Besides, the way things are going, who knows how much longer it will be here? Let me guide you to some of our cultural riches."

Angelo had been looking forward to some quiet time. Caught up in the conference, he had found little opportunity to face the issues he was hoping to sort out. But in the aftermath of his tension about his speech, he reconsidered; perhaps this jaunt would get him out of his head and loosen him up a bit. Besides, it might be a chance to find out more about Goldman.

"Okay, Avi—you're a good salesman."

"That's what I like to hear! I'll meet you in the lobby at nine."

Angelo lay back on his bed, grabbed the remote control wand, and flicked on the television. A *Baywatch* rerun dubbed in Hebrew rolled onto the screen. Strange, he thought, to hear a voice like Moses speaking through the lips of David Hasselhoff, and watch Pamela Anderson flirting in the language of the Bible.

Chapter 3

Sunday was sunny and hot; Angelo could hardly believe it was November. Along the Tel Aviv-Jerusalem Highway he observed modest Jewish settlements of limestone apartment houses rising austerely from the arid desert. As Goldman's Saab ascended toward higher country, welcome signs of greenery became visible between blue-doored Arab villages. Again the bony reminder of ongoing warfare loomed in the carnage of burnt tanks and jeeps purposely left by the side of the road since the 1948 War of Independence. Did these people keep the wreckage as a reminder of victory, or were they simply unable to see beyond conflict as a way of life?

Angelo shivered to think that at any moment the conflict could be resurrected for another round of holy annihilation. He turned his head from the macabre museum of rust, only to be confronted with an army transport truck passing on the left—one in a steady stream of military traffic moving in both directions. Goldman's car was stopped at an army checkpoint. While civilian business was ostensibly going on as usual, it was clear that at any moment martial law could displace it.

To Angelo's surprise, Michaud and Juliana, the Aryan blonde, had also been invited by Goldman to join the tour. Angelo's judgments about Michaud thickened; the man talked ceaselessly, mostly about himself. There was no doubt he was brilliant, but did he have to dangle his achievements in everyone's face? And who cared that he came from a long lineage of Alcase-Lorrainetians whose property had toggled back and forth between French and German occupation for 150 years? And did he really have to talk German to Juliana in Angelo's presence? Didn't he know that was impolite? And was it really so important that the car pull over so he could step out and field his cell phone calls in privacy?

As for Juliana, there was no getting around the fact that Angelo was attracted to her. She was vibrant and articulate, with a smile that could light up a room. She laughed easily and held her own in the midst of the group of professional men. Angelo guessed she was maybe 35, cultured, good business savvy, could play hard ball by day and be a passionate lover by night. Juliana, Angelo learned, was a reporter for *Neue Blick*, a well-known German technical magazine which advertised much of the cutting-edge European fiber optics industry. She had been sent to get the scoop on this conference, which the marketing department would parlay into lucrative advertising for their next issue. Juliana's background in the industry, combined with her striking appearance, made her a natural to infiltrate this male encampment.

Angelo sat in the front seat with his eyes on the road, listening to Jean-Claude and Juliana discussing the details of Jean-Claude's lecture. As they spoke, Angelo felt a sinking emptiness in his gut; he never had one conversation like that with his wife. He had often fantasized about being with a partner who could share in his work, yet he wrote off the possibility and restricted his shop talk to the lab. Angelo felt jealous that a turkey like Michaud had found such a stimulating woman. At the same time he was relieved that Juliana was with Jean-Claude, for if she wasn't, he would have had a hard time dealing with the chemistry he felt in her presence.

"Jerusalem is sacred to the world's three major religions," Goldman volunteered after a silence. Angelo was momentarily startled; he had gotten lost in imagining staying up into the wee hours with a woman like Juliana, alternating making love and discussing cosmology. "For thousands of years the Jews, Christians, and Muslims have identified this tiny spot on the planet as a holy and central site of their faith."

"And for just as long they have fought over the real estate," Michaud broke in, shaking the flame off a match he had just lit for a filterless Israeli cigarette.

"Indeed they have," Goldman agreed.

"Like my homeland, these borders have shifted like string in the wind," Michaud added. "During any given decade you need a referee to tell whose territory you are standing on."

Juliana stepped in: "What do you think of the political situation, Angelo?"

Again Angelo was startled. He felt honored that Juliana was making an effort to include him in the conversation. "I think it's crazy that people are killing each other over real estate," he answered. "I think their religions are causing more problems than they are solving."

The conversation went on. Goldman laid out the facts and politics of the conflict. Michaud smoked and debated with Goldman. Juliana chimed in once in a while, challenging the men with her political and scientific opinions. Angelo's attention meandered from the conversation to home, to the tense world at the roadside, to Juliana.

When they reached Jerusalem, the troupe made their way through the Arab market. Angelo was stunned to see that, with the exception of a few electric fans, he might as well have been shopping in 500 A. D. Olive-skinned merchants and their children took shelter from the sun under colorful canopies behind their stalls, while more aggressive salesmen stood on the stone pathway and tried to hawk trinkets to tourists. Clothing, jewelry, and foodstuffs were everywhere, with little order or cleanliness. Angelo almost stumbled over a half-dozen bloody lambs' heads laid out on a cloth on the sidewalk. An American sanitary inspector, Angelo chuckled, would have a heart attack beholding this scene—in many ways this place had yet to emerge from the dark ages.

At one busy corner, Angelo watched Michaud photograph an Arab child. Instantly, the boy's mother stormed Jean-Claude from behind and tried to yank the camera from his hands. Angelo remembered hearing that Arabs believed that photography robs the subject's soul. The Frenchman won the battle and niftily scampered on down the crooked sidewalk, losing himself in the motley crowd. Robbing souls—now there was a concept. Angelo wondered if he had ever felt his own soul.

The group decided to split up so that everyone could explore on their own. Angelo set out toward the curio shops and enjoyed the motley bazaar; the color, oddity, and brashness of the Arab culture fascinated him. He found his way to a little store where he saw a small carved Arabian horse he thought Jesse would enjoy. As he picked it up, he heard a woman's voice: "Are you a horse lover?" Angelo turned to see Juliana standing behind him.

"I thought my son would get a kick out of this," he answered.

"I'll bet you're a good dad," she said, smiling.

If she only knew, Angelo thought to himself. Yet his heart lifted to think that someone would think him a worthy parent.

"How much do you think this is worth?" he asked her.

"Half of whatever they're asking."

"Probably. I hate bargaining, but it's the only way you get a decent price around here."

"Would you like me to do the honors?"

Angelo started to say, "No thanks," but then reconsidered. "Sure, if you don't mind."

Juliana took the artifact in her left hand and held it up to the vendor. Then she put her right hand on Angelo's shoulder to show that she was representing him. Her touch felt good, and he hoped the haggling would go on for a while. After a few minutes of dickering she got the horse for half the price. The vendor wrapped it in Egyptian newspaper, handed the package to Angelo and told him, "Your wife, she is good businesswoman."

Angelo started to say, "She's not —" but then stopped himself. So what if the Egyptian thought they were married? The two thanked the salesman and made their way to the door, laughing. "You're good," he told her. "The next time my contract is up for negotiation, I'll call you."

"It was pure luck I found you," Juliana told him.

"You think so?"

"Yes—Avi and Jean-Claude are ready to leave. We were looking for you."

"Oh," Angelo asnwered, slightly disappointed. He was hoping she meant more than that.

On the road back to Tel Aviv, Angelo began to doze. Even in this uncomfortable little car, bouncing up and down with prehistoric shock absorbers on a pockmarked highway, he nodded out; jet lag had caught up with him.

All at once Angelo was shocked awake by the sound of sirens. Goldman pulled the car onto the shoulder of the highway to let emergency vehicles pass; three police cars and as many ambulances sped past the lineup of stopped cars and trucks. Before they could resume their passage, a half-dozen military transport vehicles streamed by, with battalions of khaki-clad soldiers leaning out, guns poised.

"What the hell is going on?" Angelo blurted out.

"It doesn't look good," Goldman answered.

"Isn't that lovely—we get to be in the middle of a war," Michaud smirked.

Juliana, sitting behind Angelo, peered over the shoulders of the men in front of her. She did not seem nervous, but poised; Angelo wondered how she had learned to stay so calm in crisis.

After a few more kilometers traffic came to a standstill. Drivers and passengers in the cars ahead had gotten out of their vehicles and were walking toward a roadblock in front of them. From the right of the highway smoke billowed, and Angelo could make out flames just beyond the buildings immediately in front of him. The group stepped out of the Saab and followed the other motorists on foot to the barricade, where they tried to push their way through a throng five or six people deep.

Angelo peered over Avi Goldman's shoulder, trying to get a view. "What's going on?" he asked.

"The Mishnayat school's been bombed," Goldman answered soberly. "*Al Sharmat* must have set it off."

Angelo watched the rescue teams move in and out of the school building, just off the road fifty yards from where he was standing. Several emergency vehicles were parked on the shoulder of the highway at the intersection of an access road leading to the school. Debris from the explosion blocked the road, making this the closest point to park the ambulances. A score of soldiers and policemen were attempting to clear the rubble as quickly as possible, but the thick shroud of smoke hampered their progress.

Then Angelo beheld a scene that hit him like a hard punch in his gut. Two paramedics were carrying an injured child to the ambulance. A little boy about seven years old was strapped to the stretcher, unconscious. The child's right arm had been torn off and he was bleeding profusely from a large gaping cavity from just below his collar bone to nearly his waist. Angelo could see portions of the boy's ribs clearly in the late afternoon sun. He couldn't tell if the child was alive or dead, but since the medics were lifting his body onto the ambulance, he assumed the mutilated form still had some life. At the last moment Angelo caught a glimpse of the boy's charred and bleeding face, a sight almost too terrible to behold.

Gasps and exclamations of horror issued from the throng. An older woman shrieked, "*Oy, Guttanu!*" and sobs began to echo through the group. Angelo heard a cry from the front, "*Meiertz Hashem!*"

Angelo felt helpless. He wanted to jump over the barricade and do something, but soldiers held the crowd back; the medics were doing all that could be done. There was nothing to do but stand there, watch, and wonder how any God could permit such an act.

Minutes later soldiers hurried another stretcher with a child on it; this time the body was completely covered, the blanket covering it wet with scarlet blood. Behind the stretcher a young mother scurried, wailing at the top of her lungs, "Gershon, my Gershon—wake up! *Please, you've got to wake up!*" But Gershon would not wake up. His mother pleaded with the soldiers to let her get to the body, beating on their backs, flailing, after a while aimlessly. There was nothing more anyone could do. Gershon was gone.

The nightmare went on for over an hour. A news crew arrived and set up ten yards away from where Angelo and Avi stood. As soon as the lights and cameras were in place, a young woman reporter rattled off the gory details of the disaster. Avi gave Angelo a running translation: "Seventeen children, ages five to eleven, were killed and eleven others were injured when a terrorist bomb exploded in the Mishnayat school. Most of the children were crushed under falling cinder blocks."

Angelo watched silently, numb, as both the survivors and the dead were carried to ambulances and other emergency vehicles. Dusk began to fall and the temperature dropped. Avi and Jean-Claude went back to the car to grab some warmer jackets, while Angelo remained at the barricade. Juliana, who had been standing several yards away, approached him. She stood at his side for a few minutes, watching the horrifying drama. Then, when it became unbearable, Juliana rested her head on Angelo's shoulder, shielding her eyes from the horror. When Juliana began to sob, Angelo put his arm around her and stroked her head in a fatherly way. There was nothing to say.

Finally the road was cleared and the stopped cars, which now numbered in the thousands, were waved on.

The remainder of the ride felt like a funeral procession. The entire group was silent. Juliana gazed vacuously out the window, an occasional tear rolling down her cheek; she gave up on her makeup. Michaud smoked continuously. Goldman kept his eyes straight ahead on the road. Angelo closed his eyes and let his head fall back, trying to get some rest, but repetitions of the horrific scene played like a torturous reprise across the inside of his eyelids. Never had he seen such tragedy and ugliness. Never had he been so disgusted by the human condition. Never had he imagined the depths of depravity to which human beings could sink.

Suddenly Angelo's work felt small and unimportant. In contrast to the carnage he had witnessed that afternoon, science seemed like a diversion from the issues of real life. What's the good of inventing time-saving technology, Angelo wondered, when humanity hasn't even learned to value the life of a child?

That night Angelo lay in his hotel bed, staring at the ceiling. That night there would be no television, no cocktails, no office work, no distractions. That night Angelo needed to be with himself. That night he asked himself questions he had not much considered before: *Who am I? Why am I here? What am I supposed to be doing with my life? Why are so many people suffering? Is there some unseen power guiding life in ways we do not understand, or is this all just a random joke?*

Angelo's mind raced out of control. No matter how hard he tried, he couldn't get the image of the dismembered child out of his head. All Angelo could think was, "My God, that could have been Jesse." He wished he were home.

Chapter 4

Angelo had been asleep only a few hours when he was awakened by a loud knock on the door. He dragged himself out of bed, struggled to pull himself together, and through the thinnest slits of eyelids he saw the clock showing nearly 8 a.m. He threw on his bathrobe and trudged to the door, where he looked through the peephole. It was Avi Goldman.

"I'm sorry to bother you so early," Avi apologized. "May I come in?"

Angelo said nothing, but opened the door and gestured to enter.

Goldman didn't even sit down. He walked over to the window, peered out over the white concrete citiscape for a few moments, and turned to his colleague.

"Angelo, I can imagine how deeply the bombing affected you. I am terribly sorry you had to see such horror. It is an awful thing, no matter how you look at it. What's worse, we Israelis have seen so much of this kind of atrocity that we are not surprised by it. But that doesn't mean our hearts are not broken and we are not outraged inside. A certain numbness is a natural psychological defense mechanism. Perhaps—"

Angelo broke in, "Avi, last night I came back to my room and stared at the ceiling most of the night. I couldn't sleep until nearly dawn. I kept seeing the little boy with his arm ripped off. I kept seeing my own son's face on that boy's body . . ."

Angelo's voice started to crack. He tried to regain his composure, but could not. Chin quivering, he continued. "Avi, that child could have been my own. My wife could have been the woman screaming to save her son."

Goldman looked Angelo squarely in the eye; he understood.

"Why her and not me?" Angelo questioned. "Why Gershon and not Jesse? With just a slight nudge on the wheel of fate, I could have been born in Israel and some cushy American could have been watching me cradle my own son's bloody corpse."

"Angelo," Goldman interrupted, "you can't think like that; it'll drive you crazy."

"But maybe I need to think like that, Avi; maybe I need a swift kick in the ass. I take my life for granted. I have a wife who has been there for me and held the fort while I've spent days and nights in my lab. I have a great kid who pisses me off to no end sometimes, but melts me more than I admit. I have a prestigious job with benefits that a third-world peon would equate with royalty, a digital mobile phone, and an eighteen-inch satellite dish that pulls in a hundred channels from an unseen universe, including twenty-four hour tennis and three grades of porno. I am insured to the hilt so that my family will be taken care of in the event of my demise, and should I survive my workaholism, I have a pension fund that will allow me to play golf until rigor mortis sets in during my backswing on the seventh hole."

"So what's the problem, Angelo? You sound very blessed."

"The problem, Avi, is that my life stinks. I have every possible amenity a modern man could desire, but my gut is a cesspool. I am riddled with fears and doubts that no one ever sees, and I take out my frustration on my child. Avi, I am seriously afraid that one day I will hurt him, and I will never be able to forgive myself. Even worse, I am afraid I will go on like this for the rest of my life and curse my miserable existence; my life, in spite of my apparent opulence and enviable success, is meaningless."

Goldman placed a reassuring hand on Angelo's shoulder. Uncharacteristically, Angelo reached up and set his hand over his friend's. "Avi, I don't know where to go or who to turn to. I thought that by coming here I would have some time to think things out, but I haven't found any more answers—only more questions. I mean, what the hell are we doing here if all we do is fight with each other over whose God has a bigger dick and who owns Jerusalem? I can't believe that God cares about some crummy hill more than the lives of the people who are bombing each other for its possession."

Goldman listened carefully, digesting Angelo's words. "Please, Angelo, sit down," Avi urged, gesturing toward one of the two chairs next to a small round slate-topped table near the window. Avi pulled a chair back for Angelo, who took a seat. Avi remained standing and faced his friend.

"In 1967 I had a wife and year-old daughter. When the Six-Day War broke out, we were stationed at a military installation near the Golan Heights. As the conflict heated up, our military advisors decided it was not safe for the women and children to be so close to the battle lines, so they decided to relocate them. Late one night they were herded into a bus and sent south toward safer ground. On their way, snipers discovered the bus and tossed half a dozen grenades into it. They were killed instantly."

Stunned, Angelo quietly interjected, "I'm sorry."

"I felt like you do now—multiplied by a thousand. I wanted to find every Arab I could, rip their throats out, and cut them in little pieces. But the war ended quickly and I had no outlet for my rage. It began to consume me. I was 19 years old, with vast quantities of adrenaline surging through my system, stewing in my own private hell. Without any outlet, my anger turned to depression, and I couldn't imagine any way out. So I decided to do it myself."

"You tried to kill yourself?"

"I locked myself in my car and ran a rubber hose from the exhaust through the driver's window. I turned on the motor, and after a few minutes I passed out."

"But you survived. . ."

"Yes, I survived. Just after I fell unconscious, the engine failed. After it happened, I thought it was a curse; now I realize it was a miracle. A few hours later my superior officer came to look for me and found me barely alive. I was rushed to the hospital and then put in a psychiatric ward."

"Avi, I had no idea. . ."

"Most people don't. . .I haven't told many people. But today it's important that I tell you." Avi took the empty chair, straddled it, and faced Angelo. "While I was hospitalized I was visited by the chaplain, a young rabbi named Isaac. He took an interest in me and we became friends. We began to have metaphysical discussions, which interested me a great deal. Then one day Isaac told me about a rabbi he had been studying with, a very wise man who had brought him great comfort. He suggested that I come to meet the rabbi. At first I resisted, but Isaac's belief in this man was so compelling that I decided to take a chance and I went. That day was the turning point of my life. The moment I met the rabbi I felt that he could see into my soul. He answered questions for me and gave me insights I could never have found in a book. I realized that destiny had brought us together, and eventually I understood that everything that had happened—including my family's death and my suicide attempt—had led to that moment. Somehow everything was connected. The fact that I am alive today, and have found a sense of peace and clarity about who I am and what I am here for, is a result of my meeting with Rav Shimon.

"Is this man still alive?"

"Yes, he is, and I would like to take you to see him tomorrow."

"But my plane ticket is for tomorrow morning."

"Would it be worth one more day here, to change your life?"

Angelo sat quietly, thinking deeply. Anything, he figured, would be worth changing his life.

Chapter 5

As Avi Goldman rounded sharp turns on two wheels, kicking up billows of dust, Angelo gripped the handle over the Saab's glove box. Goldman seemed oblivious to the scurrying sheep he missed hitting by inches. Before they reached the desert, at least a dozen drivers had honked and cursed at Avi in a mixture of Hebrew and Arabic. "I don't take it personally," Avi swore. "Everyone here takes out their frustration in traffic." Angelo decided to swallow his control obsession and kept his mouth shut.

"Have you ever heard of the Kabbala?" Avi asked after a long silence.

"Some kind of cocktail?"

Goldman laughed. "Hardly—the Kabbala is the ancient Hebrew mystical teaching passed down over the centuries through a secret oral tradition. Many great rabbis have devoted their entire lives to understanding but a portion of it. Training is given only to students who have demonstrated they are ready to learn."

"Why don't they just write a book about it?"

"Because the teachings are so powerful that, if misused, they could seriously injure the student or others. Kabbala penetrates to the very source of creation and gives the student access to vast creative power."

"Well, now you have me going," Angelo said as he rolled up his window so he could hear Avi better.

"Good—I thought this would get your attention. We are taught that no one should attempt to study Kabbala before the age of forty; only by that time may one have gained the life experience to work safely with the material."

"So what would happen if someone delved into it before that age?"

"Study without spiritual preparation could drive a man insane—or, if someone had a character disorder, he could use the power to inflict great evil. For example, Hitler learned of the esoteric teachings and probed mystical traditions so he could gain advantage in his military campaign. He even tried to collect the artifacts of Jesus—the grail from which Jesus drank, the sword that pierced his side, and the shroud of Turin, which contains the image of Jesus at the time of his resurrection. While Hitler obviously had no respect for the teachings of Jesus, he did understand that Jesus had tapped into a phenomenal source of energy. Hitler wanted that power for himself."

"How come you know so much about Jesus? I thought you were Jewish."

"Of course I am—and so was Jesus!" Both men laughed; Angelo felt the muscles in the back of his neck relax for the first time since the bombing.

"But," Avi continued, "more than anything else I am a scientist. Even from a purely scientific perspective, if Jesus did half the things attributed to him, he is worth studying as a great master. He demonstrated that there are vast untapped realms which contain great secrets that could change the world if we learned how to use them."

Just then the Saab rolled into a verdant glen, a sharp contrast to the parched wilderness the men had just traversed. A few ramshackle houses marked the presence of civilization; several children cavorted in a rudimentary school playground. At first the sight of the children lifted Angelo's heart, but quickly the memory of yesterday's disaster encroached. Angelo began to feel his chest gripped again.

"Why did you bring up this business about the Kabbala?"

"We are coming into Zvat, the ancient center of Kabbalistic studies. Those who are serious about unraveling its mysteries come here to find the real teachings. None of the schooling is advertised; it is all by word of mouth. The rabbis say that the Spirit has its own screening process. Some people spend months in this tiny town trying to find a teacher. Many go home disappointed—but they do not realize what grace they received. They were not ready, and they can't even imagine the hardship they were spared.

"Rav Shimon is a master of Kabbala. In Hebrew, he is called a *chacham*–a scholar of the highest degree. He is one of the great mystics of our time. The rabbi is very old now, and no one knows how much longer he will be with us. I try to get out here as often as I can."

Goldman parked his dented chariot in an alleyway and led Angelo past a number of art shops to a tiny old synagogue. Inside, amidst the heady smell of candles, aged wood, and musty cloth, a group of men, mostly elderly, sat around long tables with large tattered books before them. Some of the scholars silently immersed themselves in the imposing texts, while others engaged in animated discussions. A few of the men were dressed in black frocks with large round hats and long sidecurls. Others were more modernly attired, wearing knitted skullcaps. The temple was stark except for a colorful altar where the sacred scrolls were housed in a polished wooden cabinet that seemed to glow in contrast to the drabness of the room.

Goldman approached one of the men and spoke to him in Hebrew for a few minutes. Angelo figured he was inquiring about Rav Shimon. Avi returned and reported, "We're in luck–the rabbi is home, but he is not feeling well–perhaps we can see him for a little while."

Avi guided Angelo down a small winding street to a dilapidated little house and rapped on a rickety door which Angelo feared might collapse. After a few moments a forty-ish woman answered, her head covered in a red and yellow flowered kerchief; she looked pleasant enough, pretty but plain. She recognized Avi, smiled politely, and respectfully ushered the two men inside. Goldman led Angelo to a small sitting room off to the side of the parlor.

There, in a faded beige high-backed chair, sat Rav Shimon, sunlight shimmering off his high forehead. Instantly Angelo felt a sense of peace in the presence of this old man, whom Angelo figured to be at least eighty years of age. The rabbi wore a long thin white beard; just a few wispy locks of his remaining hair lay languidly on the top of his head. Though his body was bent, he projected tremendous power and dignity. Angelo noticed the rabbi's eyes; even from across the room they sparkled. Rav Shimon seemed to be peering into the next world, as if looking through a corridor of mirrors. Angelo was awed by the rabbi's compelling demeanor and felt mysteriously drawn to him.

Avi motioned toward an old brown tattered easy chair where Angelo was to sit, and then leaned over to embrace Rav Shimon. The two held each other for a long time as the rabbi patted Avi on the back. As Goldman and the rabbi conversed in Hebrew for a few minutes, Angelo looked around the room at the very simple and humble décor. The bookshelves were filled with old dusty books with faded gold Hebrew lettering on their spines. Above the bookshelf a symbol on the wall caught Angelo's eye. It appeared to be a combination of a cross and a star. It didn't look quite Christian, but it certainly wasn't Jewish. Angelo figured he would ask Avi about it when he had a chance.

Suddenly his pondering was interrupted by Avi, who began to speak in English. "Rav Shimon, this is my friend, Dr. Angelo Mann. He has come from America to address our conference. He wanted very much to meet you."

Rav Shimon reached out to take his guest's hand; Angelo was surprised to feel the old man's grip vibrant and strong. "*Shalom*, my brother," Rav Shimon greeted Angelo. "Welcome to my home." The rabbi spoke with a Slavic accent, yet his English pronunciation was quite good.

"Thank you, rabbi; it is an honor to be here."

Before any small talk transpired, Avi stated their purpose. "Rabbi, yesterday Angelo and I observed the Mishnayat bombing—"

"Yes, I heard about it. . . It is a terrible thing," the elder sympathized, nodding his head.

"Angelo is going through a hard time in his life. We were hoping that perhaps you could assist him in some way."

Rav Shimon listened attentively. Angelo had the strangest feeling the sage knew what he was going to say.

"Yes, rabbi, I am feeling much pain in my heart." Angelo stopped for a moment, surprised he was so candid and vulnerable with the rabbi so quickly. How did he know he could trust this man? He hardly knew Goldman, and here he was spilling his guts to a total

stranger. For all Angelo knew, the man could have been just some feeble old coot. Yet, for all his doubting and apprehension, Angelo felt
safe, and continued.

"Rabbi, my life has very little meaning. I have an excellent position and a beautiful family, but I don't know who I am or what I am
doing in this world. Lately science, once my first love, feels empty to
me, like an old suit that doesn't quite fit anymore. Seeing the disaster
yesterday makes me wonder if there is any hope for humanity. I
mean, what's the use of making material progress if we are morally
stuck in the stone ages? How can so many people justify killing others
in the name of God?"

The rabbi was quiet for a while, nodding his head slowly, as if
drinking in all that Angelo was laying out before him. He seemed not
so much to be formulating a response, but listening inside himself.
The silence went on for about thirty seconds, yet to Angelo it felt like
hours. Finally Rav Shimon spoke.

"Doctor, I commend you for asking the most important questions. If you were to pass through this world and not confront these
issues, your life would be shallow indeed. To ask these questions
means that you are ready for a change in your life."

The rabbi reached for some tea and sipped slowly, his hand trembling. His eyes glistened as he continued.

"To live life only at the material level brings frustration and confusion. Yet such pain and suffering force human beings to look
deeper, and many, now, are waking up. Though I live in a little town
in the middle of nowhere, I know about the great revolution occurring all over the world. My body is very sensitive; I can feel the up-
heaval that so many people are going through. It is a very difficult period, but very important."

The rabbi became quiet again, turning his attention inward.
"Thousands of years ago our prophets foretold this time. Yes, it is the
end. But it is also the beginning. Great change means great opportunity. Your feeling of emptiness means that you are clearing the way
for something new and better. But you are going to have to learn to
see through new eyes. The meaning you seek is right before you, but
you do not see it because you are trying to understand it with your old

way of thinking. That, my friend, will no longer work. You are going to have to practice a different way of thinking. It may seem difficult at first, but then it will bring you great peace. Simplify your life. Open your heart. Accept the love that is given you. Deal with what is right in front of you, and the mysteries will clarify themselves. As a scientist, you enjoy solving riddles. Why not make your own life the great experiment? Ask yourself, 'What truly makes me happy?' Then love yourself enough to do it."

Rav Shimon stopped for a moment, looked at Angelo, and added, "I'll bet that you are a very busy man."

Angelo issued a short anxious laugh, as if he had been exposed. "Busy" was an understatement.

"Play a game," the rabbi suggested. "Begin to cut away from your life what robs your joy, and add more of what brings you peace. After a month, put your hand on your heart and feel the energy there. I promise that you will thank me for this advice. . .If it doesn't work, you don't have to pay."

Rav Shimon turned to Goldman, elbowed him, and laughed heartily; clearly he got a kick out of himself.

"I have studied the Kabbala for many years," Rav Shimon explained, "and I tell you that you will not find your answers in a book. The only real power is love. Love yourself and you will see everything more clearly. Forgive yourself and the outer world will not have the power to take away your peace. Then an unseen hand will help you in ways that you could not help yourself."

Angelo was stunned by the simplicity of the rabbi's answer. For a moment he felt cheated, for he wanted an answer his mind could deal with, some kind of formula he could test. Instead the rabbi was speaking directly to his heart, a domain that Angelo had effectively sealed off. Until yesterday.

"But what about Mishnayat?"

"It is fear, my friend. Terrorists are terrified. Can you imagine how deeply alienated a human being would have to feel, to set off a bomb in the midst of schoolchildren? People who hurt others are motivated by their own pain. If you really want to change the world, begin by facing and dismantling your own fear. If you do nothing else but learn to respond to challenges with peace rather than attack, you will contribute more to humanity than a hundred Nobel scientists."

"Does that mean I should abandon science?"

"Certainly not; to the contrary—the world needs scientists with vision. Continue your work, but use your intelligence to develop technology that will help people, not injure them. Remind people that there is more to life than just survival, and make human beings aware of their vast potential."

"But I know nothing about religion."

"It is not religion I am speaking of—it is spirituality."

"But rabbi, once I leave here there is no one in my life I can go to for the kind of guidance you are giving me. What am I supposed to do—call up Moses and ask him for advice?" Angelo stopped short; he feared he had been rude to his kind host.

But instead of rebuking Angelo, Rav Shimon smiled and answered, "Why not? Moses would be glad to help you!"

"But how can he? Moses died thousands of years ago."

"My dear doctor, you make the universe much smaller than it is. Your scientific beliefs have limited your scope of life to a tiny circle. For all its glory, science has probed only the physical plane for answers. There are higher realms that make all of physical science seem Neanderthal by comparison."

"I'm sorry, sir. I don't understand."

"Then I will teach you a little Kabbala. The realm of the physical senses is a minuscule slice of the universe. In spite of all the power you ascribe to the material plane, the ideas that generate the obvious world occur on higher dimensions. For example, when you make a telephone call from, say, San Francisco. . ."

A chill ran up Angelo's spine; the rabbi had no way of knowing he was from San Francisco; the old man seemed to just pick the information out of the air.

". . .to Tel Aviv, your voice is transmitted by invisible waves up to a satellite and then down to earth again. To get the clearest and strongest signal, you must bypass the density of earth and move through a finer medium. It is the same with travel: the airplanes and rockets that go the farthest and fastest are those that fly the highest.

To truly be effective in any endeavor, you must think and act from a higher dimension."

"But what does Moses have to do with all of this?"

"When a soul leaves this world, the person does not cease to exist; they just step out of view. The person is still alive, sometimes right next to us; we just cannot perceive them with our eyes, which interpret a limited spectrum of vibration. But we have senses that we do not use. Many of our psychic faculties have. . ." Rav Shimon hesitated again and turned to Goldman for the English word.

"Atrophied," Goldman offered.

"Yes, atrophied. . .Now, getting back to Moses. . ."

Suddenly the rabbi's face flushed and he was overtaken by a coughing fit. His granddaughter hurried into the room, humbly slapped her grandpa on his back several times, gave him a sip of water, and fixed his pillows. After a few minutes, the redness in Rav Shimon's face subsided and he continued, unruffled.

"Getting back to Moses. . .The prophet is as real and alive today as he was when he delivered the ten commandments. But very few people believe in him or make an effort to contact him."

Angelo's mind began to churn. *I came all this way to hear a sermon about spooks? Next thing I know, we'll all be holding hands for a seance.*

As if he had read Angelo's thoughts, Rav Shimon added, "This is not the supernatural we are talking about; it is all super natural!" Again the rabbi laughed heartily, proud of his play on words.

Goldman seized the chance to speak. "What Rav Shimon is saying, Angelo, is that it is possible to communicate with any being, even if they don't have a physical body at the moment."

This conversation was getting downright bizarre. Angelo was tempted to write it all off as hogwash, but he forced himself to stay with it.

"Think of the physical body as a sheath, like a glove over your hand," Rav Shimon explained, lifting and working his right hand for illustration. "Because the hand is not visible, it would appear that the glove is moving itself. But it is the hand that moves the glove. The moment the hand is removed, the glove lies limp and lifeless, and serves no useful purpose." Rav Shimon gracefully flicked off the imaginary glove. "When the glove, or body, disintegrates, we call that death. But it is only the body that dies; the real person, like the hand without the glove, lives on." Nimbly he raised his hand and waved it in an artistic dance.

"So why don't more people make contact with invisible spirits?" Angelo asked. He surprised himself by taking this ridiculous conversation seriously.

"Actually, many do, but most people are reluctant to talk about it," Avi interjected. "They are afraid others will think they are wacko. Most people lead a double life; we present one face to the world and keep our more significant experiences to ourselves. Consider how different life on the planet would be if people told more truth about what they were experiencing!"

"Or if people actually talked to guys like Moses or Jesus," Angelo added. Suddenly he caught himself and wondered if he had committed a *faux pas* by mentioning Jesus in the rabbi's presence. Angelo glanced quickly at the sage, who was not flustered in the least; obviously this rabbi had space in his world for religions other than his own.

"If I ever got a hold of Moses, there are sure a lot of things I would grill him about," Angelo contended ardently.

Suddenly Rav Shimon began coughing again. This time Avi tried to comfort him. As he held the glass of water for the rabbi to sip, Goldman looked up at Angelo and stated softly, "I think maybe we should go now and let the rabbi rest."

Angelo nodded. Part of him couldn't wait to leave, while another part wanted to stay forever.

When the coughing abated, Rav Shimon beckoned in a scratchy voice, "Come closer, my friends."

Angelo followed Avi's lead as he leaned over to bid the aged sage goodbye. To Angelo's surprise, the rabbi stretched out both arms and placed the palms of his large hands over his guests' heads. In a sacred tone the elder chanted, "*Yvorechecha Adonay vyishmerecha. Yisa Adonay panav elecha vichunecha.*"

Suddenly Angelo felt a strong current course though his body. He sensed an intense heat emanating from the center of the rabbi's palms, infusing him with a wonderful tingling sensation that rippled down to his toes. This energy felt almost sexual, but it was not; it was more like a bliss that both excited and soothed his nervous system. He had never felt anything like it before, yet it felt strangely familiar. Angelo didn't want it to stop and, though baffled by the feeling, tried to absorb it.

After a few moments the rabbi retracted his arms, smiled softly, nodded, and bid his visitors goodbye. Avi and Angelo thanked Rav Shimon for his time and stepped toward the door. Just as Angelo was leaving, he heard the rabbi call him.

"Angelo—think with your heart, not your mind. You will know the truth by the peace it brings you."

Angelo stopped and nodded silently.

"—and say hello to Moses for me!"

Chapter 6

By the time the dusty Saab pulled up to the portico of the Sheraton Tel Aviv, Angelo was ready to get out and feel his feet on *terra firma* and unwind. A drink, he decided, was in order. Angelo made his way to the lounge where he found a comfortable seat in a maroon tweed chair next to a small marble table. He ordered a daiquiri, sat back, and got involved in the soccer game playing on the wide-screen TV.

A minute later Angelo noticed Juliana walk into the bar. He watched to see if she would be followed by Michaud, but she was alone. She noticed Angelo and walked directly toward him. He was excited to see her, yet a bit uneasy; he felt off balance and still did not know how to deal with the chemistry he felt in her presence.

"Hello, Angelo—what a surprise to see you here. . .I thought you were leaving this morning."

"Well, I was supposed to, but something came up; I took a little excursion with Avi."

"Mind if I join you? Unless you're waiting for someone. . ."

"No, no. . .That's fine. . .Please, have a seat."

"Actually, I'm glad I ran into you."

"Why's that?"

"I wanted to thank you for yesterday, when we were at the school. I really appreciated you being there to comfort me. God, what a tragic thing. I don't think I've ever seen such a heart-wrenching sight. As a journalist I see all kinds of strange people and events, and I've developed some thick skin, but there's no defense against a tragedy like that. I know I'm supposed to be dispassionate and all that, but I can't just turn off my feelings. . .I guess maybe you have learned how to be more objective."

"Maybe a little, but to tell you the truth, yesterday's incident got to me, too."

"How did it affect you?"

"When I saw those poor kids being carried to the ambulances, I thought about my son."

"Oh, you have a son?"

"Yes, six years old. His name is Jesse."

"So you're married."

Angelo took a deep breath and swirled his drink. His gaze fell.

"Something wrong?" Juliana asked.

"Well, we're having a hard time right now."

"Anything you feel like talking about?"

"Maybe better not. Thanks for asking, though."

"Hey, I have an idea. Let's get a bottle of wine and take a walk in the park across the street. Let's just forget about everything and enjoy this beautiful evening."

Angelo thought for a moment, trying the idea on for size. It fit. "Yes, I'd like that. I think I'd really like that."

Angelo ordered a bottle of Chardonnay, Juliana slipped a few wine glasses into her purse, and the two stepped out of the hotel into the warm and slightly humid Mediterranean evening. He slipped his light sweater off and draped it over his shoulder. The two crossed the congested street, still bustling with manic drivers, and made their way into the park, a peaceful respite from the intensity of Tel Aviv.

"How about that tree over there?" Juliana pointed. "I'll bet it would like some company."

"Sure, why not?"

The two stepped over a small foot-high white wooden fence and made their way to a grassy patch beneath the spreading limbs of an old Cypress tree. In a gentlemanly way Angelo laid his sweater on the ground to protect Juliana's dress when she sat. They sat down against the tree and let their heads lean back on the bark. Angelo closed his eyes and let the softness of the night air brush gently over his face. It seemed to wash away some the stress of the last two days.

Juliana looked up beyond the trees and told Angelo, "I used to look up at the stars all the time when I was a little girl. I used to go up to the roof of my apartment house and lay there for hours, just letting my mind drift."

Angelo offered a soft smile. He really liked the sound of Juliana's voice.

"Can you guess what I wanted to be when I grew up?" she asked.

"Let's see. . .an astronaut?"

"A spy."

"A spy?"

"Yes, I used to go up to my room with my friends and eat popcorn and watch old movies on television—you know, old war and espionage and mystery thrillers. I hardly ever saw lady spies and I thought, 'I would like to be a great lady spy.' Then I could travel around the world and leave people secret messages and escape from dangerous situations. And then when I got tired of all that, I could meet a handsome man and we could have intelligent children and live happily ever after together . . . How about you?"

"I wanted to invent a time machine. In fifth grade I read the book by H.G. Wells and I thought it was a true story. When my teacher told me it was fiction, I was really disappointed. So I decided that when I grew up I would invent it myself."

Angelo uncorked the wine bottle and filled Juliana's glass, then his own. *"Cheers,"* they toasted and smiled. "And what happened to your dream?" Juliana asked.

"I grew up and became a responsible adult and started to believe the things other people told me about what was possible and what was impossible."

Juliana sighed and slowly rubbed her hand on the plush bed of grass beside her. Then she asked, "Angelo, do you think that real love is possible, or just an illusion?"

Angelo took a moment to contemplate the question. "I think that it is real when you are in it, and an illusion when you are not."

"My," Juliana answered, "sounds like you've given the subject some thought."

"Isn't it amazing how a couple of drinks will turn even a diehard scientist into a raving poet?"

"I like to think that everyone has poetry inside them," she replied. "It just takes the right person or place or feeling to bring it out."

Angelo reached over and gently placed his hand on Juliana's. After a few moments she turned her hand upward to interlace their fingers. Angelo felt comforted by her touch.

"When I was in elementary school I had my first crush on a cute little strawberry blonde named Marie. Her parents had just moved from France, and when she walked into my classroom one day I thought my heart was going to leap out the window. That night I wrote her a love poem. I think it was pretty good. The next morning I stood in the hall by her locker and waited for her. When she showed up I read her the poem."

"And what did she say?"

"Nothing. She just stared at me like I was from Mars. The bell rang, we walked into class, and I felt like a total jerk. Then later I found out she didn't know a word of English."

The two laughed and Angelo poured another glass of wine. Juliana took a few sips and rested her head on Angelo's shoulder. The air was fragrant, hinting of some night-blooming jasmine nearby.

"Is that a bird fluttering up in the tree?" Juliana pointed.

"No, it's probably a bat."

"Oh, come on. . .what happened to the poet?"

"Okay, okay, it's a bird." Angelo smiled and leaned his head against Juliana's, looking up into the branches.

"That feels nice," she murmured

"Yes, it does," he answered, snuggling his cheek against hers.

Angelo found Juliana's eyes for the first time since they sat down. A warm feeling began to stir in his chest. He looked into her eyes for another few moments and then, as if drawn by an invisible force, their lips met. They held contact for a few seconds, not moving, just feeling the current passing between them. Just as naturally, they pulled apart.

"Sorry, I didn't mean for that to happen," she said.

"It's okay, it felt right. . ." Suddenly Angelo felt awkward. "Is it Jean-Claude?"

"What do you mean?"

"Are you and Jean-Claude, you know, an item?"

Juliana laughed, almost cackled. "Jean-Claude and I are friends. I could never be with him. The guy has an ego the size of Austria."

"But you two seemed so. . . coupled. . ."

"To be perfectly truthful, Angelo, I did date Jean-Claude a few times when I first met him—but it didn't take long to realize it would never go anywhere. I am attracted to men I can talk to. . .about my feelings. . .about my work. . .about great ideas. All Jean-Claude wanted to talk about was himself, not to mention snaking me into bed. We see each other at conferences once in a while; that's about it."

"I see," Angelo nodded, trying not to be obvious about his raging delight to hear that she was unattached.

Angelo stretched his arm around Juliana and drew her gently to him. Again their lips found each other and this time they held the kiss for a long time. This time she had to force herself to pull away. "Maybe we'd better get back; you have an early plane to catch."

Juliana stood up and extended a hand to help Angelo up. The two dusted off their clothing and made their way back from their little refuge. Angelo took Juliana's hand as they walked through the park and then threaded their way through a teeming herd of pedestrians, most of whom lived in a world where love was just an illusion.

Chapter 7

When the flight attendant woke Angelo for the kosher meal service, his head was spinning. He chuckled aloud, cynically; here he had gone to Israel to get rid of his troubles, and all he found was more of the self he was trying to escape.

Yet his evening with Juliana lingered like a sweet dream. Was it real? He closed his eyes again and recalled the softness of her lips and the comfort of her touch. She had been so welcoming, so easy to be with. Suddenly Angelo remembered he was on his way home to his wife. He winced. Angelo wondered if being with Juliana was a violation of his marriage. What makes me think I even have a marriage? he questioned. Angelo tried to remember the last time he and Claudia made love; or took a vacation together; or even had a meaningful conversation about something that was important to both of them. He came up short on all accounts. For God's sake, she wouldn't even take him to the airport.

Across the aisle a businessman was reading *The New York Times* international edition. The Mishnayat massacre was still in the headlines. To no one's surprise, the Muslim terrorist group *Al Sharmat* claimed responsibility for the explosion. The *Al Sharmat* leader, Iban Hassan, bragged that the faction was instructed by Allah to inflict the bombing to draw the world's attention to the fact that Israel belonged to the Muslims. Angelo wanted to throw up.

His indignation was sidetracked when he felt a touch on his left arm, from the passenger sitting next to him.

"Would you like my dessert?" she asked, pointing to a little packaged brownie. "No sugar for me!"

"No thanks," Angelo answered. "I'm fine with one." He held up his brownie to show her.

"They should have a little exercise room on the plane so we could stretch our muscles, don't you think?" she asked. "–Not that I would use it. . . I'm the kind of person who can't wait until New Year's so I can break my resolutions," she giggled.

Angelo liked this woman, a pleasant sixty-ish, short gray hair, round face, round maroon-rimmed eyeglasses. He found it especially endearing that she was wearing a Hard Rock Café sweatshirt; obviously this woman was more interested in being comfortable than making a fashion impression.

"My name is Harriet Pierson," she offered, extending her hand.

"Angelo. . .Angelo Mann." He reached to shake and found her touch to be motherly.

Harriet shifted her position so she could face Angelo more directly. "So how did you like Israel?' she asked.

"Oh, it was quite an adventure," he answered drolly. If she only knew. "How about you?"

"It meant a lot to me. I went on a pilgrimage."

"A pilgrimage?"

"I work with a group that practices healing. We do a lot of prayer and creative visualization."

"Creative what?"

"Creative visualization. That's when you take a situation in mind and concentrate on it as you would like it to become." Harriet reached to take a sip of coffee.

"Sort of like positive thinking?"

"More than that . . . more like positive feeling and knowing."

Angelo leaned on the armrest and rested his chin on his hand. "But how can you feel or know something that hasn't happened yet?"

"Because things often turn out the way we feel about them. If you can get a good feeling about something, you can influence it to become what you want. When you fuel your thoughts with strong emotions, they become really powerful."

Who was this lady, anyway? Had Rav Shimon hired her to sit next to Angelo and continue the lecture the rabbi had begun?

"And what was your trip about, Angelo?"

"I went to speak at a scientific conference," he answered.

"I see," Harriet answered as she got her dinner tray ready for the flight attendant to collect.

Suddenly Angelo was overcome with the strangest feeling. He felt that he should say more—not about the conference, but about himself. For some reason he could not explain, he wanted to confide in this woman. Although he had no evidence to trust her, the feeling was so compelling that he decided to go with it.

". . .and to sort out some things," he added. Suddenly Angelo felt warmth in his cheeks.

"About your life, you mean?"

"Yes, I'm having some difficulty at home, and I had hoped being in Israel would help me get some answers." Angelo could hardly believe he was saying these things to a total stranger.

"Well, I'm a good listener," Harriet offered, smiling.

Immediately Angelo felt a sense of relief. How could this be possible with someone he hardly knew?

"I am trying to figure out how to be a better father."

"How old is your child?"

"My son is six. . .Do you have any children, Harriet?"

"We have one son, Terry. He's grown now, has his own family in Richmond."

"I'm sure he's a fine young man."

"He is, but I have to tell you that we've had our moments with him. When he was little he put us to the test quite a few times. My husband L.C. (short for Lieutenant Commander)—who is the kindest, most gentle man in the world—used to get furious with our son. I never saw anyone press L.C.'s buttons like Terry did. It took him years to realize that his son was not a Navy seaman."

"So what happened?"

"Terry grew up to be a healthy, happy, and productive fellow. He loves his father and they have a very good relationship. It was all just part of growing up—for Terry and L.C. I think every parent goes through self-doubt. You get over it."

Angelo leaned back in his seat and let his head fall back. This woman had to be an angel.

Their conversation was interrupted by the pilot's voice. "Ladies and gentlemen, you probably noticed that the airplane just made a left turn. Our destination airport, Washington Dulles, is completely snowed in. We've been receiving reports of a storm that's been building since we left Europe; I waited to give you the information until we knew what our landing status would be."

A hush fell over the cabin; these passengers had been flying for more hours than most of them could count. The last thing they wanted to hear about was delay or rerouting.

"Air Traffic Control tells us that the storm moving up the eastern seaboard has stalled over the northeast, and is expanding; all major airports from Boston to Washington are socked in. The closest airport still open is Norfolk, Virginia, and that is where we are headed. Ladies and gentlemen, you will have the distinct honor of spending the night amidst the southern hospitality of Norfolk."

A cacophonous chorus of groans and curses shot out from the crowd. Most of the passengers grumbled about missing their connections, and some of them tried to convince the flight attendants that they had a special need to get somewhere soon. Angelo had flown enough to know that there was no use complaining; the airline didn't like doing this any more than the passengers.

The pilot continued, "Hopefully by tomorrow morning the eastern seaboard airports will be open again, and we will find you the next available connection to your final destination. We sure do apologize for this delay, but there's not much else we can do. When we arrive at the gate, see the agent for a hotel and meal voucher."

Another wave of protest rippled through the cabin. Americans are a funny bunch, Angelo thought. We want it all, and we want it all now.

"Well, that's wonderful!" Harriet exclaimed. "Now I don't even need to take a connecting flight."

Angelo looked at her quizzically.

"I live right in Norfolk! Nothing like service to the door!"

Angelo smiled politely.

"Where are you headed?" Harriet asked.

"San Jose."

"Oh, my, that's still quite a ways. Do you know anybody in this area?"

"Not a soul."

Harriet's eyes lit up. "I have an idea, Angelo. Why don't you spend the night at my house? L.C. will pick us up at the airport, you can have a good night's rest, and I'll make us all breakfast in the morning. That'll be so much nicer for you than staying at some impersonal hotel."

"Oh, thank you, but I couldn't do that; I stay in hotels all the time."

"Well, that's all the more reason to get away and enjoy some home cooking. We have a lovely guest room, and you'll have plenty of privacy."

"I really wouldn't want to inconvenience you."

"Oh, no inconvenience at all. Besides, you may not even be able to get a hotel room. And my husband will enjoy the company; he's an engineer for the navy, and I'll bet you guys will have something to talk about."

Suddenly Angelo's doubting mind swung into action. What if he got trapped in Norfolk and never got home? What if these people were members of a satanic cult? What if they chopped up his body in little pieces and mailed them to Taco Bells around the nation? What if. . .what if. . .what if?

Suddenly he heard Rav Shimon speak, "Go with your deepest instinct," as if the sage was sitting behind him. Angelo looked behind him to see if someone had spoken. A little girl slept with her head across her mother's lap. He turned back to Harriet, who was still smiling.

"Well, I suppose," he said.

"Wonderful, then it's settled," she answered.

Everyone in the Norfolk airport was buzzing with talk of the storm, which had rained on the city and then dropped the temperature swiftly to leave a thin sheath of ice over everything. Those who had braved the black ice to come to the airport were trading stories of the accidents they nearly missed. Sure enough, L.C. Pierson was waiting at baggage claim, unusually poised amid the throngs of rattled greeters. A career navy man, he looked the part—neatly and conservatively dressed, short hair, erect posture.

"L.C., meet Angelo Mann—our houseguest for the night."

Angelo, feeling sheepish about dropping in on the family, extended his hand. He was pleased to be met by L.C.'s firm and welcoming grip. L.C. did not appear the least flustered that his wife had invited a total stranger to be their houseguest; Angelo guessed he was used to it.

"Glad to have you aboard, Angelo. Can I offer you a hand with your bag?"

"Thanks, I think I can handle it."

"Well, then, let's shove off before the next wave of the storm hits."

Angelo followed his hosts out to the parking lot. He purposely inhaled a deep breath of the fresh air; it was quite cold, but it felt good to draw into his lungs after being cooped up in a plane for 11 hours. L.C. niftily slung Angelo's bag into the back of the impeccably clean gray PT Cruiser, and the troupe was off.

"You must both be exhausted," L.C. commented as they pulled onto the main highway.

"Oh, I'm still so buzzing about Israel," Harriet answered. Where did this lady get her energy from?

"Actually, I am kind of tired," Angelo admitted.

"Well, we'll get you to a nice bed right quick, and you can hunker down," L.C. offered in a kindly voice.

The Piersons' guest room was exactly as Angelo had imagined it: flowered wallpaper, an old walnut bed with a carved headboard and posts, and a saggy mattress with flannel sheets covered by a multicolored homemade afghan. The only anomaly was a state-of-the-art computer on an old wooden student's desk, under a wall filled with photos of Terry Pierson, the son who turned out okay. Angelo took a

minute to survey the many photos which spanned Terry's life from
diapers to his college football career to his own home and family.
Nice house, too. The Piersons seemed like a functional, happy, and
healthy family. Was there still such an animal?

After he showered, Angelo sat down on the bed and picked up
the phone on the night table. Pressing the tone buttons to call Claudia, his gut churned as he remembered his evening with Juliana.
Funny, when he was with Juliana, she seemed quite real and Claudia
a distant ghost. Now the tables were turned.

"Hello?" her voice came forth.

"Hi, it's me."

"Where are you?"

"I'm in Norfolk."

"*Norfolk?*"

"Norfolk, Virginia."

"What are you doing in *Norfolk?*"

"A snowstorm closed Dulles. They put us up here for the night."

Quickly came the expected audible sigh. Before she had a chance
to grill him, he volunteered, "I should be able to get a plane out tomorrow morning, which would put me in around mid-afternoon.
Can you pick me up?"

There was a long silence. Then, "Angelo, there's something I
need to tell you."

"What's that?"

"I won't be here when you get back."

"What?"

"I told you I didn't want you to go to Israel, and you went anyway. That shows me how much you care about me and Jesse. . .I've
had it."

"But—" Angelo started to argue, but realized it was no use. When
Claudia made her mind up, there was no changing it. He paused for
a long time, then took a deep breath. "Where are you going?"

"Susan has an extra bedroom. Jesse can get on the same school
bus with Jeremy. Maybe I can stay there for a few weeks. You and I
can talk about how we'll arrange things."

"My God, Claudia, have you thought about how this will affect

Jesse? He's had it hard enough already."

"I know—maybe if his father was home more often and spent more time with him when he was home, the boy wouldn't be so fragile. At least he'll have someone to play with after school."

"Is he there now? I'd like to talk to him."

"He's over at the Sanders'. If he doesn't come back too late, I'll have him call you on your cell phone." Click.

Angelo fell back on the bed and folded his hands behind his head. His chin began to shake, and soon the tears started to come. A wave of sadness rolled through his belly, darkened by the guilt of not giving Jesse all he could. He was angry and frustrated that Claudia did not understand that he really cared about his son. Now, with Jesse gone, Angelo would have even less of a chance to prove himself as a father. Nearly overwhelmed with a sense of hopelessness, compounded by the prospects of going home to an empty house, Angelo fell asleep, exhausted.

When he awoke and gazed at the room ceiling, he was utterly disoriented. He looked at the clock—8 p.m. I must have really conked out, he thought. Angelo forced himself out of bed and dragged his aching body into the bathroom to splash some water on his face. On his way back to the room, he heard Harriet's kindergartenteacher voice calling to him from the bottom of the stairs, "Oh, good, Angelo; you're up and about."

"Well, something like that."

"We figured you were napping and didn't want to disturb you. Would you care to join us for some coffee and cake?"

"Uh, yeah, sure. . .I'll be down in a minute."

"Take your time, dear." This lady was straight out of a '50s TV show; she had to be the prototype for *Ozzie and Harriet*.

Angelo went back into the bathroom and stared into the mirror.

"I look like shit," he thought, and began to brush his hair. As he placed the brush down, he noticed a magazine on the counter. The article on the open page caught his eye: *Who Dies?. . . Piercing Beyond the Illusion of Death.* The subject seemed remarkably similar to Angelo's discussion with Rav Shimon and Avi Goldman. Angelo picked up the magazine and read the title: *Higher Vision.* He read the lead quote above the article:

> *A Gallup Poll reveals that over eighty percent of Americans believe there is life after death, and over half of this group claims to have had some contact with a departed loved one.*

"Space cadets," he mused audibly. He scanned the article, which contained accounts by several people who had clinically died and returned to tell about their experience, or had experienced a visitation from someone who had died. To Angelo's surprise, many of the interviewees were professional people with credibility; apparently there were a bunch of people out there who had proven, at least to their own satisfaction, that *something* within us lives on after the body.

Not wanting to keep his hosts waiting, Angelo closed the magazine and made his way down the carpeted staircase bounded by the old oak railing. When he reached the living room he found an attractive spread of apple spice cake with cream cheese icing, butter cookies, gourmet crackers with camembert cheese, coffee, herbal tea, and soda. Had this woman been on the same eleven-hour flight with him?

"I see you're reading our magazine," Harriet noted.

Startled, Angelo looked into his hand and realized he had inadvertently carried *Higher Vision* downstairs with him. Funny, he hadn't meant to do that.

"Oh yeah, I found an interesting article."

"That magazine is published by the organization Harriet works for," L.C. pointed out as he swabbed his cherry-wood pipe.

"What's that?"

"The Center for Inner Development; it's in Chesapeake. It was founded by Preston Royce. Have you ever heard of him?"

"Can't say that I have."

"He was known as 'the master psychic of the twentieth century.'"

Uh—oh, here we go again.

"Royce was one of the best known intuitives in America. Before he died in the late 60's he gave over 20,000 clairvoyant readings."

Look out, Taco Bell, here I come.

L.C. finished his pipe cleaning and dipped the bowl into an aromatic mixture. He obviously enjoyed the ritual. "Royce was a sculptor who was working with his partner on an elaborate electrified futuristic sculpture for a competition in New York. While experimenting in their studio, his partner told Preston that a 220-volt line he was working on was turned off, when it wasn't. Preston grabbed the live wire and was nearly electrocuted—he was unconscious for nearly 24 hours. When he recovered, Royce discovered that he had become terrifically psychic. He knew all kinds of thing about people without them saying a word. He also could 'see' conditions in their body. Royce then trained himself to go into a sort of trance-like state, during which he gave astoundingly accurate diagnoses and prescribed remedies that proved extremely effective."

A psychic sculptor practicing medicine from a deep sleep? Give me a break.

"Most of Royce's readings are fully documented," Harriet added. "He was able to help lots of people that doctors had given up on." Without asking Angelo, she cut him a large piece of moist apple spice cake and placed it on the coffee table before him with a napkin and fork.

"A woman would come to Royce with, for example, a bad case of arthritis that doctors said was incurable. In trance he would tell her about her life patterns that led to the arthritis, and prescribe a particular herb or oil. He would say, 'There is very little of this oil available at the moment, but if you go to the Elmhurst drugstore in Gaithersburg and look on the third shelf to the left, you will find a few bottles. The patient would go to the drugstore, and sure enough there was the oil."

"That's amazing," Angelo admitted. "But as a scientist I am rather skeptical about such reports."

"That's exactly how I felt," L.C. agreed, puffing serenely. "Even

Royce's own sister, Lacie, had a hard time believing her brother's prophecies. Then Lacie fell in love with a handsome Greek man named Gregory who wanted her to move to Greece with him. Lacie thought this would be a good chance to test her brother's psychic abilities, so she asked him for a reading about her relationship. Preston told Lacie that in a past life she had been in love with this very man in ancient Greece when she was a priestess in a temple and he was a guard. When, in that life, she became pregnant with his child, she was disgraced because the two were of different social stations and, too embarrassed to admit that he was the father, she named a nobleman as the father. When Gregory—or whatever his name was then—heard this, he was infuriated. He found Lacie on a knoll near a cliff overlooking a deep valley, where she liked to meditate. He confronted her, the two began to argue, and then, in the heat of the moment, Gregory pushed Lacie over the edge of the cliff, where she and her unborn child fell to an untimely death." L.C. leaned back in his easy chair.

"And how did Lacie react to this cockamamie story?" Angelo had to ask.

"It sounded quite far-fetched," Harriet answered as she took her needlepoint into her lap. Angelo guessed that Harriet was the kind of person who had to always be doing something productive. "She pretty much wrote off the story as fantasy. But then something really got her attention: A week after her reading, Lacie found out that she was pregnant. When she told Gregory the news, he insisted that the two go to Greece to bear and raise the child."

"Now there was another interesting development," L.C. continued. "Right around the time she met Gregory, Lacie developed an irrational fear of steep ledges. Heights had not bothered her before then, but on a vacation to Hawaii she and Gregory took a mountain hike. When the couple reached a turn that took them out to the brink of a sheer cliff, she became petrified. Gregory had to literally pick Lacie up and carry her to a glen where she felt safe."

"So that doesn't prove much; it could have been a coincidence, or maybe some unconscious fear of commitment or something like that."

"Yes, it could have," Harriet concurred, working her needles. Then she looked up and caught Angelo's eyes, as if to underscore the importance of what she was about to say. "But then, about a month later, Gregory brought Lacie to Greece to see how she would like it. To her surprise and his delight, the moment she stepped off the airplane, she felt at home. Lacie fell in love with the beauty of the land and the passion of the people; she felt as if she had known them forever. Lacie considered her brother's reading, but continued to dismiss it."

L.C. stood up and began to pace back and forth in front of the bookcase, stopping every now and then to look at Angelo. "Then one day Gregory's friend Dimitri invited the couple to join him and his wife for a trip to Delphi, the site of the ancient temple where the famous oracle uttered her prophecies. As soon as Lacie set foot on the land, she felt uneasy. As her group went about a guided tour, she seemed to know where to turn, and when the guide explained what the various buildings were used for, she found herself nodding; at a few points she even shook her head in disagreement, as if to correct the guide's erroneous information.

Angelo reached to serve himself another piece of cake. He had become so fascinated with this story that he was taking bites without even looking at his plate.

"As the day went on, Lacie felt more and more edgy. At one point she felt so disoriented that she excused herself and found her way off the beaten path to a shady area away from the temple. When she peered beyond the trees she realized that she was at the edge of a high precipice. The moment she saw the drop-off, Lacie felt woozy, and had a recurrence of the panic attack she experienced in Hawaii. At that moment Gregory approached her to find out what had become of her. He reached to move her away from the cliff, but the moment he touched her she recoiled. 'Get your hands off me!' she screamed.

"But instead of stepping back or giving her space, Gregory became insulted and angry. 'What is your problem?' he yelled back. 'I'm damn sick and tired of your stupid emotions!. . .Come along and grow up, would you?'"

Harriet put down her needlepoint and continued. "This only aggravated Lacie's paranoia, and when Gregory reached to force her to come with him, she tried to slap him away. He became furious and hit her—for the first time in their relationship. He knocked Lacie to the ground and began to shake her. When she turned her head and saw that she was but inches from the precipice, she fainted. The next thing she knew, she was looking at Dimitri, who had shown up just as Gregory was assaulting her, and pulled him off. The next day, she flew home and, upon arriving, began to bleed. Lacie went to the hospital, where she lost the baby and went into a depression. She refused to talk to Gregory ever again."

"So does that prove anything?" Angelo asked, flicking a few crumbs off his lap.

"Maybe, maybe not," Harriet answered. "But there's more: After the whole ordeal, Lacie asked her brother for another reading. Without telling Preston any of the details of her trip, she asked him what was the name of the person she had named the father of her child in a previous life."

"'Demeter' he answered. "That is the origin of the modern Greek name, 'Dimitri.'"

"That still doesn't prove anything," Angelo had to say. "Could all just be coincidence."

L.C. put his pipe aside and leaned in toward Angelo. "Then let me tell what happened next, and you can decide for yourself. For several years after that, Lacie had dreams of Gregory, or his previous incarnation, throwing her over the cliff. She would wake up in a cold sweat, gasping for air. Finally she told her brother the whole story."

"And what did he say?"

"Preston told her that she needed to forgive Gregory—in this life and any other. That, Royce claimed, was the only way out of this ancient karmic pattern, and one of the major lessons she had come into this life to learn."

Harriet held her needlepoint up to the light to check it. Then she continued, "Lacie took the advice to heart, and realized that she didn't want to go on for the rest of her life hating this man and having these horrible dreams. So she wrote Gregory a long letter telling him that she forgave him and wanted to release him—and herself—from the world of pain she had built around him. The moment she dropped the letter in the mailbox she felt lighter and freer—and never had a height panic attack again.

"Then, a month later, Lacie received a letter from Gregory thanking her for her letter and her forgiveness. He enclosed a recent photo of himself at his new job. Can you imagine what he was doing?"

"I give up," Angelo answered sarcastically.

"He is a security guard at the Parthenon—the great temple that, to this day, hovers over the city of Athens."

"Now that's a good one!" even Angelo had to admit. He leaned back in his chair, folded his hands behind his head, and tried to process all of this bizarre information. His mind was spinning.

"How about another piece of cake?" asked Harriet.

"No, thank you—already had two," Angelo muttered. "What I'd really like to know is how a Navy engineer got involved with reincarnation? I don't imagine you discuss this much at your lab."

L.C. looked at his wife questioningly, as if the two were trying to decide who should speak. She nodded, yielding to him. "Eight years ago Harriet was diagnosed with breast cancer. At the time we were living near Bremerton, Washington, where I was stationed on the Olympic Peninsula, developing sonar systems for submarines. Harriet's diagnosis turned our lifestyle inside out. Her chemotherapy took a heavy toll on her and our whole family. I hated to see how sick she became after her treatments. We prayed a lot."

"Were you religious?"

"Until then my religion was science—but a life-threatening illness forces you to question your values. We started talking to God, hoping *someone* or *something* out there would hear us—sort of like SETI sending radio signals out into the far reaches of the universe and hoping for a response.

"Then I was transferred to Norfolk on short notice. I didn't want to go, since our lives had already been severely stressed by Harriet's illness. I fought vehemently against my transfer, to no avail. Within two months we were in Virginia."

"It seemed as if the universe was conspiring to disorient us entirely," Harriet continued, pouring Angelo some more coffee. "We felt lost and bereft. We didn't know anyone here, and I had no idea how long I had to live.

"One morning I felt especially dejected. My doctor told me I'd have to resume chemotherapy, which I dreaded. I pleaded with God, 'If there is any way out of this, please show me.'

"On my way home from the doctor's office I went to a little deli I liked. But that day it was closed for a Jewish holiday. So I walked a few doors down to a luncheonette and had a sandwich. On my way out, as I was rummaging through my purse for some change, I dropped the prescription I had just received. The cashier noticed the doctor's name and asked, 'Are you seeing Dr. Reisman?'

"'I just came from his office.' I told her. As I handed her a ten dollar bill she noticed that my hand was trembling.

"'C'mon, honey, we have to talk,' the cashier said. She got some-one else to take over the register and she walked me to a corner table, where she poured us some coffee. She told me that her name was Marge.

"'I know that Dr. Reisman is an oncologist,' Marge told me. 'So I know what you are going through.'

"'I'm scared,' I told her. I don't know why I would say that to a stranger; I guess I just felt comfortable with her.

"'My son Sean had a terrible case of asthma,' she told me; 'we al-most lost him a few times. Then someone told us about Preston Royce, this psychic who put himself in a trance and knew everything about whoever he was with. We studied his readings and tried some of his remedies on Sean, and he improved almost immediately; hasn't had a bout in years. We became fascinated with the material and got involved with the group.'

"'Has he had any success with cancer?' I had to ask.

"'In some cases, yes.' Marge looked at me compassionately. 'Come with me to my study group Tuesday night,' she suggested. I figured I didn't have much to lose, so I went. At first I thought the stuff was totally weird—past lives, psychic powers, prayer, creating your own des-tiny—but I found it intriguing. I started reading voraciously about al-ternative healing, immersed myself in the therapies, learned to medi-tate, cleaned up my diet, and changed my way of thinking. I've had no trace of cancer for over seven years."

Angelo's mind was churning again. All this metaphysical stuff was coming at him from all angles. Was there no escape? Just as his brain was about to surge into overdrive, his cell phone rang.

It was Claudia. "Angelo, you have to get home immediately!" she blurted out, "Something terrible has happened!"

"What is it?"

"Jesse was riding his bike home from the Sanders' and he skidded on some mud. He wasn't wearing his helmet and he hurt his head—he's pretty dazed. I'm taking him to the emergency room right now. Angelo, I'm worried; when I look into his eyes, he doesn't really see me. You have to get back here right away." Claudia's voice made no secret that she was completely unnerved.

"I'll get the first flight I can in the morning," he told her. "Do your best to stay calm. Call me if you need to, no matter what time."

As he clicked the *end* button, Angelo's gut contracted. Why is all this happening at once, he questioned. Is Jesse's accident some kind of punishment for my encounter with Juliana?

The Piersons could read their guest's concern. "What happened?" Harriet inquired.

"My son's been hurt—a bicycle accident. My wife is taking him to the hospital."

"My goodness, I hope he's all right," Harriet offered. She moved to sit on the arm of Angelo's overstuffed chair, and stretched her arm around Angelo's shoulder. Her touch felt comforting, and Angelo rested his hand over hers.

"I don't get it," Angelo shook his head. "It seems like everything is piling up on me from all angles at once."

"I know the feeling," L.C. responded. He hesitated as if he was wondering whether or not to speak further. Then he continued, "You know, Angelo, maybe something is going on, something bigger than you realize."

"What do you mean?"

"It sounds like synchronicity to me."

"Like *what*?"

"Synchronicity. It's a term that was coined by Carl Jung. It's the idea that everything that happens is connected; everyone we meet and every experience is a piece of a bigger picture, guided not by chance, but purpose."

"Yes," Harriet added. "Like you and me sitting next to one another on the plane. Just consider—of all the flights from Europe to America, and all the passengers on our flight, we ended up as seatmates. What are the chances of that, L.C.?"

"Oh, with about five hundred people on the plane, that would be about one in two hundred and fifty thousand—that's not even considering all the other flights you could have taken."

Angelo just listened; where were they going with this, anyway?

"And then consider the odds of a snowstorm diverting air traffic from Washington to Norfolk. How often does that happen, honey?"

L.C. shook his head. "Maybe one other time in the last ten years." L.C. shifted his position and leaned in toward Angelo. "From a purely scientific angle, the chances of you flying from Israel to San Francisco and ending up sitting in our living room discussing this subject with us, is maybe one in many trillions—like randomly tossing a dart into the sky and having it land on a particular star. No human being could have ever predicted it or set it up."

That's for sure.

"And then remember that you 'inadvertently' brought that magazine downstairs with you."

"Yeah, I have to admit I didn't plan on that; I noticed it only when you mentioned it."

"That's synchronicity," L.C. declared. "Imagine, Angelo, that your soul, or spirit, or self, or whatever you want to call it, chose certain key events you would experience and people you would meet. Then, even while you have been immersed in all sorts of superficial activities, your inner guidance kept you on track with the destiny you chose. *Voilà*, you show up in our living room tonight."

Here we go again. Had Rav Shimon called these people and told them he was coming?

"Then who designed this master plan? God?"

"Yes, but not a God that is separate from you. The God we're talking about is within you."

"I'm not on very good terms with God," Angelo confessed. "The God my parochial school teachers portrayed was pretty fierce. Every time I misbehaved, the nuns made it very clear to me that I was a sinner and would be punished. It's not exactly the kind of example that inspires love of God."

"So you went to Our Lady of Perpetual Guilt, too?"

Angelo laughed. "I guess you could say that."

"Angelo, most of us were taught to be afraid of God. While preachers and teachers tried to scare the hell out of us, they actually scared hell *into* us. If somebody tells you you're evil and guilty long enough, and treats you like you are, you start to believe them. Then you pass the fear onto those who come after you. It's the exact *opposite* of what religion was meant to do."

"We like to think of God simply as the voice of joy that guides you to be happy. The part of you that is God recognizes the part of everyone else that is God."

These people definitely do not have their burritos rolled very tightly, Angelo surmised. Yet in an odd way he was fascinated. "Now I bet you're going to tell me I can talk to Moses."

"You can talk to anyone you want; you are truly unlimited."

Cut the crap, already. Was this some bizarre conspiracy to drive Angelo crazy? Had one of his friends hired Candid Camera to put up the rabbi, the snowstorm, and these people to tweak his reality?

"I know this is going to sound strange, but I met a rabbi in Israel who said that I could communicate with anyone who ever lived, even if they are dead."

"We don't really die, dear; we just change addresses," Harriet added in a matter-of-fact way, as if she was telling Angelo where to find the napkins in the cupboard.

"You know as a scientist, Angelo, that there is so much more going on than meets the eye. In fact, the greatest scientists have been those who were not willing to settle for the obvious, the known, the accepted. They were the ones who busted out of conventional reality so they could discover new possibilities."

Angelo hated when people used science against him, especially other scientists. He was starting to feel irritated. He began to drum his fingers on the armrest.

"Think back just over a century ago, when Bell invented the telephone. The notion of people talking to each other over great distances was as outlandish to that culture as you talking to Moses now. Now telephones, television, faxes, the internet, and e-mail are facts of life, and most people take them for granted. Some people can't live without them."

"Like my niece Susan," Harriet broke in. "She lost her cell phone and I thought she would have a nervous breakdown."

"I think now she has the phone surgically implanted behind her ear," L.C. added. Angelo smiled. L.C. continued, "Not very long ago so much our technology was pure science fiction; in fact, most real science started out as science fiction. Did you know that DaVinci drew sketches of the submarine and the helicopter four hundred years before their invention?"

Angelo was feeling more and more agitated. The last thing he needed were a couple of cult freaks lecturing him on metaphysics—especially when he was worried about going home to an empty house, an absent wife, and an injured child.

"Tell Angelo about the *Dateline* story we saw, dear," Harriet suggested.

"We saw a TV show featuring the futuristic inventions foreshadowed on the original *Star Trek* television series. When that show came out in the late sixties, the writers tried to depict state-of-the-art scientific devices of the twenty-third century. Funny thing is, now, only thirty or so years later, many of the devices are already realities. Millions of people are walking around with flip-phone cellular communicators, medical facilities are using diagnostic instruments similar to the tricorder, and we are already doing 3-D faxing, a step toward beaming people and things around. The time between an idea and its manifestation is getting shorter and shorter; perhaps even in our lifetime we could be conversing with invisibles."

That did it. "Then why don't you and I just invent a telephone to call up the prophets?" Angelo blurted out "We could call it 'The Spook Line,' or 'Dial-a-God.' Maybe they have answering machines up there: *'Hello, this is Jesus; I just stepped out for a moment to cleanse a leper;*

leave me a message and I'll get back to you as soon as I return from my next miracle.'"

The Piersons looked at Angelo with astonishment. He was losing it, but he didn't care.

"Then the phone company could give discounts for calling selected departed friends and family, and we could set up conference calls between Moses, Jesus, and Mohammed to find out who *really* owns Jerusalem. Then we could institute a 900 phone service for guaranteed forgiven Christian confessions, and little Jewish kids could have King Solomon conduct their Bar Mitzvah over the internet. . .I mean, think of it, the possibilities are endless!"

Angelo paced up and back on the braided rug nervously. Finally he turned to the Piersons and told them, "Now if you'll excuse me, I need to be alone."

Chapter 8

Angelo closed the bedroom door behind him, feeling terribly embarrassed for making such a fool of himself. Here these people had been so kind to him, and he just got in their face. He knew the Piersons were well-meaning—deluded, perhaps, but well-meaning.

Angelo fell back on the saggy bed and stared at the ceiling for a while, trying to calm down. Suddenly Jesse's face loomed before him; God, what if he was really hurt? Angelo tried to find some peace in the maelstrom of his gut, but could not. There was no way he was going to sleep now.

He looked down onto the bed near his left hand and saw the copy of *Higher Vision*. *Did I actually carry that back with me? What is my problem, anyway?* He picked up the magazine and continued reading the article he had begun. Perhaps he could get his mind off of what a jerk he had been.

The article quoted several scientists who had tried experiments to substantiate communication with dead people. One in particular caught his eye. Dr. Arthur Dunstead, who had pioneered a company called Super Natural Communication, claimed he had made audio recordings of invisible spirits speaking to living people, and the researchers were on the threshold of capturing video images. *Yeah, right.* As Angelo read on, however, he was impressed by the technical expertise displayed by Dr. Dunstead and his associates. And the name of the company sounded familiar. *Where have I heard that before?*

At the end of the article the author listed a web site for SNC. *Hmmm.* Angelo peered over the ridge of the book to spy the computer on the desk near the foot of the bed. Harriet had mentioned that Terry had gotten her the computer so she could keep in touch with him via e-mail, and that is pretty much all she used it for. I'll bet they wouldn't mind if I logged onto the web for a few minutes, Angelo surmised.

He made his way to the rickety folding chair tucked neatly under the desk, and fired up the Compaq. He found the AOL icon and clicked on it. The familiar annoying raspy sound of the modem filled the room, and soon he was online. Angelo typed the SNC web address. Slowly the data pumped in, and after a minute it all lay before him.

It appeared that these guys had done their homework. The web site was crisp, clear, and attractively laid out. Angelo saw a button marked, "What Started it All" and clicked on that. The page downloaded and he read:

In 1983 Dr. Arthur Dunstead, a physicist, joined a three-month archaeological dig in Nepal and Northern India. There Dr. Dunstead encountered spiritual masters who displayed extraordinary powers. He observed these yogis heal the sick, manifest food and material supplies out of thin air, and display knowledge of events before they occurred. Dr. Dunstead was told these adepts were members of an esoteric order called the Sar-Mun Brotherhood.

One of the yogis, Ram Ananda, offered Dr. Dunstead a private consultation which changed the course of his life. During this strange session the yogi verbalized intimate details about Dr. Dunstead's life, none of which the yogi could have possibly known. Even more astounding was Ram Ananda's knowledge of Dr. Dunstead's deceased parents and his son Randolph, who had died as an infant. For a portion of the interview the yogi served as a vehicle through which Dr. Dunstead was able to converse with his parents and son as if the three were sitting in the very room with him. In the face of his training as a critical scientist, Dr. Dunstead was shaken to the core of his being, and grew determined to understand how living persons could communicate with invisibles. Upon his return from the east, Dr. Dunstead chose to devote the remainder of his life to develop technology that would enable human beings to communicate with those in *the next dimension.*

Angelo whistled aloud, astounded by the similarity between Dunstead's encounter with the yogi and Angelo's meeting with Rav Shimon. Rapidly he clicked on the other pages within the web site. Page after page revealed testimonials from people who had come to the SNC labs and used the technology to converse with their deceased friends and relatives. Some of the conversations had been recorded on digital audio, and visitors to the web site could listen to short clips of some of the conversations. Eagerly Angelo clicked on the icon to hear a conversation, and heard a garbled but unmistakable voice say, "The time has come for us to meet again." Angelo felt a shiver ripple up his spine and he exited the page immediately.

Rattled and embarrassed that he was listening to such drivel, Angelo abruptly arose from the desk and scurried nervously to the bedroom window, where he looked onto the street and pondered the strange information he had fallen upon. He had sat through all kinds of weird movies, but this voice sounded *real.* Angelo composed himself, took a deep breath, ran his hand through his hair, and looked again at the computer, which loomed before him like a slot machine. Well, maybe one more try.

He clicked on several of the less spooky pages on the site, trying to glean some of the physics behind the technology. But the web site was primarily geared to lay people, and the authors made little effort to explain how they did it. Or perhaps the whole thing was a sham.

Suddenly Angelo was jarred by the ringing of his cell phone. He looked at the caller ID. It was Claudia.

"Angelo," she blurted out, "It's me. . .I'm at the emergency room. . .Jesse isn't waking up. . .I'm really scared."

A wave of adrenaline coursed through his system; instantly his neck and back tightened.

"By the time I got him here he was very sluggish; I had to carry him in. He just isn't responding."

"What does the doctor say?"

"He won't say anything. . .They're running tests. Angelo, I can't handle this by myself. You have to get home *now.*"

"Okay, just try and relax. I promise I'll get the first flight I can in the morning. Call me again if you need to."

Angelo sat back in the chair and let his head fall back onto the thick backrest, his mind careening. He tried to take a deep breath. Could the universe possibly pile anything else onto his plate?

In the morning Angelo was awakened by the savory aroma of frying bacon. He got dressed and made his way downstairs. Angelo walked into the kitchen, where he found a huge spread of hot blueberry pancakes, bagels, cream cheese, three types of jam, orange juice, coffee, and a fruit salad. L.C. was reading the morning paper while Harriet stood at the stove turning over the sizzling strips of bacon.

"Good morning," he announced himself, feeling quite self-conscious.

"Good morning, Angelo," Harriet called above the loud crackling at the stove. L.C. smiled and nodded. "Please, sit down," L.C. offered, pointing to a chair at the table.

Quietly Angelo took a seat. "I'm sorry about last night—I was tired and upset."

"That's all right," Harriet answered quickly, without even turning her head. "We know you have a lot on your mind. . .Would you like some cream?"

"Sure, thanks," he answered as he covered his lap with a linen napkin.

Harriet opened the refrigerator and picked out a container of half-and-half. As she set it down in front of Angelo, she read the concern on his face. "Are you all right?" she asked.

"My wife called me late last night . . .My son is in the hospital. . . . He's unconscious."

L.C. put down his newspaper. Harriet turned off the flame and sat down next to Angelo. "What have the doctors said?" Harriet asked.

My Father's Voice

"Nothing. They're doing tests."

"We went through something like this ourselves," said L.C.

"Really?"

"When Terry was in high school he went out with some kids after a football game and got into a bad car crash. He was in the hospital for a week, and his mother and I were pretty nervous. . .We worried ourselves silly, but he weathered the ordeal. Came out of it with a couple of small scars, but nothing serious."

"Somehow kids bounce back from all kinds of injuries," Harriet added. "I'm sure your son will be fine." She smiled as she placed her hand softly on Angelo's.

Angelo took a deep breath and felt his solar plexus let go. His appreciation for these people deepened; he wondered if he had ever known two people who were so generous of spirit. How could they be so kind to him after he had teed off on them?

"You know," L.C. suggested, "Preston Royce did a number of readings for people in co . . . people who were unconscious."

"And what did he say?"

"He said it was a safe place that a person chose to retreat to, like a cocoon, where they could make a decision about their life."

"But Jesse is only six. What kind of a decisions could he have to make?"

"Children have all kinds of things going on inside of them that we adults are not aware of," Harriet suggested. "Is he in any kind of conflict?"

Angelo cringed as he flashed on the times he had come down heavily on Jesse. Now he had been away from his son, halfway across the world, for over a week.

"Who knows?" Angelo answered quickly. "Kids think of all kinds of stuff." Scrambling to change the subject, he announced, "I have a confession to make. Last night I couldn't sleep, so I booted up your computer and surfed the web for a while. I hope you don't mind."

"No problem," answered L.C. "That's what it's there for."

"I found a web site by this guy who claims he has a machine that can communicate with people in another dimension. A bunch of people say they have made contact with the deceased."

"That's pretty good, since a lot of people I know have yet to make contact with the living," L.C. noted dryly.

"Oh, come on, honey," Harriet chastised her husband; "Angelo is being serious."

"Okay, okay."

"Have you heard anything about this machine, L.C.?" Angelo asked.

Without a word L.C. stood up and walked to the bookcase in the living room. He scanned the shelves for a minute, then pulled out a tattered burgundy hardcover volume that Angelo figured was at least fifty years old. L.C. dusted off the cover and returned to the kitchen, where he placed the book on the table in front of Angelo. "Just this," he stated in a serious voice.

Angelo picked up the ancient tome. *Journey Beyond the Known*, by Andre Velanovich. He opened it and began to finger the pages. Lots of physics, technical stuff. "How about a capsule summary?"

"Velanovich was a Russian student of Nikola Tesla—Are you familiar with him?"

Angelo wrinkled his forehead. "Wasn't he a European electronics researcher?"

"That, and much more. Tesla was a full-blown genius and mystic, way ahead of his time. He had an amazing ability to put lofty metaphysics into practical application." L.C. stood up and walked over to the food prep island in the middle of the kitchen. He unplugged the blender, held up the plug and asked, "For example, Angelo, who do you think most people would say is responsible for developing electricity as it is used in the modern world?"

Angelo crossed his arms and leaned back. "Edison, of course."

"That's right—that's what most people would say. But it was Tesla who discovered and developed alternating current electricity. Edison was trying to develop direct current, but AC has far broader applications. Have you ever been to Niagara Falls?"

"Went there on my honeymoon."

"Well, if you go to this park on the New York side of the Falls, just above the largest bank of electric turbines in the world, you'll find a huge bronze statue of Nikola Tesla. If it weren't for his vision and intellectual prowess, you and I might be trying to power our houses on flashlight batteries."

"So what does this have to do with the machine?"

L.C. sat down and set his hand on the book. "In this text Velanovich describes the experiments he helped Tesla conduct on what they called a 'Subtle Image Recorder.'"

"A what?"

"A 'Subtle Image Recorder.' It was a device that could go into any time and place in the past and make a photographic and audio recording of any event."

"Are you serious?"

"Here, see for yourself." L.C. leaned over and began paging through the fragile leaves. After a minute he opened the book flat and swiveled it so Angelo could read clearly:

> Our initial image was that of the building of the Great Pyramid of Giza. This was especially exciting to us, since there has been so much mystery and speculation about how the pyramids were constructed; to this day no one has proven how this great task was accomplished, or been able to replicate it with modern technology.
>
> To our surprise, the photo did not indicate hundreds of thousands of slaves heaving the huge stones with brute strength, as some have suggested. Nor did the photo depict elaborate systems of pulleys and ropes, as others have postulated. To the contrary, the image portrayed perhaps four or five hundred Egyptians, both men and women, surrounding an enormous block and lifting it with: sound.
>
> Yes, these people were using their voices to raise the stone. In addition, a number of individuals were holding wind instruments up to their lips, instruments akin to a modern flute or oboe; some held instruments that were longer and larger, like a bassoon or Australian didgeridoo.
>
> The chanters were standing erect, their hands facing the stone, which incredibly was hovering a few feet off the ground; our photo was even a slight bit blurry, indicating that the stone was clearly in motion.
>
> As we gained an audio track of the event, our assumptions

about the sound element were confirmed. The men were chanting a deep resonant tone, like the Hindu "Om," while the women were emitting a very high pitch. In a similar fashion, the larger instruments generated a low earthy tone, while the smaller instruments were toning a high, shrill sound.

We were most impressed by the focus and reverence demonstrated by the chanters. The expression on their faces was one of utmost intention, and they certainly appeared to be summoning some higher force. I cannot describe the exhilaration I felt upon observing this most historic and illuminating scene.

"That's amazing!" Angelo uttered. "Do you really believe this?"

"It makes perfect sense to me," answered L.C. "Consider what our current technology can do with light and sound. Lasers can restore a person's eyesight in 20 minutes, read a license plate from a satellite, and cut a man down at a distance of a thousand yards. We use sound to clean teeth, change television channels by remote control, run the entire internet, and polish diamonds. If the technology were applied properly, lifting huge objects shouldn't be a lot harder."

"So," Angelo postulated, "this machine would allow you to go into any time in history, see and hear any person who has ever lived, study significant events, and find out what really happened."

"Bingo." L.C. slapped his hand on the table.

Angelo's eyes came alive. "That means that anyone could watch an original Shakespearean play, be there as Van Gogh put the finishing touches on 'Starry Night,' or hear Jesus deliver the actual Sermon on the Mount."

L.C. began to get excited, too. It was the first time Angelo had seem him so animated. "Your son could watch the expression on his grandparents' faces as they stood on the bow of their steamship as it passed the Statue of Liberty welcoming them to America."

"That's incredible!" Angelo proclaimed, drumming his hands on the sides of his chair.

"Oh, it's quite credible," added Harriet as she placed a fresh container of warm maple syrup on the table. "In the eastern tradition it is called the 'Akashic Record'—the sum total of all knowledge and experience that has ever existed and ever will take place."

"And you really believe this?"

L.C. leaned over to adjust the venetian blinds to allow more of the morning sunlight into the kitchen. Then he answered, "Think of it this way: You walk up to an airline reservations agent to check in for a flight. The agent presses the appropriate keys on her computer terminal and *presto*, all the information about not only you and your flight, but every passenger on every flight, is at her fingertips."

"That's how a good psychic can tell you things about your life that they have no other way of knowing," Harriet added. "A clairvoyant has access to the Big Computer."

"So now I suppose you are going to tell me I should find the nearest gypsy fortune teller and have her read my tea leaves, right?"

"Not necessarily," Harriet laughed. She finally sat down with the two men. "Like any profession, there are many different grades and qualities of psychics. Some are bogus or have limited talents, and some are wired to the Mind-at-Large with hardly any interference."

"Like Preston Royce."

"People like Royce are simply making use of the potential we all have. Take *déja vu* for example, the eerie feeling that what is happening now has happened before; you know that the person sitting across the table from you is going to look at her watch, mention that she needs to get home to feed the dog, and then, as she stands up, bump the table and knock the salt shaker onto the floor. In *déja vu* your field of awareness opens up for a brief moment, and your circuitry into the mainframe is activated."

Angelo leaned back and folded his hands behind his neck, elbows out wide. "So if we're so omniscient, then why doesn't everyone remember more?"

"Let me turn the question back on you, Angelo," Harriet answered. "What have you felt when you have experienced *déja vu?*"

"It is exciting, a feeling of great power. But then it's sort of frightening—I don't like being out of control."

"Exactly. Fear causes us to shut down," L.C. explained, taking a final sip from his glass of orange juice. "To reconnect with the Big Computer, we have to walk past our fears and tell the truth about what is happening *inside* of us."

"Okay, then, if we all know so much, why are so many people in so much pain? Why are our lives so broken? Why don't we live what we know?" Angelo leaned back, crossing his arms as if to indicate he was confident that he had made a strong point.

"We are born knowing, Angelo," L.C. answered, leaning in toward Angelo. "Children, until the age of six or seven, are terrifically psychic. Many children have 'imaginary' playmates who aren't so imaginary; sometimes they see departed relatives, angels, or nature spirits."

Suddenly Angelo's face grew soft and childlike. "Now that you mention it, I remember that when I was about five years old, my grandmother died. A few months later I saw her face come to me just before I went to sleep one night; I felt that she was right there in my room with me."

"Did she say anything to you?" asked Harriet.

"She told me she loved me and that she would watch over me. She didn't really speak in words; it was more like thoughts from her mind to mine."

"Did you tell anyone about this?"

"The next morning I told my mom."

"And what did she say?"

"She told me, 'That's nice dear; just don't tell your dad.'"

"And your response?"

"I knew exactly what she meant. My dad had no patience for anything he couldn't touch. So I didn't tell him—or anyone else, for that matter—I didn't want to be a weirdo."

"Did you ever see your grandmother's face again?"

"No."

L.C. took a napkin, dipped it in a glass of water, and wiped down his place mat. "You are a perfect example of a child who was programmed out your natural perceptions. When children are punished for expressing their psychic impressions, they shut down. This world has never treated mystics very kindly." Harriet got up again and brought the remaining dishes to the dishwasher, proving Angelo's theory that she could not sit still more than five minutes.

"Yes," L.C. inserted, "we have access to know everything that God knows because, on the most essential level, our mind *is* the mind of God."

"Now hold your horses right there, Bucko," Angelo interrupted, his chin jutting forward. "People have been burned for less!"

"Of course they have; people who are connected to their higher power are extremely threatening to those who are living superficially. Try Buddha, Jesus, Gandhi, and King for starters—they were all silenced when they made a stand for what they knew. And in the back of our collective psyche we remember the fate historically dealt to those who speak their inner truth. That's why many people, especially women, are so reluctant to disclose their psychic experiences. If in a past life you were burned at the stake for telling your truth, you wouldn't exactly be champing at the bit to tell everyone what you see in their aura."

"So you're saying there's a whole culture of closet clairvoyants walking around?"

L.C. stood up and leaned against the island counter. "We're living in world of wounded souls who have forgotten the power of their own experience," he declared. "If you got most people to relax their defenses, they would privately tell you of their precognitive dreams, past life impressions, unexplainable healings, UFO sightings, visions of angels, or at least the experience of thinking about someone and having that person telephone them shortly after they thought of them."

"You're making our culture sound like *The Emperor's New Clothes*—everyone is agreeing to a big lie, but no one is willing to tell the truth that would expose it."

"That's quite so—but now there's a growing conspiracy to tell the bigger truth—and with the advent of the internet and rapid communication, the tide is turning so that a spiritual reality is becoming more accepted. Angelo, we are in the midst of a huge consciousness revolution."

"Yes," interrupted Harriet. "Just walk into any Borders or Barnes and Noble and you will find that half of the top ten best-selling non-fiction books are about spiritual growth or relationships."

L.C. continued, "The theme for the last thirty years has been, 'no more hiding.' All the unthinkable issues we shoved under the rug for centuries are being held up to the light—child sexual abuse, mental and physical handicaps, political corruption, and the double lives of various gurus, preachers, politicians, and cultural heroes. Consider all the celebrities we have worshiped as gods, only to discover they are human beings with faults and even more problems than us—JFK, Elvis, O.J., Michael Jackson, Princess Diana, Bill Clinton. The intense spotlight on our heroes' humanity has forced us all to become more honest about who we are. Just consider the news reports about Monica Lewinsky's dress; if anybody had dared to talk about the President's semen in public just a few years earlier, it would have been scandalous. Suddenly it becomes table talk for everyone in America!"

Angelo laughed; he had to agree.

"Seriously, Angelo, the more truth we tell, the more psychic we become, until we discover that we are all connected, and we all can know anything there is to know." L.C. grabbed an apple from the bowl near his hand and began to munch on it.

"So how does this machine fit into all of this? And how would it work, anyway?

"As you know, all communication devices capture invisible frequencies of sound or light, and translate them into images that physical eyes and ears can recognize. Just as a television camera records events happening at a far distance, a more subtle apparatus could pick up events happening at a distant time. Such a machine could be attuned to a particular time/space matrix in the past, and like a fax machine or hologram, replicate it on the physical plane."

"If that's true, it would be the most monumental invention in history," Angelo declared. "And this book says that such a machine already exists?"

"*Existed,*" L.C. underscored. "When Tesla emigrated to the United States in 1884, he knew that if he brought the Subtle Image Recorder he would be considered a lunatic, so he left the machine for safekeeping with Velanovich, with the hope that when Tesla had established his reputation in the new world, the machine could be introduced to the public. But the Russian authorities had been monitoring Tesla's work, and when they found Velanovich with the machine they destroyed it and imprisoned him. Several years later he escaped—rumor had it that Tesla's students formed a posse to free him—and he fled to England. There he showed the text to the now-famous Theosophical Society. They realized its huge import and published it."

"Well, then, I'm surprised other people haven't tried to replicate the machine."

"Actually, some have—but they all seemed to mysteriously disappear. Colin Wilcox, the man who translated Velanovich's text, set out to document experiments by several British researchers who got hold of the book, but he hit a dead end every time. It's as if anyone who digs into this, falls into a big black hole and no one ever hears from them again. There's even a controversy over whether Wilcox's death while boating was an accident."

"That's bizarre," Angelo noted. "But I don't believe in this conspiracy malarkey." Angelo reached over and pulled the Velanovich text toward him for another look. He opened up to the dog-eared page about the pyramids and flipped to the next page. There he read:

> *We were fascinated to observe the prevalence of a small symbol which the Egyptians had imprinted on some of their clothing, the musical instruments, and even the pyramid itself. The symbol resembled a star with a white space in the center, overlaid by two intersecting diagonal lines. Below is our best attempt to replicate this obviously important symbol:*

"I've seen that symbol before!" Angelo exclaimed, holding his jaw and cheek with his hand.

"Where was that?" asked L.C.

"I don't remember exactly. Let me think. . ." Angelo closed his eyes, placed his hand over his chin and mouth, and tried to concentrate. L.C. and Harriet waited eagerly for Angelo's response.

"Rav Shimon," Angelo said, opening his eyes and dropping his hand. "That was the symbol I saw on Rav Shimon's wall. I remember it because it didn't look like all the other Jewish symbols. I meant to ask him about it, but I forgot. Do you have any idea what that symbol means?"

"Yes," L.C. answered, "That's the symbol of the Sar-Mun Brotherhood."

Angelo sat up straight and opened his eyes wide. "The Sar-Mun Brotherhood?" Angelo exclaimed. "That's the name I saw on the web site I found last night; it's the order of spiritual masters Dunstead met in Asia."

"Are you serious?" L.C. asked incredulously. The two men locked eyes. A world of communication passed between them without a word. Seconds later, they were on their way up the stairs.

"You go ahead and navigate," suggested L.C. as he sat on the edge of the bed and offered Angelo the desk chair.

"Okay," Angelo answered, "I think I remember the key words." Quickly he typed in "Super Natural Communication." The pair sat and waited for the search engine to scan the World Wide Web. Then a stark message appeared in bold black letters:

The page you requested is no longer available.

"That's weird," Angelo declared. "This is where the page was last night. . . I'll try it again." Quickly he punched in the same search request. Seconds later, the message appeared:

The page you requested is no longer available.

"Try the guy's name," L.C. suggested. "What was it?"

"Dunstead, Arthur Dunstead. Okay, here goes." Angelo typed the name into the search engine and waited. The response came:

No entries were found matching your request.

"I can't believe this!" Angelo complained. "They had a whole site! Now there is nothing—*nada.*"

Feverishly Angelo typed in various spelling possibilities for Dunstead, the company, and any other variation on the theme he could imagine. All yielded the same result. Ten minutes later Angelo leaned back, threw up his hands, and sighed. "I don't get it, I just don't get it."

L.C., who by now was puffing away on his pipe, became very still and looked Angelo squarely in the eye. "Maybe the web site went the way of Colin Wilcox and his predecessors."

"Oh, come on, L.C., you don't give any credence to this conspiracy bullshit, do you?"

"Let's put it this way: In eighteen years of doing classified research for the navy, a number of top secret documents have crossed my desk. Personally, I wouldn't put anything past our government. You've heard about flight 800."

"You mean the TWA flight that blew up just after leaving JFK?"

"That's right. There were quite a few rumors going around, suggesting that the explosion was not a malfunction or terrorist bombing. Pierre Salinger brought forth some documents indicating it was a misfired missile from a nearby U.S. Navy destroyer."

"Well, is it true?"

"Let's just say that there are things going on that most people don't know about. I wouldn't be surprised if that is what happened to your web site."

"So what about this machine? Do you think it could be replicated?"

"Sure, if someone had the balls to have a go at it."

"Well, then, can I borrow your book?"

Chapter 9

As they approached the door to Intensive Care Unit Room 3 at Lucile Salter Packard Children's Hospital, Claudia turned and looked at Angelo nervously. "I don't know if I can do this," she said, her voice on the edge of cracking. "I'm glad you're here. . .for Jesse."

Angelo nodded. He had hoped she was glad to see him. . .for herself.

As the two entered the room, Angelo stopped to gather himself. Claudia hurried to the bed. There lay their son, the bandage on his head covering most of the right side of his face, a few light blood stains seeping through. The boy looked as if he was sleeping. He looked peaceful. Angelo remembered Harriet telling him that when the body sustains a traumatic injury, the spirit removes itself to allow the body to heal. Angelo took comfort in the thought that somehow, somewhere, Jesse might be all right.

The I.C.U. had grown even more complex since the last time Angelo had visited one. Peering through a jungle of plastic tubes, color-coded wires, blinking LCD displays, I.V.'s, and beeping monitors, Angelo wondered how many more machines they could hook up to one patient. Flashing back to his time in Israel, he considered that Jesus had effected many remarkable healings without even one machine. Would science one day come full circle and discover that a focused mind could accomplish all that technology sought to achieve?

A young doctor wearing a white lab coat entered the room. His shiny black hair was combed back neatly, accented by thick eyebrows that almost touched over the bridge of his nose. Not very tall, he wore round silver-rimmed eyeglasses, carried a patient's log, and sported a Ronald McDonald button on his lapel, compliments of the clown who had just visited the third floor. Angelo looked down and noticed he was wearing Reeboks. Somehow Angelo liked him and felt at ease in his presence.

"Hello, Mr. and Mrs. Mann. I'm Dr. Kravitz. I've been evaluating Jesse since he arrived last night."

Angelo felt Claudia's hand grip his arm a little tighter.

"What can you tell us?" Angelo asked abruptly.

"When Jesse fell off his bike he hit the lower back of the right side of his head, which created a bruise on the underside of his skull. In medical terms, it's called a 'subdural hematoma.' In plain language, it's a blood clot on the brain. His comatose state is due to the unusual pressure on his brain and nervous system."

"Comatose?" Claudia blurted out. "Jesse's in a coma?" Her face turned to a shadow as the tears started to flow.

"Yes, Mrs. Mann. Jesse is in a coma."

Angelo's gut began to sink. But he was not surprised. He had a sense this was coming. "What are his chances of regaining consciousness?"

"That's hard to say. Sometimes the body manages to dissolve the clot through its own cleansing processes."

"How long could that take?"

"Usually we see signs within the first 24 hours after the injury. Jesse's been here for about 18 hours and so far he is stable—no worse, but no better. We're watching him carefully. Customarily in a situation like this we would go in surgically and do what we can to ease the pressure. In your son's case, we have an impediment. Here, let me show you."

The doctor guided the worried couple to a small consulting room just down the hall and found a large manila envelope with Jesse's name printed by hand in large thick black letters. The resident carefully pulled out some x-rays and clipped them up against a light screen.

"This dark blotch right here is the blood clot that has rendered your son unconscious. As you can see, it is lodged very close to the spinal cord, almost right where the brain stems into the cord. We can't get to the hematoma without disturbing and probably damaging the spinal nerves, which could leave Jesse partially or fully paralyzed. Surgery in this situation would be just too risky. I'm afraid we have no choice but to just let Jesse be, and hope his body fights off the clot by its own methods."

Claudia, utterly frazzled, squeezed Angelo's arm again and looked at him for reassurance. He tried to give it, but he knew that his wife knew he was as frightened as she was. Where was his ability to fool her when his facade might actually have helped her?

"I can promise you we'll keep a close eye on your son," Dr. Kravitz said. "All we can do now is watch and wait." He paused for a moment and looked both parents squarely in the eyes. Angelo saw that Dr. Kravitz, too, felt more than he was letting on. "I know how hard this must be for you. Page me if you have any questions. I'll be checking on Jesse again in a few hours." Dr. Kravitz offered a small but kind smile and turned to talk to a nurse.

Claudia looked up at Angelo: "What do you think?"

"I think we just heard it from the horse's mouth. We don't have much choice but to wait and pray."

"Did I hear you say, 'pray?'" Claudia asked. "I don't think I've ever heard you say that word before."

"You haven't." Angelo looked down for a moment, then up to her eyes. "Claudia, I've been doing some thinking lately. . .We need to talk. . .about us."

"Oh, please, Angelo, not here. . .not now. Jesse has me so worried that I just don't have any energy to deal with us."

"But maybe we can help each other through this."

"I think it's a little too late for that, Angelo. Where were you when Jesse was up and walking around? At the lab until nine or ten every night. And where were you when Jesse's psychologist wanted to talk to both of us? And where were you when Jesse came home hysterical after some kid punched him in the balls and it took a whole night to convince him to go back to school the next day? Honestly, Angelo, I wish you had thought 'maybe we can help each other' a little earlier than tonight."

Angelo could feel the blood rushing to his neck. "Why do you always have to keep going back to the same things?" he asked. "You know that I have projects with deadlines. I love Jesse as much as you do, but I can't just walk out in the middle of something that's due the next day." Angelo shook his head and threw up his hands in exasperation. "Jesus Christ, Claudia, it's always the same thing, over and over and over. . .I wish you'd just get over it already!"

"I don't have to put up with this, Angelo. Our kid is lying in there half alive . . ." Claudia's voice began to crack as more tears welled up in her eyes. ". . .and you want to talk about our relationship. Please, just do me a favor and keep your distance. I can't handle this now."

Claudia turned and walked briskly to the elevator.

Chapter 10

Coming home to a sparsely decorated apartment was even more devastating than Angelo had imagined. As much as his communication with his wife had broken down, he liked that she was there. It wasn't as if he needed her to cook or iron for him; he just liked knowing that Claudia was in the same place that he was. But now she wasn't.

In the two weeks since Jesse's accident, Angelo became vocationally impotent. He came into the lab a few hours a day, but couldn't concentrate. He would pick up a few papers, look at them, and then look at some more, not doing anything about any of them. Papers, papers, papers. He sat down at his desk and glanced at the spindle next to his telephone. There were at least a dozen messages he needed to return. Inches away his inbox was brimming with correspondence he didn't know when he would get to. He wished he could just let someone else communicate for him. He wished he could just let someone take over his life.

Angelo reached to the intercom and pressed the black *call* button.

"Yes?" Lin's voice answered.

"Do me a favor and hold my calls for now. I have a mountain of stuff to plow through here."

"Check," came the voice.

Angelo reached for the phone and noticed the picture he had kept on his desk for a long time, a photo of Claudia and Jesse and himself at Jesse's kindergarten graduation. God, the kid was cute. And Claudia looked radiant. She was gazing at Jesse with such pride, her arm around Angelo's waist. It was a moment that Angelo cherished, one he went back to when he felt alone. Today, though, he could hardly bear to look at it; both Jesse and Claudia seemed light years away, and he didn't know if he could stand being reminded of the nightmare his life with them had become. Carefully he took the photo and placed it in his lower right desk drawer, the one he hardly ever opened. He closed the drawer.

Through his partially open door he heard Lin's phone ring. "Dr. Mann's lab," she answered in a businesslike way. . ."I'm sorry, Dr. Mann is not in at the moment. May I take a message?. . .Miss Brauer?. . . And how do you spell that, please?"

Angelo picked up the phone and intercepted the call. "That's okay, Lin, I've got it," he told her firmly. . ."Hello, this is Angelo."

"Hello, Angelo," the soft voice spoke. "How have you survived your return to the U.S.A.?"

"Juliana, it's good to hear from you. You sound like you're right next door. Where are you?"

"I'm in San Jose at the Marriott, covering a conference on DSL technology."

"That's not very far from me."

"So, tell me how have you been?"

"To tell you the truth, it's been a wild ride. Lots of changes—sometimes I feel like a little pebble cascading down a huge waterfall. I have no idea where I'm going to land."

"I understand. I really want to hear more about what is happening with you, Angelo. I can't really talk much now; I have an interview in a few minutes."

"Maybe we could meet for a drink or walk."

"I'd like that."

"How about tomorrow night? I could pick you up in the Marriott lobby at, let's say, eight o'clock?"

"Okay, sounds good—see you then."

Angelo placed the receiver back on the telephone and leaned back. He hadn't expected to hear from Juliana so soon. He felt a wave of angst roll through his solar plexus. Am I just digging my trench deeper? he questioned. Yet there was something about Juliana that felt so safe, so soothing, like a quiet park in a huge crazy city.

Alan Cohen

The Marriott lobby was bustling with internet tech heads buzzing with conversations about the latest breakthrough in data rates. Angelo arrived a few minutes early and took a seat on a leather couch facing the elevator, watching each load of passengers pour off in search of one great little restaurant or another. Each time the door opened, his heart jumped into his throat; funny how this woman had him going. The elevator door opened yet another time, and out walked two fellows who worked in the same building as Angelo; quickly he grabbed a magazine and buried his head in it.

Finally she appeared. Even in jeans and a pullover sweater Juliana was radiant; Angelo liked the fact that she could dress to kill in a professional setting, and come off like the girl next door after hours. Angelo rose and took her hands. "It's so good to see you," he told her.

"I'm glad we could meet, too, Angelo. Thanks for coming over." The two embraced (almost too politely, Angelo thought, considering their evening in the park).

"So what do you feel like doing?" he asked as he took her hand and walked her toward the door.

"I'll just let you be my guide."

"There's a great little jazz club a few minutes from here. We could get a few drinks and catch up."

"How did you know I love jazz?"

"I didn't—this just happens to be my favorite place."

Angelo ushered Juliana to his car and opened the door for her. As she slipped into the passenger's seat, Angelo felt a pang in his heart as he remembered when he used to open the door like that for Claudia. Suddenly he heard that voice again, the voice of Rav Shimon, the voice he found both haunting and healing: *"Just deal with what is in front of you."*

The club was dark and smoky, and the two found a table in a quieter area near the back of the room. They both ordered Harvey Wallbangers and leaned in to hear each other. Angelo could almost feel the warmth of Juliana's cheeks.

"So you said you were going through big changes," she said, brushing her hair back with her hand. "Like what?"

"Like my wife and I separated."

"Really?" Juliana wrinkled her forehead.

"Yes, Claudia and I hit a wall. She has to be the stubbornest woman on the planet. And it doesn't help that I am the stubbornest man." Angelo didn't want to make himself look bad, but he wanted to be honest with Juliana.

"Do you want to get back with her?"

"Things are so messed up right now that I can't really see how that would happen. When we first got together we had a great connection, but since we've had Jesse, things have changed. She thinks I'm an irresponsible father." Angelo sighed, looked down into his drink, and then, after a moment of thought, found Juliana's eyes. "I know I haven't been there-as much as I could, but I really do love my son." He took a deep breath. "And something else happened. Jesse was in a bicycle accident and he hurt his head. He's been in the hospital for two weeks. He's unconscious."

Juliana placed her hand on Angelo's arm. "Oh my goodness, Angelo, I'm so sorry to hear that."

"It's been pretty intense; the whole ordeal has put a huge strain on our relationship. Claudia was going to get her own place, but now she says she wants the house for when Jesse comes home. So I took an apartment. It's just a hole-in-the-wall, but it's okay. Now she hardly talks to me at all. Frankly, I think it might be better this way; not talking at all feels better than her criticizing me at every turn. I have a lot of self-confidence when it comes to my work, but with her I feel like a little boy who always just did something wrong." Suddenly Angelo felt vulnerable and self-conscious, and wanted to change the subject. "How about you?"

"I've been terribly busy with work. I don't have much of a social life. I have virtually no friends I can talk to about what I do. I miss that."

"That's exactly what I have missed with Claudia; she has no interest in my work. I come home brimming with excitement about some new discovery, and the most I'll get is, 'that's nice.' But for me it isn't 'nice'—it's *outrageous*. I sometimes fantasize about coming home and talking into the wee hours with a woman who can stretch her mind with me into the unknown."

Claudia held Angelo's eye contact and nodded. My God, she was really *listening*.

The band went into a soulful version of *Unchained Melody*. "It sounds like they've slowed the music down," Angelo noted. "Would you like to dance?"

"I'd love to."

The pair made their way to the crowded dance floor, hot under multi-colored lights. As Angelo drew Juliana to him, he remembered their tender moments at the school and in the park. Her body seemed to fit so perfectly next to his; he was glad the dance gave them an opportunity to touch.

"You're a good dancer," she told him.

"Not bad for a scientist," he answered, smiling.

Juliana snuggled her head into Angelo's shoulder and he held her closer. He could feel himself melting into her. He couldn't remember the last time he felt so at ease with a woman. His brain, which usually rambled at a hundred miles an hour, started to decelerate and he became aware of the changing colors of the lights as they brushed lightly over Juliana's fair skin. As if sensing his gaze, she looked up and their eyes connected. At first he felt a bit self-conscious, wondering if she could see the pain and frustration he had been feeling. But as Angelo forced himself to stay present with Juliana, he sensed that she was not seeing any of that; she seemed to be seeing something good and worthy within him. Angelo felt a huge sense of relief. He felt accepted by Juliana for who he really was. He wanted to kiss her right there, but restrained himself.

The song ended and the two began to walk back to their table, hand in hand. With an impish smile, Juliana told him, "I have to confess I've had some fantasies about you, Dr. Mann."

"Really? What kind of fantasies?"

"I know this is going to sound weird, but. . .sometimes I imagine us. . . working together."

"Whew. . .You had me going for a minute there. . .I thought maybe you were going to ask me to dress up in a lab coat or something."

"No, not for now. . .That's next week," she teased. "But I must admit when I heard you speak at the conference, your flexible concatenation grabs in a sonet frame got me going a bit."

"Well, if you think that's a turn-on, wait until you see my vertical cavity surface emitting lasers with 12-fiber ribbons." Both laughed.

When they arrived back at the table, Angelo held the chair for Juliana to sit. "Seriously, Juliana, I'd be happy to show you what I'm doing in my lab if you like."

"Yeah, right. Do you have etchings there, too?"

"No, but I think you'd be interested in my short-reach optical interfaces."

"Really? I thought you'd never ask."

Angelo flipped the switch and flooded the laboratory with light. The sophisticated electronic equipment seemed to sparkle in a magical way. Juliana's eyes opened wide as she laid eyes on the differential mapping comparator. Like a little girl in a candy store, she moved from workstation to workstation fingering the equipment. "Is this a sonic histogram recorder?"

"Why, yes," Angelo answered, surprised. "How did you know that?"

"I did an internship at Syracuse University," she answered. "We had two sonic parameter mappers which I got to use as part of my senior project; they were just about to come out with the histogram recorder when I left."

Angelo leaned back against the counter, watching Juliana incredulously and shaking his head.

"If I had the time and inclination," Juliana added, "I would do a VR visibility analysis from a multi-camera viewpoint."

"Well, go figure," he responded. "That's a component of the data-flow paradigm grant I just submitted for funding. . .I can hardly believe you know all about this."

"Oh, there are a lot of things about me you would hardly believe, if you knew," Juliana came back coyly.

The pair moved to a counter where Juliana picked up a bitscope driver disk and studied it for a moment. As she placed it back on the table, she fumbled the disk and dropped it onto the floor. "Oh, how clumsy of me!" she exclaimed, embarrassed. She and Angelo stooped at the same time to pick it up, and the two came face to face just below the countertop. They stopped and looked at each other. Angelo leaned over, pressed his lips against Juliana's, and savored their sweetness. She responded and melted into his kiss.

Without opening their eyes or parting lips, the two stood up and embraced. God, it felt good to feel her whole body against his. The two began to breathe together, first slowly, then more rapidly. Spontaneously Angelo lifted Juliana to sit on the countertop and he leaned into her.

"My data rate is increasing, Dr. Mann," she whispered.

"I love it when you talk scientific to me," he answered.

Chapter 11

Thursday afternoon on his way to the hospital Angelo stopped at an offbeat second-hand bookstore in Palo Alto to find out what he could about Preston Royce. While paging through some tattered old texts he came across a book by French philosopher Teilhard de Chardin. The quote on the back cover caught his eye:

> One day, after conquering the winds, the tides, and the waves,
> man will harness for God the power of love, and then,
> for the second time in history,
> he will have discovered fire.

No shortage of fire in my life, Angelo thought as he slipped the book back into its slot on the shelf. He kept searching and finally found a used book by Royce—*More than Meets the Eye*. He looked through the book for a few moments and noticed his watch; he was late. Angelo grabbed the paperback and headed for the checkout. Greeting him was an emaciated young clerk with orange-highlighted hair, a small gold ring piercing his right eyebrow, a tattoo of Sinead O' Connor on his exposed navel, and a huge round name tag button proclaiming, "Hi, I'm Shawn." Angelo glanced furtively out the window to make sure that no one he knew was seeing him, then rushed through the purchase. As he turned hastily toward the door, he bumped into a woman behind him, knocking over the books she was holding. Embarrassed and flustered, Angelo bent over to help her pick them up. He read one title, *The Man Who Saw Afar*.

"Thank you," the woman responded. Angelo breathed a sigh of relief, concerned that she would be justifiably upset.

"What's that book about?" he asked.

"Oh, it's fascinating—it's about Ted Kohler, a man who takes mental pictures of things thousands of miles away."

"Seriously?"

"Yes, he's been tested in laboratories and documented by many authorities."

"How does he do it?"

"He takes a camera with unexposed film, holds it up to his chest, gets an impression in his mind, and concentrates for a few seconds. When the film is developed it contains a photo of what he saw in his mind."

"Is this guy for real?"

"Just look at these pictures." The woman paged through the book and opened to an inset showing two photographs. "The picture on the left came out of his camera after he concentrated," she explained. Angelo studied the photo of an American city skyline. The image was slightly fuzzy, yet all the buildings were unmistakable and defined.

"That's the Chicago skyline," she told him. "So is the one on the right."

Angelo shifted his attention to the opposite photo, which was almost identical. It was clearer and more focused, yet the two pictures were undeniably the same image, taken roughly from the same vantage point.

"Did Kohler take the one on the right, as well?"

"No, that was taken by a Chicago newspaper reporter; it's a real photograph."

"And this man Kohler just produced the photo on the left with his mind?"

"He was in Santa Fe when this picture came off his Polaroid. He had never been to Chicago."

"Excuse me," Angelo said abruptly, and hurried back to the shelves. In short order he returned with his own copy of *The Man Who Saw Afar*.

As Angelo fumbled through his wallet for the second time in five minutes, Shawn pointed to a bowl next to the cash register and invited him, "Go ahead, pick a card."

"Some kind of drawing?"

"No, these are guidance cards; the one you pick will have a message for you."

"Sort of a new age fortune cookie?"

"Something like that."

Angelo, embarrassed to be playing a parlor game, reached into the bowl anyway and pulled out a card. He stuffed it in his shirt pocket and dashed out to his illegally parked car.

Angelo made his way past the fifth floor nursing station where the receptionist, sporting a Santa Claus hat, was opening a box of Godiva chocolates she had won in a grab bag. "Hello, Dr. Mann," she called out. "Hello. . ." he answered, embarrassed that, after coming in nearly every day for three weeks, he still didn't know her name.

On his way down the hall, Angelo looked through the window of a large ward, where he saw half a dozen children being entertained by a petite storyteller in a green tights and a purple elf's costume. Three kids in pajamas were sitting on little chairs on the floor; one little boy lay in bed with his leg in traction, while another, his arm bandaged as if it had been burned, sat up in his bed. The elf approached the bed of a little girl with no hair and her arm hooked up to an I.V.; the elf stroked her forehead, and she smiled. Angelo felt touched when he considered the elf's gift to the kids; then he started to contract as he realized Jesse was unable to enjoy such a show.

He walked into Jesse's room and saw Claudia sitting in the chair where she always sat, reading and looking up every few moments in hopes her son would show some sign of life.

Angelo walked to the night table and placed an Obi-Wan Kenobi action figure next to the Luke Skywalker and Darth Vader figures already there.

"Another one?" Claudia asked.

"It's Hanukah. Jewish kids get a present every night; why not

Jesse? He'll be surprised when he wakes up."

As he set the legs of the figure so it would stand up, Angelo remembered the afternoon Jesse had put a rubber Spiderman in the blender and ruined the blades. He could see Jesse's shocked face as his enraged father cast the mess at him and told him he had just lost his allowance. Now he looked at his son's ashen face and limp form and felt like an utter idiot for making a kitchen appliance more important than his child.

"Dr. Kravitz wants to talk to us," Claudia reported. "He asked me to have him paged when you got here."

Angelo nodded, reticent to make any conversation other than what was necessary. He knew that the slightest provocation could ignite an argument.

But Claudia spoke: "I hope this doctor knows what he's doing. He does look young."

"I sort of like the guy," Angelo responded. "He seems to be on top of things."

"Maybe we should—"

Claudia was interrupted by Dr. Kravitz entering the room. "Hello, Jesse's parents," he greeted them with a slight smile. "Let's take a little walk."

The doctor ushered the couple to a lounge at the end of the hall. Angelo was pleased to find a coffee dispenser, where he drew a cup for himself and Claudia. The two sat on an uncomfortable couch while the doctor took a seat in a chair facing them.

"Mr. and Mrs. Mann," Dr. Kravitz began, "I know you are very concerned about Jesse. We've been keeping careful track of his condition which, as you know, has changed very little since he first came to us. I know how hard it is to watch him and not know if or when he will wake up. I can—"

"Get to the point, doctor," Angelo interrupted coarsely. "What is really happening?"

"Unfortunately, we don't know much more than you at this point. A coma is still in many ways a mystery to the medical profession. For some reason the patient stays in a state of limbo for what could be a very long time."

"What are his chances of coming back?"

"We can't say exactly. I would say that if we do not see any signs of improvement soon, he may remain like this indefinitely."

Claudia winced and began to weep. Angelo leaned over and put his arm around her; he was surprised she did not push him away. The doctor reached into the flowered Kleenex box on the coffee table, and handed her a tissue.

Angelo felt helpless. God, how he hated to be out of control, powerless. His thoughts raced to the last time he had seen Jesse, when he was leaving for Israel. Running late, Angelo hardly said good-bye; he gave a hurried wave as he stepped onto the shuttle bus. Now how he wished he had taken the time to give the kid a hug.

"The hospital runs a support group for families in your position," Dr. Kravitz said. "You might want to give the facilitator a call. She's—"

"Come on, doctor," Angelo broke in. "Level with us, would you? Tell us if our son is going to wake up!"

Claudia grabbed Angelo's arm. "Angelo, please. . ."

"Quit beating around the bush, would you? You've seen enough coma cases to know what's going on. We don't want to be shuffled into some weepy-waily support group with a bunch of sniveling parents singing 'poor me' on command. Just lay it on the line, doctor. Should we leave Angelo's Christmas presents out, or are we going to be tramping in here for the next twenty years, foolishly hoping we'll see the color in his eyes again? Why the hell can't you just cut the bullshit and tell us the truth?"

Angelo turned his head away and nervously scratched the side of his neck. Claudia, though used to Angelo's outbursts, still looked embarrassed when he flew off the handle in public.

Dr. Kravitz remained cool. He lowered his head a bit and lifted his right hand as if to say, hold it. "Mr. Mann. . .Angelo," he spoke calmly. "I know this is a terribly trying time for you. Believe me, if I knew more, I would tell you. One thing I will tell you: I don't pull punches; this morning I had to tell the young mother of an only child with leukemia that this would be her daughter's last Christmas. Do you think that's easy?"

Angelo nodded his head; he was listening.

"If I had to take a guess I would say your son has a fifty percent chance of recovery. Beyond that I cannot and will not play God. We'll just have to watch and wait."

Angelo hated that word; he was never good at waiting. He always felt impugned when someone suggested he should.

"I would like you to consider this support group; you're not the only ones in this predicament. If you'd like the number, I can give it to you."

Angelo looked at Claudia for some kind of response. Her tears had abated, but her eyes were still red and wet. She nodded.

"Okay," Angelo responded, "Sorry about my barrage; when I feel helpless, my MO is to attack."

"I understand." Dr. Kravitz reached into his jacket pocket for his pen, but discovered he had left it at the nursing station. Angelo reached for his own and gave it to him. With the pen emerged the card he had picked up in the bookstore. As Dr. Kravitz scribed the phone number, Angelo read the card:

Do not be fooled by appearances.
Trust your hopes, not your fears.

Chapter 12

He sat in the chair opposite Jesse's bed and opened the book he had borrowed from L.C. Angelo felt anxious about what he might find. This metaphysical stuff was starting to sound plausible, and although he would not have admitted it to the Piersons, a lot of what they said made sense. On some level Angelo knew that if he got into this material, it might overturn his entire belief system, and he was having a hard enough time dealing with the changes already on his plate. Already his laboratory projects and his conversations with his fellow scientists felt boring, a waste of time. Angelo felt adrift in a huge unknown sea. If it weren't for his daily e-mails with Juliana, Angelo might have felt utterly lost.

As he opened to the table of contents, a nurse entered the room. "Good afternoon, Mr. Mann," she greeted him. "Reading anything interesting?"

"I'll let you know if I understand anything," he quipped.

"Is your wife still here?"

"No, she left. We're. . .We're on different schedules."

"Now that you mention it, I don't think I've seen you here much together."

Angelo said nothing and went back to reading. *The Subtle Image Recorder: Cases and Applications.* That sounded interesting. He opened to page 183. Velanovich, though scientifically deft, droned on and on about a case he had observed, in which a man made contact with his deceased grandfather, including numerous details about his grandfather's home and his family relationships. Okay, already, Angelo thought, losing interest as he went. The warmth in the room was starting to get to him, compounded by the weight of lunch in his belly. Before long Angelo started to fade, half reading and half dozing.

As if looking through a foggy window, Angelo saw the word "coma." That got his attention. He sat up with a start and began to read:

Contact with a Coma Patient

On September 17, Mr. George Petrovsky, a friend of Mr. Tesla, asked if he could employ the Subtle Image Recorder to attempt contact with his elderly father, Sergei, who, after contracting an unidentified virus, had fallen into a coma. At the time, Sergei had been in a comatose state for approximately one month. As Mr. Tesla had not previously considered this application of the device, he deemed this a worthy experiment, as well as a potential service to his friend, and granted Mr. Petrovsky use of the apparatus.

To the surprise of Mr. Tesla, Mr. Petrovsky was able to engage in a direct communication with his comatose father. In spite of the fact that Sergei Petrovsky lay inert in a bed, utterly unable to communicate with anyone physically, he was fully conscious on a spiritual level and, via the Subtle Image Recorder, participated in an animated conversation with his son. The following is an excerpt from the recording:

George Petrovsky: Father, I want to communicate with you.

Sergei Petrovsky: And I with you.

George: Can you hear me?

Sergei: Yes, very well. I am very pleased that you are able to speak to me in this way.

George: Father, where are you? What kind of place are you in?

Sergei: I am in my place, son. I am in a good place. You need not fear for me. I am resting.

George: Is there any way I can help you? Can I do something to revive you?

Sergei: No, and you need not. I have chosen this experience for a purpose. I am preparing to go on.

George: You are going to die?

Sergei: I am old and I have done all I wish to do. Please do not hold on to me. Let me go.

George: *Then why did you not simply pass on? This coma is a torture for our family.*

Sergei: *I am sorry if I cause you any pain. I needed this time to think about what I wanted to do. I am ready to go on.*

Sergei: *We will miss you very much.*

George: *I will still be with you. Are you not communicating with me now?*

Three days later, Sergei Petrovsky died peacefully.

Angelo clamped the book closed. "It wasn't an accident" he whispered aloud. *This machine is how I will contact Jesse.*

Angelo marched into his office, smiled at Lin as she talked on the phone, and slid his arm across her desk, scraping all of her papers into the trash can. Lin gasped, then began to stutter and sputter, "Uh. . .Ah. . .Could I please call you back, Mrs. Bouchard? Something just came up here that I need to handle immediately. . .Yes, thanks a lot, I'll get right back to you."

Lin banged the phone down and asked, "What the hell are you doing?"

"I want you to scrap those projects."

"What are you talking about? Have you gone completely insane?"

"No, my dear, I am approaching sanity—for the first time in a long time."

"Angelo, would you please explain what is going on here?"

"This, my dear, is our new project. First priority." Angelo threw a book down on her cleared desktop.

"'*The Man Who Saw Afar?*'—'*Capturing Remote Vision on Film?*' Angelo, what's gotten into you? Did you shack up with Shirley MacLaine this weekend?"

"No, I shacked up with myself."

"Oh, that explains it. Now would you like your latté? Come on,

Angelo, let me in on what you're up to—I may be a lowly r.a., but I still have a right to some human dignity."

"I want you to find the author of this book and get me a meeting with him ASAP. Then I want you to get copies of every book and article he makes reference to. And then every book and article the references refer to. Put everything else on a back burner until I find out everything I need to know about Ted Kohler and how he develops pictures with his mind."

"But the Garrison report is due by the first of the year. Donnely's been breathing down my neck to make sure we're going to comply. If we don't keep hustling on that paper, there's no way we're going to meet the deadline."

"I don't care—tell them anything. The whole experiment is bullshit, just another clever ruse to keep their Defense Department contract on life support. The primary purpose of that project is to keep their CEO in six figures."

"Why are you so interested in this new age stuff all of a sudden?"

Angelo leaned over and stared Lin in the eyes, his nose inches from hers. "Lin, there is something I need to find out. If my hunch is correct, it could change my life forever—and who knows, maybe even alter the course of life on the planet. If not, I'll go back to kissing Garrison's ass. For now, my hunch is infinitely more interesting. Wanna play?"

Lin held his stare. Slowly her lips turned into a slight smile and she nodded. "Okay, I'm game. If you go down, life won't be very interesting around here. Besides, Garrison's a big bore and Donnely is the Anal Retentive Poster Boy. At least you're fun—compulsive, maybe, but bearable."

He floored the gas pedal of his rental car and pulled as quickly as possible onto the on-ramp on the northbound lane of I-17. Lin had not been able to secure an appointment with Kohler, but she had located the small institute Kohler had founded on the north side of Phoenix. Angelo fought his way through massive highway construction and arrived at the office around 4:30. There he found a plump, conservatively-dressed middle-aged secretary with henna hair, shutting down her computer.

"I'm looking for Ted Kohler," Angelo told the secretary without introducing himself.

"I'm sorry," the woman answered mechanically, "Mr. Kohler won't be back until next week."

"Would you mind telling me where he is?"

"He's up in Sedona on a personal retreat."

"Is there any way I could see him?"

"I'm afraid not—he's given me strict orders not to disturb him."

Angelo bit his lip and thought for a moment. "I see. Would you mind if I looked through some of your literature?"

"I'll be closing in just a few minutes."

"That's okay—just kick me out when it's time."

"Suit yourself."

Angelo turned to a shelf displaying a half-dozen different pamphlets describing classes offered by the institute, and paged through them nonchalantly. When the secretary got up to take the trash can down the hall, Angelo scurried to her desk and began feverishly flipping through the Rolodex. *K. . .K & J Carpet Cleaning. . .Klaus, Anne Marie. . .Krusnik, Henry, Attorney-at-law. . .*"Damn—no 'Kohler,'" Angelo muttered. He looked down the hall; the secretary had dumped the garbage and she was halfway back to the office. He had about thirty seconds. Think, man, think. . .

Angelo's eyes shot to a photo of Kohler on the wall behind the desk. "To the best staff in the world. Thanks for a great job!—Love, Ted."

Love, Ted . . .Ted . . ."—T!"

Ravenously Angelo picked through the Rolodex. *Tamblin, Charles, CPA. . .Telephone Repair. . .Ted, home.* "That's it!". . .No, it was a Phoenix address. . .Next card. . .*Ted, Sedona. . .37 Painted Wagon Drive.* Bingo! Angelo grabbed a pencil and began to scribble the address on the brochure he was holding. Then he heard the sound of the secretary's heavy gait as she approached. He grabbed the Rolodex card, tore it out of the holder, and slipped it into his hip pocket just as the secretary trudged through the door. Quickly he turned back toward the rack and tried to assume a nonchalant posture.

"Well, thank you very much; I guess I'll stop back another time," he told her as casually as possible. Damn, I'm good—should have been an actor, he silently complimented himself.

"All right, have a nice day."

Angelo had heard about Sedona from his nephew Scott, who had worked at a resort there. *Enchantment* was a posh retreat nestled (to the chagrin of Native American sympathizers) in the heart of sacred Indian land. Scott used to rave about the massive red rock formations towering over the town. Reports were that UFO's regularly buzzed the area; even the saltiest old ranch owners had become believers. Angelo had written it all off as hogwash; now he was beginning to wonder.

He arrived after dark and, tired from his journey, pulled into the Bell Rock Motel and got a cheap room. After downing a couple of raunchy tacos at a Mexican dive next door, he grabbed a handful of rack cards describing local tourist attractions and headed for his room. After stripping to his underwear Angelo opened a can of beer, turned on the TV, and with half a mind began to read the rack cards.

Apparently this place was a Mecca for psychics, channelers, religious zealots, crystal aficionados, extraterrestrial abductees, and assorted weirdos. The big attraction was an array of natural vortexes, or energy power points, at half a dozen huge rock formations around the town. Several makeshift companies offered vortex tours, the most prominent of which was the *"Indy Jones Vortex Adventure."* For just $35 an experienced "sensitized" guide would escort you and your party to most of the major vortexes at which you could "align with the mystical power." Angelo hummed a few bars of *The Twilight Zone* theme, smiled, and cast the advertisements into the wastebasket. If only Claudia could see him now.

Ah, Claudia. The woman he once thought to be the love of his life, was fading quickly, becoming untouchable. Is there any reason to hang in there, or am I just hitting my head against a brick wall? And Juliana—could the universe have sent her as a comforting angel to give my life hope and meaning through this crazy time? God, I feel like I love her. But Jesse is my priority now, Jesse is my priority.

Angelo promised himself he would get up and brush his teeth, but, so exhausted he could hardly move, he surrendered his head to the cheap foam pillow. Shortly he was transported to a field behind the house he grew up in, where he saw Jesse playing in the high wispy grasses. Suddenly the earth began to rumble, and everything trembled; the trees, the old wooden fence, even the rocks at the base of the ravine quaked wildly.

Below Jesse's feet a huge crevasse began to open along the entire length of the field. It was widening rapidly, and within moments the boy would have to jump to one side or the other. Behind Jesse stood an old man with a red face and white stubble—Lorenzo. He was screaming at Jesse, chastising him for all the things he had done wrong, berating him for everything he was not. Lorenzo's voice became so piercing that the child covered his ears, cowered, and began to cry. The earth beneath Jesse was starting to give way, and the boy had to either jump to the ground where Lorenzo was, or leap into the dark chasm and face oblivion. Then the intensity of the scene escalated—the rumbling, the old man's horrible shrieking, and the widening gap that made it impossible for Jesse to remain where he was. Everything in the universe was forcing Jesse to choose; there was no other alternative.

Angelo awoke screaming, sweat covering his face. He felt the terror of his son's plight. The boy had nowhere to turn and no one to help him; the child was being torn apart like a wishbone.

Angelo forced himself out of bed. He staggered into the bathroom to splash the perspiration off his brow, and looked out the window. Beyond a closed Jack-in-the-Box and Exxon station across the road, all was pitch black.

He began to think about his dream. Why was his father chastising Jesse? Lorenzo had died the year before Jesse was born. Was he haunting his grandchild from the grave, as he had haunted his own son in life? And what was on the other side of the abyss? Would Jesse do better to jump?

Angelo tried to go back to sleep, but couldn't. The dream had been too real, too alive, too close to home. He feared that if he closed his eyes again he would return to the quake and Lorenzo; yet part of him wanted to continue so he could conquer the demons, or at least understand the symbols. But there was no going back; his mind and gut were too agitated. He looked at the blue numbers on the clock, piercing the dark. 3:30. What the hell, he thought. I'll get a head start on the day.

A hot shower soothed Angelo's neck and shoulders; yesterday's flying and driving had twisted his upper torso into one massive knot. Then the water temperature kept turning from hot to cold and back again. So much for the Bell Rock Motel.

He stepped in front of the mirror to shave. After filling the basin with hot water, Angelo lifted the blue plastic razor to the lower left side of his neck, the place he always began. But when he looked in the mirror, the whiskers he was shaving were white. He squinted and looked again; maybe it was just the play of the cheap fluorescent light. But the bristles were still white. "What the hell—?" he muttered aloud. Angelo had some gray hair over his temples, but his beard was still black—or so he thought. He looked again, and this time he saw not his face, but Lorenzo's. Gasping, he dropped the razor in the sink and started to turn away. But after a moment's thought, he forced himself to keep looking, staring intently into the eyes.

Then Angelo Mann beheld his worst nightmare: he could no longer tell the difference between his father and himself. He had become the man he despised. Every ounce of his father's venom and vindictiveness coursed through his own veins. It was not Lorenzo who tortured Jesse, as the dream had suggested—it was Angelo. It was his own rage that had pushed his son into the pit, perhaps never to return.

"No!" he shouted with the fury of an angry bull, cornered and piqued. He picked up his shaving kit and hurled it at the mirror, cracking it into a spider web pattern. "Shit!" he grunted as he thought, *There is no escape from him. He is in me. The one I most fear, the one I most hate, walks as me.*

Then Angelo began to sob. Like a warrior spent after a long and frustrating campaign, he sat naked on the edge of the seedy bathtub and cried like a baby for a long, long time.

Chapter 13

A single finger of pink light found its way through the louvered glass over the toilet and brightened a small patch of discolored ivory tile on the bathroom wall. As the warmth of the sun penetrated Angelo's chilly crucible, he realized that he had finally faced the invisible vampire that had sucked his life force nearly to the bone for most of his stubborn life. He had allowed himself to feel all the loathing for his father that he had stuffed in his gut and turned against himself. Angelo realized that he had never escaped Lorenzo's wrath by hating him; instead he had recreated it and passed it along to his own child. He felt crushed, sick with hypocrisy, and utterly alone. Not once had he seen his son as he was, without the heavy shroud of resentment he carried toward Lorenzo. For all the time he had spent with Jesse, he did not know who the boy was; for all the times he had told Claudia he had loved her, he did not know her; for all the times he had looked in the mirror, he had never seen himself.

Spent, purged, and dazed, Angelo stood up to look in the mirror again. He started to turn away to avoid Lorenzo's visage, but suddenly he realized that something was different. This time he saw his own face. He saw the wounded boy he had denied, the child that dreamed and trusted. He saw the boy who could put his head in his mother's lap and let her comfort him. He understood that his presentation was but an empty fortress, a bullying defense, the rampage of a wounded wolf. He saw how much of his life he had spent trying to distance himself from his father, meanwhile binding himself to the very thing he resisted. Every time he reenacted his father's abuse, he brought history to life and made it ruler of the future. What frightened Angelo the most, however, was the knowledge that—if he lived—Jesse would continue the dark cycle unless something radical happened.

Then Angelo thought he could see another face in the mirror, hovering over his shoulder. He turned with a start, but found no one there. Again he peered into the looking glass, at the face of Rav Shimon.

"It was only natural," he heard the rabbi speak.

"Natural?"

"It was only natural for you to develop a thick hide," the rabbi reiterated. "You lived under a constant siege. You had to protect yourself."

"Yes. . ." Angelo whispered.

"But the real you has not died," Rav Shimon explained; "It has just been buried. You are innocent, Angelo. You must know that. You are innocent."

"I am innocent," he repeated, dazed.

He looked in the mirror again and saw his face as a little boy. He hadn't looked upon that countenance in a long time, except in a few old family photographs.

"Jesse is your key,' the rabbi said.

"What do you mean?"

"He is your innocent self in a form you can look at, speak to, touch. He is who you were before you learned to protect yourself. . . and everything you can become if you decide to drop your mask. He is your childhood revisited, a second chance to forgive what you have condemned and free what you have imprisoned. Free him, and you will free yourself."

Rav Shimon's countenance faded, and Angelo again saw only his own face.

Chapter 14

He grabbed a cup of coffee at the Circle K on the corner and bought a street map of the town. Painted Wagon Drive was on the north side of the main strip, about fifteen minutes from the motel. Angelo threw his overnight bag into the trunk and turned left out of the parking lot onto Route 119.

As soon as he pulled onto the highway Angelo beheld a sight that practically knocked him over. It was not so much the scene as the feeling. A few hundred yards down the road towered a massive rock formation in the shape of a giant bell. Angelo was so stunned by the energy emanating from the structure that he slowed almost to a stop, craning his neck to get a full view. Within seconds a piercing honk from the car behind him jarred him, and he pulled onto the shoulder.

God, the thing was amazing—it looked like a gigantic sculpture. Was it really a natural formation? Angelo got out of the car and leaned against the passenger's door, trying to take it all in. A few hikers were making their way up a trail on the east face. The morning sun was beginning to bear down on the formation, highlighting the deep red even more dramatically. Angelo had never seen or felt anything so overwhelming.

He stayed at Bell Rock for about fifteen minutes, then reminded himself that he was on a mission—he had to catch Kohler before he went out for the day. Continuing through the heart of Sedona, Angelo laid eyes upon even more formidable red rock spires, close to town and at a distance. He realized why so many people were drawn to this place and wished he had time to explore.

Angelo found Painted Wagon Drive easily enough. Despite its

mushrooming fame and rampant development, Sedona was comprised of a surprisingly small number of streets. Kohler's house was a small gray ranch with a black shingled roof. A rusty blue Ford Explorer sat in the driveway while a wood-colored Ridgeback lazed in the sun next to a small bed of thirsty Desert Verbena.

Angelo parked across the street, shut off the engine, and took a deep breath, hoping Kohler would be willing to see him. He was just about to tug on the car door handle when the front door of the house opened and a man walked out. It was Ted Kohler, the man who saw afar. He looked older than his picture on the book; his hair was thinner, his face more drawn. But it was him nonetheless.

For some reason Angelo stopped in his tracks. He had an urge to override his hesitation and accost Kohler, but he decided to sit tight. He watched Kohler get into the Explorer and pull out of the driveway. Without thinking, Angelo turned on his engine and followed him. "I'm becoming a friggin' spy," he mumbled aloud, shaking his head. Suddenly Angelo wondered what Juliana would say if she saw him now—would she be proud, or laugh?

The Explorer rambled down the hill and turned left onto the main drag; Angelo stayed close on Kohler's tail. After a few stoplights the truck turned into the parking lot of a restaurant called *The Coffee Pot*. Angelo followed suit. The lot was so crowded that Angelo had to drive around the back for a parking spot. Why was this restaurant so popular?

Kohler approached a table near an outdoor courtyard, where a man and woman were waiting for him. Both rose, the man shook Ted's hand, and the woman gave him a friendly hug. The group sat down and began conversing intently.

Angelo took the only open table with a view of Kohler. A harried young waitress tossed a menu onto Angelo's table and told him she'd be right back. *"The Coffee Pot,"* Angelo read, *"Home of the Famous 101 Omelets."* Angelo was astounded to count exactly a hundred and one omelets on the bill of fare, many of which defied his imagination, from peanut butter and jelly to asparagus, imitation crab, and Swiss cheese. He ordered a guacamole, sour cream, and hot chili omelet. "When in Rome. . .," he told himself.

The tables were so crowded together that Angelo could overhear several nearby conversations. The couple next to him was debating the merits of tantric sex, whatever that was, while the two men on the other side were discussing the energetic qualities of a mineral called Moldavite. Many of the customers were alternative culture types, with long hair and casual dress. Angelo thought of the bar scene in *Star Wars.* "I don't think we're in Kansas anymore, Toto," he whispered audibly. In another booth he saw a few conventional-looking couples, obviously older tourists on vacation, and he felt a little safer.

A fair-skinned man with long sandy hair in a pony tail sat down at an electronic keyboard and began to play some soft instrumental compositions. "Bubble music," Angelo assessed the set, which reminded him of the subtle music wafting amid blinking neon lights through the underground walkway at O'Hare Airport in Chicago. In spite of its hippie nature, Angelo found the music soothing, especially after the catharsis he had undergone during the night. When the keyboard player offered his rendition of the theme from *Close Encounters of the Third Kind,* he received a loud round of applause. "Definitely not Kansas," Angelo said under his breath again, all the while keeping a close eye on Kohler and his party.

By ten o'clock Angelo had heard enough bubble music to cushion him through every airport in America for a lifetime. That was when Kohler's friends rose and made their exit. Now was his chance.

As Kohler was leaving a five dollar bill for the tip, Angelo approached him. "Excuse me, aren't you Ted Kohler?"

Kohler looked up and nonchalantly answered, "That's right."

Go ahead, spit it out. "I'm wondering if I could have a few minutes of your time."

"Actually, I'm on a personal retreat and I'm not seeing anyone until I go back to Phoenix next week. Perhaps you could make an appointment with my secretary."

"I don't mean to bother you, Mr. Kohler, but I have come all the way from San Francisco to see you—it's very important."

Kohler thought for a moment, then reclaimed his chair. He motioned to Angelo to have a seat. Angelo grabbed it quickly.

"Mr. Kohler, I'm aware of your work and I have some information that I think could take what you are doing to the next level. . . and possibly alter the destiny of this planet."

"No small proposition—shoot."

"Are you familiar with the book, *Journey Beyond the Known?*"

"Read it years ago."

"Then you may remember Andre Velanovich's reference to the Subtle Image Recorder."

"Yes, but as I recall, there was no real information about it; most people claimed it was just a theory or hoax or wishful thinking."

"Mr. Kohler—Ted—Some friends and I are interested in developing that device; we believe we have the technology and expertise to do it."

"What are your credentials?"

Angelo reached into his wallet, pulled out a business card, and tossed it onto the table in front of Kohler. It landed neatly on an angle just under Abraham Lincoln's face on the bill. Angelo wondered if it was a synchronicity that Lincoln was one of the historical figures he hoped to contact.

Kohler fattened his lower lip, raised an eyebrow, and murmured, "Hmmm."

"These are my colleagues." Angelo reached into his wallet again and tossed out the cards of Avi Goldman and L.C. Pierson. Suddenly Angelo thought that maybe he should talk to Avi and L.C. before committing them, but he wasn't about to tell that to Kohler now.

Kohler raised his eyebrow again. "No meager lineup. What makes you think you can pull this off?"

"You do."

"Me?"

"If you can record still pictures of objects a thousand miles away, moving pictures are the next step. And if your mind can transcend the limits of space, time should not be a barrier either."

"Keep talking."

"I met a Kabbalistic scholar who displayed the most extraordinary wisdom," Angelo explained. "He said it would be easy. He said we already have the technology; now all we need is to believe it is possible."

Kohler pondered for a moment, then said in a matter-of-fact

voice, "Let's take a ride." He motioned toward the door, and before Angelo could make sense of what was happening, he was sitting on the torn bench seat in Kohler's funky old truck, bouncing west on Route 89, toward God only knew where.

Ten minutes outside of town the Explorer turned left and pulled onto a scenic overlook with a clear view of an impressive formation Kohler called "Cathedral Rock." Instantly Angelo was awed by this colorfully sculpted spire hovering over the entire southwest portion of the town. Ted told Angelo this was the vortex where he felt the most energized and came to do his best thinking. Angelo was so stunned by this huge natural monolith that he had a hard time focusing on Kohler.

"Why do you want to do this?" Kohler asked. "Profit factor? Fame?"

"No, I am already well known and well paid." Angelo kept talking as the two looked straight out at Cathedral Rock. "My six-year-old son is in a coma, utterly incapacitated. I need to be able to communicate with him. There are things I have to say to him that could make the difference between whether he lives or dies. If this machine can help me contact him, it would be worth everything I own and know."

Angelo paused, turned to the man who saw afar, and looked him squarely in the eye. "Look, Mr. Kohler, I hardly know you, and as far as you know, I could be just another fruitcake. But I know that when I saw your book I felt utterly compelled to find you. I believe you have the power to help me."

Without a word Kohler walked to his truck and returned with a Polaroid camera. He grasped it in both hands and asked Angelo, "Where did you grow up?"

"Boston, mostly."

Kohler held the camera in front of his chest just below his chin, closed his eyes, and concentrated. Suddenly the wind intensified and whipped up so adamantly that Angelo had to hold down his wind-breaker to keep it from flapping against his head. Then, just as quickly as it had surged, the gust died down and left the pair in an eerie silence.

Kohler pressed a button on the Polaroid, and a white photo template whirred out of the camera's underbelly. He tore it off and gave it to Angelo, who watched it develop. Over the course of a minute a form began to emerge. Angelo studied the film intensely to see if he could identify the image. As the lines and colors defined themselves, he began to recognize it vaguely, but couldn't place it exactly. Then it became clear—Boston Common.

A chill ran up Angelo's spine. "That's incredible!" he exclaimed. "How did you do that?" The scientist's mind began to run wild. He wondered if Kohler had pre-loaded the camera, or somehow known Angelo was coming. Maybe Kohler's secretary had figured out that Angelo had stolen Ted's Rolodex card and phoned ahead. But then she had no way of knowing he grew up in Boston. In about five seconds Angelo's mind tested every possible theory and explanation, then shorted out.

"All minds are connected," Kohler explained dryly. "Everything that has ever been seen, felt, or known by anyone—or ever will be—is available to everyone. It's the Mind of God."

"You mean the Akashic Record?"

"Exactly. When I concentrate, I open myself to the subject matter you suggest. If anyone has ever seen the object on which I place my attention—even in their imagination—I can see and record it."

"So if someone has ever registered the image of Boston Common in their mind, you send a mental pipeline to them and draw from their experience?"

"Something like that. You could also think of it like the probes NASA sends out into space to photograph the moons of Jupiter, for example. The probe receives a visual impression, translates it into radio signals, and transmits the image back to the command center, which interprets the signals and regenerates the picture." Kohler paused as he gazed out over the panorama before them. "Scientific inventions simply replicate our natural faculties. We have invented devices to do for us what we are capable of doing for ourselves with no instrumentation. One day we will throw away all the machines we have manufactured to substitute for our innate abilities, and live from our inner power, not external objects."

As Ted finished the thought, a dark green Aerostar van pulled up to the lookout. A healthy-looking couple with two blonde children emerged and began to savor the view. The father, a young Robert Redford look-alike, hustled back to the van, returned with a camcorder, and began videotaping his wife and sons standing before the backdrop of Cathedral Rock. As quickly as they arrived, the family packed up and drove off, leaving a billow of dust in their wake.

Ted continued as if the family's visit had been a planned scene in a well-orchestrated play. "Consider the popularity of camcorders, Angelo. When we were children, only a small percentage of families owned 8-millimeter home movie cameras. Taking the movies, getting them developed, and showing them was a major project. Do you recall the time your dad showed home movies and forgot to secure the take-up reel? Remember how astonished he was to find a hundred-foot snake of gnarled film on the floor?"

Angelo started to laugh and then stiffened to wonder how Kohler knew about that scene. Was he reading Angelo's memory bank, or was it just a common experience?

"Now home movies seem Jurassic by comparison. Anyone can make a movie anywhere, and the video is ready to watch the moment it is recorded. Your mind can do the same."

"My mind?" Angelo asked incredulously. "You mean I could do this too?"

"Wanna shot at it?"

Angelo felt anxious, put on the spot. But he was up for the adventure. "What do I do?"

"Take the camera and create an image yourself."

"What should I think of?"

"Anything you want—or, if you like, you can just relax your mind and see what comes out."

The scientist was hooked. Mimicking Kohler's procedure, he held the camera up to his chest, closed his eyes, and took a few deep breaths. He felt awkward and wondered if he was being set up for a joke. Almost comically he looked around to see if anyone was watching; luckily, no one else was in sight, and Angelo was relieved. He looked back at Kohler, who was dead serious, almost reverent. Angelo turned his attention back to the camera. No particular scene came to mind, so he simply relaxed and mentally asked for an image to come forth. After a few moments he clicked the shutter and opened his eyes.

Out whirred a new plate. Angelo was rapt; if Cathedral Rock disintegrated that minute, he wouldn't have noticed. His eyes were glued on the developing photo. Angelo had done ten thousand science experiments, but none were as engrossing as this one.

The image began to take shape, and like the other one, it was initially fuzzy. Then Angelo saw a light green color begin to emerge, bordered by a long gray section running diagonally across the upper left portion of the photo. After a few more seconds Angelo could make out a small figure next to the dark area, and to the right of the small figure was a larger one. The seconds seemed like hours. Why was it taking so long to develop?

As the green darkened, Angelo could make out a rolling meadow. The gray area seemed to be some kind of valley. Angelo started to feel anxious when he saw it, but didn't know why. Then he understood. The chasm was a split in the earth, and the small figure standing next to it was Jesse. Angelo's gut began to churn. Then the larger figure took form. His fears were confirmed—it was Lorenzo. Angelo was holding in his hands a picture of his dream the previous night.

Angelo paled and dropped the photo. "No way!" he exclaimed in a low voice.

He turned and stared at Kohler in bewilderment. "That picture is an exact image of a dream I had last night—there is no way you could ever have known about that."

"But you knew," Ted answered, "and that is all that was necessary."

"You mean that camera can read my mind?"

"The camera is just an instrument. It picked up on the most predominant energy in your subconscious. It doesn't lie."

"But that experience was not real; it was a dream."

"Dreams are just as real as the waking state when you are in them—sometimes more so. Your subconscious does not distinguish between waking and dreaming. When you concentrated, you accessed a part of your mind below the threshold of your awareness. This dream is pointing you to something inside you calling for your attention."

Angelo felt weak-kneed and sat down on a rock. Kohler walked back to the Explorer and brought the disoriented scientist a canteen of water. Angelo held it up to his lips, then hesitated—maybe it was laced with LSD. But what the hell, he figured, this trip was already unbelievable. He drank.

Kohler, who seemed sensitive to what Angelo was going through, walked to the edge of the bluff, giving Angelo some time to relax and deal with his astonishment. Ted stood with his hands on his hips, surveying the panorama. Angelo felt as if he had just undergone major surgery.

After a few minutes Kohler returned and asked, "Feel like you're ready to go?"

"Just promise me we won't be abducted by a couple of bug-eyed aliens poking needles in my groin."

Kohler smiled and motioned to Angelo to come along. As Angelo slid onto the worn seat he realized that, bizarre and outrageous as this man was, he trusted him.

For most of the ride back to town Angelo remained quiet, watching the scenery go by. As the two approached the outskirts of Sedona he asked, "If I can generate the picture I just did, why aren't other people doing it?"

"Everyone can," Ted answered assuredly, "but most people don't believe they can. Plus, the fact that I was with you makes a big difference."

"You mean you have a special power to make it happen?"

"No, I act as an amplifier. Because I have done it so many times and I know the power of the process, I serve as a jump starter—I push the energy over the threshold for manifestation. With enough practice, anyone can make the photos. One day it will be as commonplace as making a home video."

"And then every Sunday night millions of people will be glued to their TV sets watching 'America's *Funniest Psychic Photos?*'"

Kohler laughed. "You're actually not far off. It won't be a long time before many people trust their psychic faculties to make important life decisions. Some are even starting to do it now. I am training a group of Exxon executives to do management by intuition. The results have been phenomenal."

"But that could put the *Psychic Hotline* and a lot of other services out of business."

"There will still be a place for helpers—but by and large people will be looking *in* for answers, rather than out. Do you know the definition of a consultant?"

"What's that?" asked Angelo.

"A consultant is somebody who borrows your watch to tell you what time it is."

Angelo smiled. "We all have good watches; we just haven't been using them. . .Hand me that Polaroid, would you?"

Angelo passed the camera to this enigmatic man, who held it beside his chest with one hand and went into his focusing mode. When the Explorer stopped at a red light, Kohler closed his eyes for a few seconds and clicked the shutter. Angelo, now familiar with the process, tore off the photo and watched it develop. By the time it revealed itself, Ted was steering the Explorer into *The Coffee Pot* lot.

Kohler pulled up behind Angelo's car and put the truck into park. Angelo opened the door and stepped onto the rough asphalt, almost losing his balance as he studied the photograph. After staring at the fresh image for a long time, he lifted his head and closed the door. His face was wrinkled in consternation. Angelo leaned through the open window and with intense curiosity asked, "Hey, will this really happen?"

"That's up to you," Kohler answered earnestly. Then the man who saw afar stepped on the gas, leaving Angelo to deal with the photo and himself.

Chapter 15

Her voice was as familiar as apple spice cake with cream cheese frosting, and just as sweet.

"Hello, Harriet?" he greeted her. "This is Angelo Mann. . .Yes, it's nice to hear your voice, too. . .Well, things are a little crazy here, but exciting. . .No, my son is still in the hospital, no real change. . .We're hoping for the best. . .Yes, thank you very much for your prayers. . .I was wondering if L.C. is home?. . .Oh, good, sure I can hold. . .Take care."

"L.C. here," the voice came.

"L.C., it's Angelo Mann."

"Well, well, Angelo, how goes it?"

"It goes fast. . .My life is on fast forward, and there's no turning back. . .L.C., I'm calling to let you know that I am ready."

"That's great. . .Ready for what?"

"Ready to go for contact."

"That's great. . .Contact with whom?"

"With Jesse. . .with anyone out there who wants to communicate."

"Is your son out of the coma?"

"No, that's just the point. I don't want to wait until he wakes up. I need to talk to him now. There are things I need to say. I'm not willing to sit around and hope."

"And how do you plan to do this?"

"With you."

"With me?"

"You know that Velanovich book you loaned me?"

"Of course."

"I've studied it. I've studied it a lot, and I believe the communicator is plausible."

"That's what I told you."

"I know, but I had to come to that conclusion myself. I met Ted Kohler, you know the book *The Man Who Saw Afar?*"

"Yes, of course; it's a classic—You met Kohler?"

"Yes, and he gave me some key ideas. I want to move ahead, and I want you to work with me."

"And just how do you propose we do this?"

"We're both experts in our fields and we have state-of-the-art labs."

"Now hold your horses, Mr. Enthusiasm. May I remind you that I work for the United States Navy? Most of my projects are classified. If the Navy ever found out I was involved in a project like this, my butt would get deep-sixed, no questions asked. That would be the end of Mrs. Pierson's apple spice cake for both of us."

Angelo replied quickly, "I have the same kinds of risks, L.C. My lab building is a fortress. We have all kinds of military contracts, and anybody entering the building has to pass more security checks than a presidential bodyguard; Christ, they make *Mission Impossible* look simple by comparison. I know what security is, L.C. But none of that seems important to me now. Right now all I want to do is get my son back, beginning with talking to him. If you could help me do that, I would be more grateful than you could ever know—not to mention all the other people we could help."

A long silence followed. "Well, let's say I had a moment of madness and said yes. How would we fund this research? I can't go to the Department of Defense, you know."

"I can get the funding," Angelo assured L.C. "I know I can. I have all kinds of contacts. If you would promise to help me with the technical pieces, I'll find a funder."

L.C. Pierson sighed and answered, "It's a long shot, Angelo."

"Is it any longer a shot than me sitting next to Harriet on the airplane and ending up in your living room? Wasn't it you who told me about synchronicity? I came to you for a purpose. It's no accident I am asking you to do this. I believe you and I have a purpose. What do you say?"

L.C. thought for a moment and answered, "Well, I was getting kind of tired of the navy. . .and besides, I missed the sixties. . ."

Angelo grabbed his Palm Pilot and accidentally pressed "M" for "money" instead of "L" for Henry Lehman. Perfectly Freudian, he deduced. He corrected his request, got Lehman's number, and picked up the phone to get him before he left his office for the day. Stutter tone; message in. Angelo pressed his voicemail code and waited. Static, must be long distance. Then a very welcome voice. "Hello Angelo, this is Avi calling you from the Land of Holy War. I hope you are doing well. I just came back from a visit with Rav Shimon. He told me to call you. I have no idea why he told me that, but I have learned not to question his intuition. He said it would be important. Give me a buzz if you have any idea what he meant. Shalom."

"Holy shit," Angelo muttered aloud. "This stuff really works."

Quickly Angelo dialed Avi's home number, and he answered.

"Avi, this is Angelo," he announced gleefully.

"Shalom, my friend."

"Avi, I know why you called me."

"Good, please let me know why I do things like that."

"I am ready to proceed with my project, and I want you to be a part of it."

"Certainly! Now just tell me which project that is."

"Are you familiar with the work of Andre Velanovich?"

"Velanovich? I studied with him."

"You studied with Andre Velanovich?"

"After Velanovich's book was published in England, he became a man on the run. Everything you have heard about the authorities trying to squash Tesla's work—and subsequently that of Velanovich—is true. With headhunters from three countries on his tail, he fled to

Israel shortly after we became a nation. He was Jewish, and figured he would get asylum in his own country. He sniffed out Zvat as the center of mysticism, took an assumed identity, and lived out his years there in seclusion."

"How did you get to study with him?"

"He became a student of Rav Shimon."

"Are you serious?"

"Yes, mystics always recognize one another. The two developed a deep camaraderie and Rav Shimon convinced Andre to share his knowledge with the students in our group. I heard Velanovich lecture half a dozen times."

"That's incredible!"

"Nothing is incredible, my friend. I think it would be incredible if things like this did *not* happen. . .Now, what are you up to?"

· "I want to replicate the Subtle Image Recorder."

"It's about time."

"You mean you think it can be done?"

"One night while Velanovich was lecturing, I asked him if he thought anyone would recreate the device."

"And what did he say?"

"He said that the technical part would be easy, especially since it had already been done. But the world would have to be ready for it. Someone would have to be sufficiently motivated to overcome the resistance that would follow in its wake. He said such a machine would totally change the world, and too many people had an investment in the world as it is, to allow it to reach the masses.

"Then that very night something strange happened. Rav Shimon, who had been listening to our conversation, tapped me on the shoulder and whispered in my ear, 'Maybe you should do this, Avi.' At the time I thought he was just kidding—I had just been with the rabbi for a short time—but later I learned that he never made off-the-cuff comments unless he meant something."

"So how come you never did anything about it?"

"I never had the motivation. But your call tells me that this could be the time. Why are you so interested?"

"Jesse was in an accident. He can't talk. I want to communicate with my son."

"Then count me in."

"Really?"

"No accidents, Angelo, no accidents."

"Thank you, Avi. Thank you." Angelo hesitated, then continued, "Avi, there's one more thing."

"What's that?"

"Money. We'll need funding and manpower. Can you help?"

"I wish I could. But, as you well know, the whole country is geared up for war. All research grants are on hold. You know, war and generosity make poor bedfellows. . .You may have to carry the ball there."

"Dr. Lehman will see you now," the stylishly-suited secretary motioned to Angelo. Clumsily he set down his coffee cup, grabbed his briefcase, and strode briskly toward the open door, where he was met by the burly sixty-ish Nevadan. Lehman extended his hand to Angelo and deftly ushered his visitor to the chair facing the imposing black metal desk. Lehman's plaques on the wall glittered in the afternoon sun; obviously they had been polished recently.

"Good to see you, Angelo," the administrator offered in his gravelly voice. "It must be a year since the Dallas meeting."

"Gosh, has it been that long?"

Lehman, true to form, got right down to business. "So what can I do for you today?"

"Henry, I need your help with something."

"Shoot."

"I have a project—a fairly unusual one—and I am going to need some funding and manpower." Angelo searched the veteran scientist's eyes for a response, but found none.

"Keep talking."

"Well, I've been doing some traveling lately, and I've met some, let's say, unorthodox thinkers. We're speculating on developing a device with some fairly serious ramifications."

Again Angelo tried to pierce Lehman's stone face. Nothing. Angelo leaned forward, folded his hands on the desk, and caught Henry Lehman's eyes, hoping to convince the salty old dog that he meant business. "My colleagues and I believe we have the technology to create a machine that can make audio and possibly video recordings of past, and possibly future events."

"Excuse me?"

Angelo tried to remain cool, but couldn't mask his nervousness. "You heard me correctly, sir. . . I know this sounds wild, but I have come upon some literature that indicates that such a machine has already been invented, and I believe that with the right people and financial support, we can replicate it."

"Sort of a time machine?"

"After a fashion—not that we plan to ride in it like a rocket ship; it's more like taking pictures from a distance."

"Oh, yeah, something like *Bill and Ted's Excellent Adventure?*" Lehman asked. "My grandson used to watch that video at my house; he'd sit mesmerized in front of the TV for hours."

Angelo sat up in his chair. Thank God the man had some notion of the possibility.

Dr. Lehman reached into his desk drawer, pulled out a sheet of letterhead, and began writing. Fabulous, Angelo thought—a hit on the first at-bat.

When he finished writing, Lehman twirled the sheet around on the desk and slid it toward Angelo. It read, "*Keith Ragone, 17 Grant Ave., Menasha, WI 56831.*"

"Who is this?"

"It's my grandson—maybe he'd be interested in working with you."

"Is he a scientist?"

"No, he does landscaping—but maybe you could kick some ideas around. He reads a lot of science fiction."

Angelo's gut clenched. "But this is not science fiction, Henry—it's a very real possibility."

"Sounds like science fiction to me. . .Look, Angelo, all kidding aside—you're a well-respected man in the scientific community. If I were you, I wouldn't be telling a lot of people about this. You know as well as I do that grant monies are drying up. If anyone in the association got wind of this, you'd be on the shit list in no time. Save yourself some embarrassment and stick with plausible research."

Angelo took a deep breath. He searched the ceiling for a while, trying to decide whether or not to continue. He did. "There's one more thing, Henry."

"What's that?"

"My son is ill; he was hurt while bicycling, and he's in a coma. I have no idea if he will ever come out. I believe this machine can help me contact him."

"You want to invent a machine to help you talk to your son who's in a coma?"

"That's right."

Henry Lehman tossed his pen onto his blotter and leaned back. Then he said, "Angelo, we know each other fairly well. We've worked on a number of projects over the years. You know how much I respect you. Even more important, your reputation in the research community is impeccable. I hate to see you go through this. This must be very stressful for you. Have you thought about seeing a psychiatrist?"

"I'm not crazy, Henry," Angelo returned vociferously, standing up. "Upset, yes. Confused, yes. Vulnerable, yes. But I'm not crazy. In fact, I feel more sane and alive than I have in a long time. I don't need a psychiatrist. I just need some support. I need some funding. Will you help me?"

Lehman paused. "I'm sorry, Angelo, it's not something I could justify."

That was it. Angelo knew Henry Lehman well enough to know that any further discussion would be a waste of time. Angelo stood up, drew a deep breath, and tried one last time to pierce the Lehman veneer. *Nada*, Angelo concluded; the man was a brick wall in a business suit.

Sometimes he thought he heard Jesse calling to him from the kitchen. Sometimes he thought he saw him on the soccer field with his friends. Sometimes when Angelo got a takeout from the pizza shop he would walk next door to the Baskin-Robbins shop and buy a fudge nut pistachio ice cream cone, just as Jesse liked to do.

He placed Jesse's photo in a gold frame on his desk in the lab. He made a copy and set it on the nightstand next to his bed. He put another picture on his refrigerator, and taped one on the dashboard of his car.

Sometimes when he went to work he would reach into his lower right desk drawer and gaze for a minute at the photo of himself with Claudia and Jesse. Sometimes he wished his life were easier.

"Why did you want to meet at Denny's?" Larry Ellsworth asked Angelo as the waitress took their menus.

"Well, it's sort of a personal thing."

"Family problem? Hey, man, I'm here for you."

"Thanks, Larry, but it's not that."

"Then what?"

"I just wanted to bounce an idea off you."

"Bounce away."

"I want to invent a machine to talk with spirits."

Silence. Wait. Watch. Gulp. Wonder.

"Like dead people?"

"No. . .Yes. . .Well, sort of. . ." Angelo began to nervously tap his fork against the table top. "Dead people and living people who are incommunicado. Like my son Jesse."

"Jesse is incommunicado?"

"He's in the hospital. He's unconscious. We don't know what's going to happen."

"My God, Angelo, I had no idea. . ."

"I've met a few people who are into metaphysics. They say that people don't really die and that even if someone is unconscious, they can be contacted. I want to—I have to—find out."

Ellsworth stared.

"Larry, we've been around the block together. If anyone knows I'm not a lunatic, you do. What do you think? Are you interested in playing?"

Ellsworth slumped back in his bench seat and let out a long exhale. Just then the waitress delivered Larry's Diet Coke and Angelo's coffee. After some pleasantries with the girl, Larry leaned forward and spoke in a hushed tone. "Angelo, I think I have some idea of what you're up to. But it's a long shot. I'm not saying you couldn't do this, or at least make some headway. I'm just concerned about how this would affect your position. Are you sure you want to put it all on the line for something like this?"

Angelo leaned in and whispered back to Larry, mocking his style. "Funny thing is, Larry, my life is *already* on the line. I'm just not impressed anymore with the world I've created. I don't know how much longer I can go on doing something I don't believe in."

Angelo sat back and returned his voice to normal volume. "Do you remember the night we went out drinking just before graduation?" he queried.

"You mean the night we met those two blonde coeds and played nude volleyball on the beach until two in the morning?"

"No, not that time, testicle brain—I mean the night we stayed up late talking about Galileo and Copernicus and Wilhelm Reich. You were the one who told me how all of these men were great geniuses who were ahead of their time and that they were silenced or jailed or killed or written out of the history books because they scared the hell out of the powers that be."

"Sure, I still think so."

"Then why would you think I am off the wall?"

"The truth is, Angelo, I don't think you're off the wall. If anyone could pull something like this off, you could. But, to be quite honest, I wouldn't want my name associated with it. Diane has been in and out of the hospital with back problems and Ricky will be going to college next year. I'm not about to put my ass on the line. I've invested too much time and work getting where I am to risk it all on the X-files."

Ellsworth stirred his soda and gazed into the swirls. Then he lifted his eyes and looked seriously at Angelo. "I'm sorry, Angelo, I wish I could help you. Have you tried Henry Lehman?"

Angelo opened his e-mail template and typed,

Dear Juliana,

I have no idea where you are today or what you are doing. Wherever you are, I want you to know that I am thinking about you. My life is a tornado; everything is changing at once. I don't know where I will end up. But I do know that when I think about you, I feel happy. You have become like a bright spot of happiness in the midst of a dark and turbulent night. I am so grateful that you showed up in my life; I think my world would be unbearable without the thought of you. Our time together meant everything to me, and our e-mails are like a lifeline to me. I can't wait until we see each other again. Let's make it soon.

Angelo

Angelo's only remaining hope was Sara Bartner. Angelo had met Sara at the fall faculty meeting three years earlier. He liked her sassy,

no-bullshit attitude. Sara was a successful lawyer cum poli-sci instruc-
tor who had grown to command significant respect at Stanford. Sara
had well-positioned connections with funding agencies, and regularly
rubbed shoulders with people who could pull strings at high levels.
Oddly, Sara was rumored to have dabbled in parapsychology, mostly
in association with her ex-husband Kenneth, a therapist who had
studied at Duke under famous occult investigator J. B. Rhine. Angelo
had always found Sara intriguing, partly because she wielded power
like a man, and partly because she had great legs.

The law library seemed like an odd place to meet about a long-
shot metaphysical enterprise, but when Sara insisted that was her only
available time slot, Angelo figured he would take what he could get.
He found Sara sitting at a carrel surfing the net on a law update web
site. As Angelo approached, she saw him out of the corner of her eye
but she said nothing and kept her eyes glued to the screen. He took a
seat in the carrel next to hers and, in spite of feeling insulted that she
did not acknowledge his entrance in the slightest way, waited with in-
sincere patience.

After another minute Sara closed out the screen she had been
studying and turned to Angelo. "Stupid suckers," she sighed, "all
they had to do was attack Jensen's credibility, and they would have
had him by the balls. . .When will they ever learn, when will they
ever learn?"

Sara spun around on her chair and faced Angelo squarely. There
were those great legs. Don't go there, he thought, don't even *think*
about going there.

"So how is the renowned Dr. Mann these days?"

"Dr. Mann is looking for some help."

"Legal advice?"

"Not exactly. . .I have a project that needs brainpower and funding and I thought maybe you or Kenneth could help me make some
connections."

"Maybe I can. As for Kenneth, you'll have to talk to the bastard
yourself; we haven't spoken since he claimed poverty on his six-figure
income. Funny how he teaches people to get along with each other. . .
What's that saying about the shoemaker's kids?"

Angelo smiled politely, but was anxious to get on with the meeting. "Sara, have you ever read a book called *Journey Beyond the Known?*"

"I haven't, but I remember seeing it sitting in Kenneth's bookcase. I never got much into the woo-woo stuff. That was Kenneth's department. He was great in bed, and what he did in his free time was up to him."

"Well, the book has given me an idea for a rare invention. . .a machine that would enable people to visit the past and future and talk to people who have been here before and maybe even after us. Maybe even reach people who cannot communicate verbally."

Sara was silent for a few moments, then pursed her lips, closed her eyes, and shook her head. "Angelo, I think you may be talking to the wrong person about this. You know me. I deal in the real world— you know, murders and rapes and power plays and infidelity and class actions and all the stuff that keeps the ten o'clock news on the air. I admit that for a while I got into talking with Kenneth about this stuff, and some of it was interesting. But Kenneth turned out to be an arrogant airhead—not to mention asshole—and all those lovely theories went down the tubes with our marriage. The guy didn't live what he taught, and I have no respect for a hypocrite. There are lots of people out there with real problems, and I am not about to suggest reincarnation as their answer."

Angelo felt cut off at the knees. He had come to this woman for help, and he got a lecture. He did his best to squelch his ire, but could not hide it. Truth be told, the real dagger was his fear that Sara was correct; in some sector of his own brain he still questioned his sanity.

"Okay, Sara, I get your point. But maybe you could give me some names of some people I could contact who would be more sympathetic."

"Maybe I could, but I won't. Not because I don't want to help you—but because I do. Angelo, do you have any idea of the kind of legal and moral implications you are playing with here?"

"Legal implications? Is there something illegal about trying to help people?"

"Plenty of people have gotten into big trouble for doing things that started out to be helpful. Here, let me show you one. . ." Sara turned back to the computer, still online. She clicked onto a search engine and typed the words "assisted expression." Within a few seconds, a screen full of matching results popped up. Sara clicked on the third one and tilted the monitor so Angelo could see. He leaned in to see a copy of a newspaper headline which read, *"Educator Loses All After Invention is Debunked."* Angelo read the first paragraph of the article that followed:

After four glorious years in the sunshine of national praise, Dr. Sanford Statler today resigned his position at the University of Minnesota, dissolved his Foundation for Assisted Expression, and declared corporate and personal bankruptcy. "When I was being touted as a revolutionary hero in the field of education, I had no idea it would ever come to this," Dr. Statler stated at a press conference in Minneapolis' Hyatt Regency hotel.

"What happened to this guy?" Angelo asked.

"Statler worked with autistic kids and invented a machine that supposedly translated their innermost feelings and experiences into words and pictures. Can you imagine the kind of relief and peace this brought parents and teachers who had struggled for many, many years—sometimes a whole *lifetime*–to reach children who were written off as unreachable?"

Angelo listened attentively. *Where the hell are we headed now?* he wondered.

"Within a short time Statler rose to national prominence as a sort of savior. At national conventions he demonstrated his apparatus for autistic children and adults, and even his biggest skeptics were impressed. Then NEC got in on the action, invested megabucks in streamlining the design to make the machine accessible to anyone, and marketed the puppy."

"Did people go for it?"

"Big time. I mean, BIG TIME. If you had an autistic kid, how much would you pay to bring your child back to the real world?"

Suddenly Angelo thought of Jesse. "I would give everything I own."

"Some people did. The man and the machine became a national phenomenon in the field of autism. People who could afford the machines bought them before they were even produced, and those who could not afford them formed support groups, chipped in, and shared them. People were so *happy* to get their lost children back. It was the prodigal son coming home."

"So what happened?"

"Some cynics hired a laboratory to conduct independent testing of the device. What they found was a bombshell: the communication was being influenced by the people who operated the machine. You see, someone—an adult other than the child, usually the parent —had to run the machine while the autistic child was 'communicating.' The experiment revealed that the operator was unconsciously causing the machine to express what the operator wanted to hear. Now it makes perfect sense that the child's parents would want him or her to be communicating, especially loving and sensitive thoughts, which is mostly what they got. So all the machine was picking up, according to this study, was the intent of the parent."

"Did people believe the study?"

"At first they didn't—they didn't want to; who, after having their beloved child rescued from the abyss, would want to cast them back into it? But then as more and more people began hearing and talking about the study, the tide of opinion turned and a mob psychology ensued. All of a sudden the people who had worshipped Statler, hated him. Overnight he went from being a savior, to the devil. Man, was it *ugly!*"

"And how did Statler deal with the lynch mob?"

"He stuck to his guns. He claimed that the invention was for real, and his detractors, old-guard educators and psychologists, were threatened by his innovation, and just sought to discredit him. But it was too late. Too many people already had Statler on a cross, not to mention the financial losses and claims against NEC. The man was ruined and became a laughing stock."

Angelo leaned back, shaken. He folded his hands behind his neck and bit his lower lip.

"Now here's my point," Sara continued. "I believe Statler was sincere. He really wanted to help. I think he really believed in this invention and thought it could do wonders for autistic kids and their families. Jesus Christ, maybe the thing *was* for real. But he was bucking a system that had a huge investment in their way of doing things, and just as he had tapped into the emotions of people who wanted to be helped, his debunkers played on their fears. Angelo, I know enough from talking with Kenneth—the turd—to realize that anything is possible. But you're dealing with people, and people can get really crazy. I'd hate to see you set yourself up to be the next whipping boy."

Angelo kept a poker face, stood up, and dryly uttered, "Thank you for your time." As he turned toward the library exit, he didn't even notice Sara Bartner's legs.

When Lin turned on the light in the office at 7:30 p.m., she found her boss submerged in the tweed couch with his feet up on the coffee table. His body was twisted into the cushions, his head cradled back. The floor was cluttered with papers at the foot of a quarter-full Johnny Walker bottle next to an empty glass. Angelo's blue pinstriped shirt was hanging untucked, his cheeks and chin shadowed with dark stubble; he was pinching the bridge of his nose below his wrinkled forehead. Lin, startled, blurted out, "Sorry— I didn't know you were here."

Angelo didn't bother to move or even open his eyes. "That's okay," he answered in an uncharacteristic drawl; "What are you doing back?"

"I'm on my way over to my niece's house for her birthday; at lunchtime I got her a baseball mitt—go figure, that's what she wanted—and I forgot to take it home. What's your excuse?"

"My excuse is stupidity. I actually imagined that I could communicate with my son, make something better of my life, and offer a contribution to humanity. Unfortunately, I'm insane. Everyone I ask for help looks at me as if I have a large green penis protruding from my forehead. Can you see anything there?" Angelo brushed aside the hair hanging over his forehead.

Lin snickered, "Well, I've been accusing you of thinking with your dick for a long time, but I don't think it's gone that far."

Angelo pursed his lips and shook his head slightly.

Then Lin grew serious. "Excuse me, but aren't you the physics professor who came into my class one day and quoted Einstein: 'Great ideas have always been met with violent opposition from mediocre minds?'"

Angelo pulled a throw pillow over his face and shook his head more adamantly. From under his shield he murmured, "I hate it when my students take what I taught them and use it against me."

Lin sat on the arm of the sofa, looked motheringly at her boss's wracked figure, and stroked what she could find of his forehead. "C'mon, big guy, it can't be all that bad."

"Oh yeah—maybe you should try going out and hustling venture capital from a bunch of tight-assed bureaucrats. You know the first law of physics: 'To produce a diamond, give a piece of coal to an administrator and have him hold it in his butt.'"

Lin snickered again, then spoke softly: "Angelo, I know the guys you're talking about; I work with them every day—remember? I also know that in a hundred lifetimes not one of them will ever come close to what you have going for you. These last few weeks I've seen you come to life in a big way. I don't know about all this spiritual stuff, but it sure is a pleasure to see you excited about something. For the first time in as long as I know you, you're really alive. Angelo, you can't quit now—you might really be onto something."

Angelo peeked one eye out from under the pillow. The lady wasn't kidding.

Lin reached for the phone, set it on the coffee table next to her boss's feet, and began tapping some numbers. "What are you doing?" he asked.

"I think it's time for a call to the holy land, mister. You need a dose of Matsah-Man."

"You're calling Avi?"

"It's morning there, and we should be able to catch your buddy."

As Lin listened to the fuzzy ringing on the line, she motioned to Angelo to sit up and pull himself together.

"Hello? This is Dr. Angelo Mann's office in San Francisco calling for Dr. Goldman . . .Yes, I'll hold on. . .Thank you."

Angelo grumbled as he raked his hand through his hair.

"Hello, Avi?" Lin said in a perky voice, "I have someone here who wants to talk to you. Hold on just a moment. . ."

Lin made a stern face at Angelo, as if to say, "Get it together, man." Angelo grimaced like a five-year-old being forced to take cough syrup, and took the phone.

"Angelo!" the buoyant voice rang out. "How is our project going?"

"Hi, Avi. . .to tell you the truth, things aren't going so well here. I've gone to half a dozen people I thought I could count on, and every single one has shot me down. I'm starting to wonder if I *have* gone wacko. I hate to sound like a quitter, but I just don't know where to go from here. I am really confused. Maybe it's the kosher food."

Avi's familiar laugh exuded from the handset and spilled throughout the room.

"Seriously, though," Angelo continued, "I wonder if maybe we are just too far ahead of our time. I don't think the world is ready for us yet."

Avi's voice came back, this time more serious: "No inventor ever had it easy, Angelo. People believe a new idea only when they see it proven and working. We're in good company with every dreamer who ever wanted to change the world for the better."

"But how are we supposed to do anything without the Almighty Dollar? We can't do this alone— we need equipment and manpower. I'm about ready to throw in the towel, Avi."

"Listen to me, Angelo. I think we're being tested. Do you remember Dunstead's story of his exploits in Asia, the one you found on the web site you told me disappeared?"

"Sure."

"I am well aware of that expedition; Velanovich told me about it. He and Dunstead were in communication for a while." Avi stated.

"Really? And what did Velanovich say?"

"He said that Dunstead's expedition was not all fun and games. They pushed through lots of muck you didn't read about, and he worked hard to sustain his entourage. He also struggled with doubt."

"Yes," Angelo argued, "but, like the book says, he had the Sar-Mun Brotherhood working on his behalf. He had access to help from amazing unseen powers."

"And what makes you think we don't?

"Well, he was right in the midst of all that mystical stuff. You know, yogis and adepts and healings and miracles and all that."

"And why are we any different? Just because we wear suits instead of loincloths and eat bread instead of rice, does that mean that the power of God is any farther from us?"

He had him there. "Well, I guess not."

"Angelo, don't let fear stop you now. We are headed in the right direction. Rav Shimon taught me that whenever I get stuck, that is the time to go within and connect with the Source. I think that's what we need to do now. We need to remember that the power of the entire universe is behind us."

"Yeah, yeah, okay," Angelo answered, somewhat annoyed by Avi's positiveness, yet more inspired by it. "I'll call you in a couple of days."

Lin, satisfied that Angelo had received what he needed, bid him a polite salute from the door as she rushed out, mitt on hand, leaving Angelo to rejoin the land of the living.

As soon as the door closed, Angelo picked up his original copy of *Journey Beyond the Known*. He leaned back on the couch, rested his head on the soft cushion, and plopped the book over his face, making a little tent against the glare of the overbearing fluorescent light. He breathed a long sigh and started to close his eyes.

On the inside of his eyelids he saw an after-impression of the page he had looked at. It was the symbol of the Sar-Mun Brotherhood:

The image vibrated on his inner field of vision, as if it was blinking on and off. Intrigued, Angelo opened his eyes and read the page:

> *After they had passed their initiation, members of the Sar-Mun Brotherhood were taught the meaning of their sacred symbol. The intersection of the vertical and horizontal lines symbolizes the meeting of heaven and earth. The diagonal rays represent the invincible power that emanates when wisdom is combined with pure love and infused into the world. The clear space in the center represents the inner clarity which is the source of all right action and healing.*
>
> *Members of the brotherhood carved this symbol into trees or rocks where the brotherhood had met. If a member wished to call a meeting of the brotherhood, he would carve or paint the symbol in a conspicuous place. By the Law of Attraction those who were intended to know about the meeting would be guided to see it and come.*

Angelo took a pen and began to doodle the Sar-Mun symbol on his notepad. He drew the symbol over and over and over again, each time with more intensity. After he nearly broke the tip of his pen, he picked up the telephone and dialed.

"Hello, Bill? . . .This is Angelo Mann. . .Fine, and you?. . .Good, glad to hear it. . . Bill, how long would it take you to build me a web site?"

Chapter 16

Claudia was sitting with Jesse when Angelo walked into the hospital room. "Oh, you're still here," he said.

"I got here late." Claudia began to gather her purse and jacket.

"How is he?" asked Angelo as he approached Jesse.

"The same."

"And how are you?"

"I've been better." Claudia stood up and went into the bathroom, where she stood in front of the mirror and touched up her make-up.

"Would you like to go down to the coffee shop with me and have a talk?"

"I don't think there's much to talk about, Angelo," Claudia snipped. She stepped out of the bathroom and faced Angelo directly. "And why would you want to talk to me, anyway? You have someone to talk to."

"Excuse me?"

"You heard me. Don't play dumb, Angelo. I know you're seeing someone."

Angelo was stunned. Okay, he thought, no use denying it. "How did you know?"

"Karen Kuczinski's husband saw you at the Marriott." Claudia turned and looked Angelo directly in the eye.

"Okay, so maybe I am seeing someone. Can you blame me? I just need someone to talk to. I need someone who understands what I'm going through."

"Well, I'm going through the same thing. I didn't run out and find a concubine."

"She's not a concubine." Angelo stood up, angry, and faced Claudia. "She's a good person who supports me. We have a lot in common."

"Well so do we, Angelo. He's lying right there." Jaw clenched and her chin jutting forward, Claudia pointed to Jesse. Suddenly her face wrinkled like a little girl who had been stung by a bee, and tears brimmed in her eyes. Claudia turned and walked out.

Shaken, Angelo walked to the window and looked out on the city. He was shocked that Claudia had found out about Juliana. But maybe it was better that this was out in the open, anyway.

As he looked down on the busy street below, he began to think about Claudia's words. Yes, they did have Jesse in common. What a huge "in common" that was. Angelo remembered when Jesse came home from the hospital right after he was born. For years Angelo had resisted having a child, fearing that the responsibility would tie him down. But when he saw the little guy, he knew it was right. With the baby, Angelo fell in love with Claudia all over again. Maybe even for the first time. They were so happy together, the three of them. Jesse gave his life dimension, and Claudia felt it. They talked a lot then. Angelo felt safe. He wasn't so involved with the lab then; he was just getting into his research career, and he didn't have an empire to manage. Now he didn't mean to hurt Claudia; the marriage just wasn't what it used to be.

Angelo walked back to the bed and looked down at his son. Jesse looked much as he had for the last two months. The child's body lay limp, breathing shallow, connected to a Medusa-like web of tubes and apparatuses. His white fluffy stuffed dog Sammy lay next to his head, a silent but devoted friend, while a Mylar balloon floated above the bedpost, dancing lightly in the breeze wafting softly through the half-open window. Hanging onto life by a mysterious thread, the child drifted in some bizarre limbo.

Angelo spent a minute stroking Jesse's forehead, imagining that the boy's eyes were opening and he was greeting him. But soon the reality of his son's absence encroached on Angelo's hopeful reveries. He sat down in the uncomfortable chair and let his head hang back against the wall. The waiting, the waiting, the waiting, was taking its toll on Angelo. While he was at the lab he distracted himself from his heartache, yet with each visit to Jesse's bedside he became more distraught. Will I ever see my son put on his yellow day pack for school again? Where is Jesse? Is he living an unseen life in some other dimension? Is he trying to communicate?

Angelo dozed for a while, and awoke when the nurse walked into the room to check Jesse's vital signs. Angelo looked at his watch— almost 2:15. He savored another long look at Jesse, took a deep breath, and stood up. Angelo touched his son's soft hand, turned, and trudged down the long corridor. Every day the elevator seemed a little farther away.

Chapter 17

When Lin unlocked the office door, she found Angelo already sitting at his desk, nearly obscured by a mountain of books, magazine articles, papers, and several used coffee cups. She looked up at the clock. 7:58 a.m.

"I've never seen you so busy at this hour," Lin remarked. "What time did you get in?"

"Six, I think," he muttered without even raising his head.

Lin approached his desk and casually picked up one of the books. *Nikola Tesla: The Man and the Mystery*. Then another: *Alice Bailey on Reincarnation*. Then another: *Tesla's Black Box*. "You're really into this Tesla guy, huh?" she asked.

"It's weird," Angelo responded. "The more I read about him, the more I feel like I know him."

"Well, that's sort of natural."

"Yes, but it's more than that."

"How so?"

"Have you ever felt like you knew someone from the inside out? Like you knew their thoughts and their feelings, and you could actually *be* that person?"

"Well, maybe."

"Everything I am reading about Tesla's life feels so familiar, like I was right there. . ."

Lin looked down at Angelo's desk and saw another book: *Many Lives, Many Masters*. "Oh, come on, Angelo—you're not going to try to tell me that you *were* Nikola Tesla in your past life."

"Don't you think it could be possible?"

"I guess anything's possible. But do you know how many people claim to be Cleopatra? Oprah could do shows for a month with that crowd alone. I know Cleopatra was quite a woman, but hey, I don't think she could spread herself *that* thin."

Angelo picked up *The Man and the Mystery.* "Consider this: Tesla died in 1943, 15 years before I was born. In this biography Tesla told the author that he wished he had more time to complete his work. He said, 'My only regret is that I was born in a time and milieu quite unready for the technology I envision. I firmly believe that, had I been born even a few decades hence, I could complete my work and make the kind of contribution my soul longs to achieve.'"

Lin shrugged her shoulders and answered, "Well, Angelo, maybe this stuff is true and maybe it isn't. I don't really know. But I do know that I like being around you a lot more since you've gotten into this, and if thinking you are Nikola Tesla makes your boat float, I'm not gonna try and sink it. Just don't ask me to learn Yugoslavian." Lin smiled and walked out of Angelo's office.

Angelo leaned back in his chair, stretched his arms, and tried to suck some fresh oxygen into his brain. Until the intercom buzzed. "Someone is here to see you," Lin announced.

"Tell them I'm busy."

A few moments later Lin's voice came again: "She says she came all the way from Germany and wants to know if you think she is worth a few steps to your door."

A look of disbelief washed over Angelo's face. "Juliana?"

By then she was standing at his door. "I can't believe you're here!" he exclaimed, pushing the door closed behind her. Angelo wrapped his arms around her and held her for a long time. Juliana closed her eyes, surrendered to the embrace, and drank him in.

"They sent me to New York, then Japan on short notice. On my way back I had to change planes in San Francisco, so I took a day layover and decided to drop in. I hope it's okay."

"Okay? I wouldn't have it any other way!. . .Would you like to go out for a cup of coffee?"

"Yes, let's."

Angelo took Juliana to his favorite outdoor café across the street
from the park. As soon as they were seated, he reached across the table and took Juliana's hand. It felt strong yet soft. "It's great to see
you," he said.

"I couldn't imagine passing by here without connecting," she replied. "I love your e-mails, Angelo. You may be a scientist by vocation,
but you really are a romantic."

"Funny, I never thought of myself in that way. I think you bring it
out in me."

Juliana smiled and moved the plastic flowers on the table out
from between her and Angelo. "So bring me up to date on what's
been happening."

"Well, Jesse is the same. I go to the hospital every day and sit with
him. I talk to him in my mind, but I'd sure like to hear him talk
back."

"And Claudia?"

"Claudia has retreated into her own world. I've never seen her
like this before. She won't even talk to me, except when we have our
medical consults." Angelo took a deep breath. "She knows about us."

"She does? How?"

"Somebody we know saw us the night I picked you up at the Marriott."

Juliana shifted her position; she began to look very uncomfortable. "And how did Claudia handle it?"

"Not well," Angelo answered. "But she doesn't handle anything
well these days. She's angry. This is another log on the fire."

Juliana leaned in and looked down at the table, then up at Angelo. "Angelo, you know I care about you a great deal. But if this is
going to make your life or Claudia's any harder, I don't want to do
that."

Angelo felt frightened and irritated. "Well, if I had a marriage, we
could discuss that. But Claudia is gone, Juliana. She walked out on
me. She won't even talk to me. She shuts me out every time I reach
out to her. And that didn't start with you. She was gone before I got
involved with you. If Claudia and I had something real or beautiful or
alive, I wouldn't be sitting here with you now. Maybe her moving

away from me cleared the way for me to be with you. . ."

At the worst possible moment, the waitress arrived with their coffees and pastries. "Well, here we are for both of you," she said as she placed the plates on the table. "My, those are some big honkers of croissants!" Obviously the waitress didn't have a clue about how obtrusive her perkiness was in the face of the gravity of the conversation. Fortunately, she disappeared quickly.

Juliana continued their conversation. "You know how important you are to me, too, Angelo. "I think we have something really good going here. I want to give it every chance. I don't want it to hurt you or Claudia. And I don't want to sneak around." Juliana suddenly looked pained. "God knows I hate that."

Angelo took Juliana's hands. "We don't have to sneak around. I don't want to do that either. Look, Claudia and I are separated. She knows I'm seeing you. We have nothing to hide. I believe that what we are doing is right."

Juliana sighed. "All right, thanks for telling me."

Eager to dislodge them from the mucky feelings that had been stirred, Angelo added, "Something else has happened that has given me hope."

"Oh, good. I want to hear about it."

"Well, it's a little far out. . ."

"That's okay. If it's important to you, then it's important."

"Okay. . .here goes. . .Are you familiar with the work of Nikola Tesla?"

"Of course; Europeans know a lot about him. He invented all kinds of things like x-rays, fluorescent lights, radar—even the radio."

"That's right. He also invented a device that was never publicized."

"Which was. . .?"

"He called it a 'Subtle Image Recorder.' It was capable of communicating with people in the spiritual dimension."

"Seriously?"

"I told you this was far out. Now here's what really got my attention: this device could also facilitate communication with people who were incommunicado—like those in a coma."

"I can't believe I never heard about this." Juliana wrinkled her brow.

"You're not the only one. When the government got wind of this, they did everything possible to squash it."

"Well, that doesn't surprise me. . .So you want to reinvent this device to communicate with your son?"

"That's right," Angelo answered with a sparkle in his eye. "Do you think I'm wacko?"

Juliana smiled softly. "No," she told him in a kind voice. "I think you love your son very much. I'm sure that if I were in your position, I would do the very same thing."

Angelo became very still and leaned back. He felt relieved. "Thank you for not thinking I'm a lunatic, Juliana. . .Thank you for believing in me."

"That's easy," she answered. "I have never known anyone like you, Angelo. If anyone can do this, you can."

Angelo felt deeply touched. "Juliana," he said, "I can hardly believe that a woman as wonderful as you has shown up in my world. If I was a person who prayed, I would say that you are an answer to my prayers."

"I know exactly how you feel," she answered. "I feel the same way."

The two were silent for a minute. Then he said, "You know what? . . .I have been working my butt off for weeks. I think I deserve a day off."

"I agree!"

"Let me take you into San Francisco. I'll give you a private tour. . .museum. . .ferry to Tiburon. . .then a romantic dinner overlooking the bay and the city skyline at night."

"I'm all yours." Juliana smiled.

Chapter 18

The e-mails came fast and furious. Spiritual seekers, curiosity hounds, intellectuals, and science fiction buffs responded to the message. Angelo and Lin culled through 127 the first week and tried to make sense of who would be right for the project. "Maybe we should take them all," Angelo suggested offhandedly.

"No way, "Lin answered. "It would be a circus. There's definitely a sampler of space cases in this crowd."

"Yeah, you're right," Angelo concurred.

"Let's narrow it down to a handful. A few focused and talented people are all we really need." She had a point there.

Angelo and Lin set about the task of returning e-mails and phoning the candidates. Many of those inquiring were sincere, but unskilled. A few were living just the other side of any known reality. Some just wanted to talk. Some were qualified, but had no time or money to come and participate. And some were looking for cybersex. By the end of the week, Angelo and Lin were glad the screening was over. After a lengthy discussion, they agreed upon three people who fit the bill and invited them to a meeting at Lin's apartment.

When the auspicious evening arrived, two men and a woman sat on Lin's sofa, faces brimming with questions. As Angelo greeted them, he felt excited that the project was finally under way, yet terrified that he was going out on a huge limb. He was fully aware that his entire career and reputation were on the line; it was succeed or bust. Part of him wanted to get up and run out the door, but it was too late. He had called this gathering, and now he had to see it through. He took a brown metal folding chair, turned it so he could straddle it, leaned forward on the backrest, and began.

"I'd like to thank you for coming," he opened in a pseudo-confident voice. He looked at Lin and knew that she knew he was scared shitless. "You have come here with a little information and a good deal of faith. So to minimize your discomfort, I will get right to the point.

"You are here because you saw the symbol of the Sar-Mun Brotherhood on the internet. I imagine that you are all familiar with it, as well as the work of Dr. Tesla as recorded in *Journey Beyond the Known*."

The three nodded.

"Since the web site posted no words except for the symbol and the e-mail address, I assume that you are willing to follow your intuition. That was our first screen. We are looking for some courageous people to undertake an experiment with potentially huge risk, but possibly huge reward and monumental importance. I briefly discussed the nature of the project with each of you over the phone. Tonight you will receive more details. But before I go on, I am eager to find out about you. Who would care to begin?"

An uncomfortable silence ensued as the guests looked at each other to decide who would speak first. The woman, African-American, attractive face, more than modest make-up, slightly plump, a pack of Virginia Slims protruding from her handbag, no apologies, began: "My name is Carol Wilkins. I am a professional intuitive. I do personal readings and I also consult with police departments to help solve crimes and find missing people. I read *Journey Beyond the Known* a long time ago and loved it; the book opened my eyes to a lot of things that I knew were true, but couldn't find anyone to talk to about. I knew that at some point the book would affect my life in a deeper way. I also knew that when the time was right, I would know it. When I saw the Sar-Mun symbol on your web page, I knew I was supposed to come tonight."

Angelo thanked her, then nodded toward the younger man, who appeared jittery. His skin was sallow, chestnut hair thinning, and he wore less-than-stylish plastic brown-rimmed eyeglasses. Yet, despite his nerd-like demeanor, his eyes bore a certain resolution.

"Hi, I'm Jerry Abramson. I work — or should I say *worked* – down the road at Microsoft as a programmer. After 10 years there I was laid off due to the downsizing; I'm sure you're aware of the turmoil the trust-busting has created. But in retrospect I suspect that my layoff was an answer to a prayer. You see, Andre Velanovich's book has been my Bible since I was in grad school. I'm not religious, or even very spiritual, but as a scientist I know that the universe operates according to lawful principles. I know those principles point us to possibilities far beyond anything we have created. Tesla and Velanovich have tapped into those laws in a way that nobody else has, and I want to see them come to life."

Angelo clasped his hands together behind his head and leaned back, taking in his guests' accounts. His scientist's mind was busy sizing up each of the candidates. He was hopeful that he had attracted a group of geniuses, yet simultaneously fearful they were lunatics.

Attention shifted to the older gentleman, who had sat politely, hands folded in his lap. He was tall, with salt-and-pepper hair, a ruddy complexion, and gentle eyes. His soft blue cardigan sweater reminded Angelo of Mr. Rogers.

"My name is Al Conklin. Most people know me as 'Father Al'— I'm a Roman Catholic priest. Now before you form any expectations, you should know that I'm not your traditional clergyman—never have been, never will be. I believe in Jesus and I believe in the church, but I have always been a closet mystic. I know there's a lot more going on in life than meets the eye. *Journey Beyond the Known* means a lot to me because it presents Jesus—and Buddha, and everyone else, for that matter—not as remote gods to be worshiped, but role models, elder brothers who are showing us how to walk in our own magnificence. The Jesus I met in that book seemed believable and available, and he helped me a great deal in my faith. I am here tonight because I want to deepen my connection with the man who embodies the power of true love."

Angelo waited a moment and scanned the three again. He was feeling more relaxed and confident. "Thank you. Now I will tell you more about this project. Perhaps I should begin with myself. Though I am a research scientist by profession, I have recently discovered the spiritual path that obviously all of you have been on for a long time. I have become very interested . . ."

"—Try 'obsessed,'" Lin interjected.

". . .Okay, whatever. . .in Tesla's work, especially the machine called the 'Subtle Image Recorder' that Velanovich refers to."

"Yes," Abramson broke in excitedly. "When I read about the recorder, I wrote to the publisher and asked for more information about it. All I got was a form letter saying the book was out of print and they knew nothing."

"And so did a lot of people," Angelo added. "But I'm not willing to just stop there. My colleagues and I may have access to the skills and materials needed to recreate the Subtle Image Recorder." Abramson's eyes opened wide. Lukoff's lips turned up in a slight smile and she nodded slightly. Father Al was harder to read.

"I have some grant monies I could funnel from projects I am already working on—not a lot, but enough to get us started. If you decide to get involved, this project will require a deep commitment. We are venturing into uncharted territory, and if what I have seen is any indication of public reaction, we are not going to be the most popular kids on the block. We will need time and energy and skill and belief. If this is not something you can do, I will understand. And if you are game, we could change our lives—and maybe the world—forever."

Angelo looked over at Lin, who was beaming at him proudly.

"Now, let me tell you some of my ideas, and when I am done you can tell me if you want to play. . . ."

Chapter 19

Within two weeks the lab was teeming with computers, oscilloscopes, sophisticated imaging equipment, and state-of-the-art digital recording hardware. The desks and tables were strewn with texts that had rarely, if ever, seen the interior of a scientific fortress. *The Tibetan Book of the Dead, Psychic Discoveries Behind the Iron Curtain,* and *Life after Life* proclaimed their unconventional themes, along with what had to be the most complete collection of Tesla's writing ever assembled, along with that of Preston Royce.

"I'm going out for some rations," Jerry Abramson called to Angelo from the lab door. "Want anything?"

"Pastrami sandwich and Coke," he called back. "Extra mayo."

Angelo turned to Avi, who was sitting at the communicator imbedding some core programming. "Thanks for coming on short notice, Avi," he told him. "I can hardly believe this is all coming together so quickly."

Avi smiled. "It's *kairos,* my friend."

Angelo looked at his friend inquisitively. "*Kairos?*"

"*Kairos* is a Greek word from the first translation of the Bible."

"I can't believe you know all this stuff," Angelo said, shaking his head. "Okay, what about *kairos?*"

"In that translation the Greeks use two different words for our word "time." They used *chronos,* which is equivalent to our idea of time—you know, minutes, seconds, hours—dividing life up into little segments for measurement."

Angelo put down his papers and wheeled his chair to face Avi.

"*Kairos,* on the other hand, is much more fascinating. The best way to translate the word would be 'at the right time' or 'in God's time' or 'when the moment is ripe.' *Kairos* indicates that life does not operate by the hands of the clock, but by the hand of God. For example, spring shows up when the time is ripe. It doesn't go according to a date. The flowers don't say, 'Okay, it's March 21st—time to pop out now !'"

Angelo laughed.

"Instead, the flowers appear when all the conditions are right. Sometimes that is as early as February, and maybe as late as April. And then there are flowers that thrive all year round in warmer climates, or just show up for a short time in more frigid regions. The point is that everything in life has a right timing, and if we attune ourselves to that rhythm rather than the numbers ticking next to our bed, we are in our right place at the right time, and the right things happen."

Once again Avi blew Angelo away with his insight. The discussion piqued a question in Angelo. "Do you think *kairos* applies to relationships?" he asked.

"*Kairos* applies to everything," Avi answered, dead serious.

"I met a woman," Angelo said. "Actually, you know her."

"Really?'

"It's Juliana."

"Ah, Juliana," Avi smiled. "A rare flower. Beauty and brains. Good taste, my man."

"I feel like my relationship with Claudia is dead, Avi. I think it has been dying slowly, gradually, over a long period of time. We've drifted apart. I think maybe Juliana showed up to remind me how dead my marriage has become, and how I really want to feel with a woman."

Avi put his computer on standby and shifted to face Angelo.

"What do you think, Avi? Do you think I'm doing the right thing?"

"That's not for me to say, Angelo. I think you have to look into your own heart for that answer."

Angelo felt disappointed. He was hoping that Avi would give him some clue as to what he was supposed to do.

Then Avi continued. "I do know that passion is an important element in a relationship."

"You mean sex?'"

"No, I mean passion. Sex is an expression of passion, but there is a lot more to passion than sex. Passion means that you really want to be with this person, and that you are with them by choice, not routine. It means that you spark each other to be as creative as you can be as individuals. It means that you are more alive with each other than without. It means they remind you how good life can be."

Well, that was pretty much a no-brainer, Angelo thought. "So you don't think I'm a turkey for falling in love?"

Avi laughed. "I think you would be a turkey if you ran away from love."

Avi took a breath and got serious. "Look, Angelo, I know this is a big one for you. If you feel that you can salvage your marriage, then I would say, do it. But if not, you have to be true to yourself."

"Claudia has said that it is over; she wants no part of me."

"Well, maybe *kairos* is operating according to plan." Avi smiled and went back to his computer.

Angelo felt comforted, relieved.

At that moment—maybe it was *kairos*—Carol walked in from the meditation alcove, which just a week ago had been a small stock room. "How's our 'sacred space?'" Angelo asked, just a tad sarcastically.

"It's great and getting better," Carol answered. "You can make fun of it if you like, but you'll see how important it is. When we're ready for transmissions, we're going to have to really focalize our minds. If your thoughts are all over the place, we ain't gonna draw in nobody worthwhile. Maybe some creepy Ouija Board dudes. So you better get your concentration practice going, mister, or else I'll kick your butt."

Everyone laughed. Angelo had come to appreciate Carol's bawdy sense of humor.

Carol softened and turned to Avi, who was still smiling. "How long will you be with us, Avi?" she asked.

"I have to go back to Tel Aviv on Monday. I'll need a few weeks there to finish the semester and tie up some loose ends before I return indefinitely."

Angelo added, "Even more important, Avi is going back to see Rav Shimon."

"Yes," Avi responded. "I believe he can help us in a big way. I've been recording questions I think only he can answer."

"By that time L.C. should have made some progress on the sonic resonator in his own lab. He said he would come as soon as he figured out that piece." Angelo took smug delight in knowing the Navy was contributing to the project.

Angelo returned to the book before him, Manly Hall's *Secret Teachings of All Ages*. Ten minutes later Jerry returned from the deli. "Lakers kicked ass last night," he noted as he dropped a copy of the *Chronicle* on Angelo's desk with his sandwich. "Parker scored 37 points, then fouled out."

Angelo glanced briefly at the sports section, then gave the paper back to Jerry. But the front page headline caught his eye: *Lebanese Troops Poised at Israeli Border*. How long would the threats keep escalating? The tension was becoming torturous, and Angelo did not envy Avi going back the middle east.

As Abramson opened up his sandwich he asked Angelo, "So how long do you think you can string the funders along?"

"Maybe another few weeks," Angelo answered, taking a bite of his dill pickle. "Garrison still thinks I'm working on their OC-48 span grooming interfaces. We have a report due at the end of the month, and if it's not to their liking, they'll pull the plug for sure. If we don't come up with some data to get new funding for this project by that time, we can kiss our little adventure goodbye."

In the week that followed, Angelo Mann lived and breathed this project. He thought about the communicator when he showered, ate, and sat on the toilet. The communicator—and Jesse—dominated his consciousness as he drove to the lab, talked on the telephone, read magazine articles, and met people in the hall. Angelo became like a vacuum cleaner, sucking up any and all possible information that would make this outrageous vision a reality.

While he was analyzing some data camera evidence graphs, the phone rang. Angelo reached over and put the phone on speaker. "Mann," he grunted.

"Shalom from the Land of Milk, Honey, and Scud Missiles!" an amiable voice rang out amidst crackling static.

Excited, Angelo grabbed the receiver and exclaimed, "Holy Moses, Avi, I was just about to call you!"

"I am amazed that synchronicity still surprises you. Haven't I told you a hundred times that the movie is always rolling?"

"Did you see Rav Shimon?"

"Yes—and now I know why I needed to come here. He was more helpful than I ever imagined." Avi paused for a few seconds, then added, "Angelo, he gave us the missing piece."

"The missing piece?"

"There was one crucial piece of information I needed before we could make the link. He gave it to me."

"What was it?"

"I can't go into it now. Let's just say that I believe we finally have everything in place. When I arrive next week I will explain it to you, and then it will be only a matter of time until our first transmission."

Angelo grew very serious, like a ten-year-old boy batting in his first little league game. "Good, Avi, good work. Take care—I'll see you soon."

Angelo hung up and turned to Abramson. "We have it," Angelo exclaimed. "We have the technology for the link-up."

✳

Early the next morning Angelo stood in his personal sanctuary, the shower. He loved to take long hot showers on winter mornings, sometimes until he felt dizzy. The steaming stream tingled every inch of Angelo's stiff back, opening up tight pores almost to the point of pain. With only four hours' sleep, the brisk cascade was oh, so soothing. Suddenly the water went cold. That hadn't happened before.

Angelo stepped out of the shower and reached for his oversized maroon towel, wondering what the problem was. As he was drying his back he heard the television he had left on in the bedroom. Usually there was an interplay between male and female hosts' voices; this morning only men were speaking. Angelo thought he heard the word "Israel" mentioned several times. Still dripping, he hastily wrapped the towel around his waist and hurried into the bedroom to investigate.

". . .widespread damage in the northeast sector of the city," the newscaster reported. "At this time we have no idea of the extent of the casualties. Early reports indicate that the Ramat Aviv area has suffered heavy shelling."

"Oh, shit!" Angelo whispered. He sat on the edge of the bed and leaned forward to raise the TV volume.

"Israeli civil defense officials admit they were not prepared for the bombing of civilian populations. Generally such strikes are directed at military installations. Some speculators believe the missiles may have been intended for an Israeli Air Force base approximately thirty kilometers north of Tel Aviv. If so, the missile strike was off target just enough to land in the heart of one of the most populated areas of the city. General Mordecai Havi, Commander-in-Chief of Israeli Armed Forces, has confirmed to CNN that, in the wake of the declaration of war, all Israeli military personnel have been mobilized, and air strikes are currently being launched upon Lebanon. . ."

Feverishly Angelo grabbed the telephone and called the lab. Lin answered.

"Have you heard about the war?"

"Everyone here is glued to the TV. It doesn't look pretty."

"I need to call Avi to make sure he's all right."

"I've been trying him ever since the news came on," Lin answered. "All I get is a busy circuit signal. The lines are all tied up."

"Then try the international operator. . .I'll hold."

Angelo paced up and back on the rug between the bed and the

television, still wet from the waist up, the towel around his waist disheveled. He nervously tapped his fingers against his leg. Why was it taking so long?

Finally Lin came back on the line. "I got the operator. She said they have no better access. Everyone is trying to call. We'll just have to wait."

"We can't afford to wait!" Angelo ranted. "We have too much riding on this project. Avi has to be all right."

"I know, Angelo, I know."

The next three days Angelo spent most of his time in front of the television and on the phone, frantically trying to find Avi Goldman. Most of his calls ended with the instant and annoying rapid busy circuit signal. Several times his call made it through to Israel, but he was disconnected; apparently many of the telephone lines in Tel Aviv had been sundered by the missile attack. He tried e-mail, fax, and even Western Union, but every channel was blocked. He might as well have been trying to reach Jupiter. The communicator, Angelo reasoned, would have come in handy right about now—all the more reason to resurrect it.

Angelo hoped that Avi would have the presence of mind to call him to reassure him that he was all right, but Angelo figured that Avi, too, could not find an open line. If there was only some way to communicate without a telephone line. Angelo remembered Avi telling him that Rav Shimon had predicted that one day, when we reclaim our psychic faculties, we would not need telephones to communicate. One day . . .

On Friday morning Lin discovered that a fax line had opened up, and she fired a fax to Avi's office.

No response. More waiting.

When he came into his office on Tuesday, Angelo found a fax on his desk. It was handwritten with awkward English letters, just barely legible.

> *Dear Dr. Mann,*
> *I regret to inform you that Dr. Avi Goldman was killed in last Tuesday's missile attack on Tel Aviv. All hell has broken out here. May God rest his soul, and protect ours.*
>
> *Shoshana Birnbaum, Administrator*
> *Department of Physics*

Angelo crumpled the fax and furiously cast it into the wastebasket. Then he picked up his coffee mug and hurled it at the wall, smashing it into a thousand pieces. Angelo turned to see Lin standing in the doorway. Her face was filled with anguish. She had received the fax. "I'm sorry, Angelo."

"Sorry? What good is 'sorry' going to do? He's dead! And so is the key to this whole fucking project! What are we going to do without him? He was the glue that held this entire thing together!"

"We'll catch up, Angelo."

"No, Lin, we won't catch up. You don't understand."

"Understand what?"

"When Avi came to set up the communicator, he coded the primary hard drive with core programming which only he knows. And I picked a password that only I know. We did that as a failsafe so that no one could misuse the communicator. We need both pieces if we are ever to replicate the machine or explain it to anyone else."

"But can't you have someone go in and decipher what he did?"

"That's just the point. He programmed it so that if anyone ever tried to crack the code or even copy the program, it would immediately generate a virus that would disable the entire computer."

"So that means that if anything ever went wrong with this machine, that would be the end of the communicator?"

"Exactly. We never counted on Avi being separated from the project this soon."

"Oh, man. . ."

"Not to mention our time crunch. Who knows how much time

we have before Garrison pulls the plug? If we don't get any results soon, we're dead meat." Angelo looked at Lin inquisitively, hoping she would argue with him. But she couldn't; she knew as well as Angelo that the team was living on borrowed time.

"Maybe I can go find Rav Shimon myself," Angelo blurted out impulsively.

"Get real, Angelo. The place is a war zone. They've suspended all commercial flights indefinitely. This thing isn't going to cool down in time for you to go trotting around the desert. You may be an Italian stallion, but you're not Lawrence of Arabia."

Lin was right. The team was left to their own devices. If there was any synchronicity in the universe, it sure wasn't apparent now.

Chapter 20

I know it's after midnight," he said apologetically, squeezing the phone to his ear with his shoulder, "but I really wanted to talk to you."

"Angelo?"

"Yes, Juliana, it's me."

"Oh, Angelo. . .You don't ever have to worry about waking me."

"I just needed to talk."

"Is everything all right?. . .Is it Jesse?'

"No, it's Avi. . ."

"What happened?"

"He was killed in the war."

"Oh, my God—that's terrible."

"It's more than terrible. . .I know this sounds awfully selfish, but this whole project depended on him. . .I don't know where we go from here."

"I know how important this is to you, Angelo. . .I wish I could help you somehow."

"I just wish I could hold you, feel you, be with you."

"I know. . .I feel the same way. . .Being with you was wonderful. . .It was more than wonderful."

"Then come back. Come back to be with me."

"Are you serious?"

"Yes, Juliana, I am. I want you here with me. I want to look into your eyes and feel your body against mine and laugh with you and talk about the mysteries of the universe with you. I don't want to do it by telephone half a world away. I want to fall asleep with my arms around you and wake up to your smile. I don't want to wait a month

to see you again. You're too important to me. I want you to be a part
of this project. I want to share my life and my work with you."

"God, Angelo, I don't know what to say. . ."

"Just say yes, Juliana, just say yes."

Then a long pause, longer than Angelo could measure. He felt as
if his guts were hanging out. But he didn't care—he said what he had
to say.

"But what would I tell them at the magazine?"

"Tell them you have a lead on a story that could turn science inside out, and this is a once-in-a lifetime chance to get the scoop."

"Angelo, are you sure you aren't really some kind of salesman?"

"If that's what I have to be to get you here, then that's what I'll
be."

"Then it's yes, Angelo. . .It's yes."

Chapter 21

Bearing the awful burden of Avi Goldman's demise, the Beam Team, as they had dubbed themselves, pressed on, desperately trying to fill the void. Avi's insight, they quickly recognized, incorporated so much more than technical knowledge; it was the culmination of 30 years' intimate tutelage with a rare mystic sage—not the kind of knowledge you find in a book or gather in a month.

Angelo hit a dead end; every experiment led the group in circles. In the week since the team learned of Goldman's death, they had made no progress. The funders and university were starting to give Angelo ultimatums, and by his best guess they had a week on the outside. To make matters worse, Juliana called and told him she would have to stay in Germany longer to complete a project before she left for America.

Exasperated, Angelo cleared a mess of papers off the small couch in the lounge next to his office, and lay down. He picked up his original copy of *Journey Beyond the Known* and reread a few paragraphs describing the original imaging device. Suddenly he began to wonder if this was all just a fantasy, some romantic myth. Maybe his critics were right; maybe he was a fool. Maybe, he considered, I should quit before I'm totally embarrassed and turn out like the guy with the machine for autistic kids.

As Angelo turned the pages, the final photo Kohler had given him fell out of the book. Angelo looked at it long and hard, and took a deep breath. He still could not believe what he saw. He placed the photo back in the book and dozed off.

In a flash Angelo found himself in a college guidance counselor's office. He was about 20 years old, being interviewed for a job by several representatives of a prestigious scientific equipment company. When the interviewers described the job qualifications, Angelo shriveled and heard himself answer, "I don't think I can do this job; I don't have the proper credentials."

The reps asked Angelo to please step outside while they conferred. Angelo couldn't imagine why they needed to discuss him; he had just admitted he was not qualified for the job.

When the young Angelo walked into the lobby, he found Avi Goldman sitting on an old, deeply-wrinkled brown leather couch with thick armrests. The two were delighted to be reunited. They hugged warmly and Angelo felt his eyes well up with tears. Avi looked great, and Angelo told him so.

"What are you doing here?" asked Goldman.

"I'm applying for this job, but I don't think I'm going to get it," Angelo answered.

"Why not?"

"I don't have the qualifications; if I took the position, I wouldn't have the slightest clue what I was doing."

"Don't worry," Avi answered. "You have friends in high places."

Angelo awoke with a start. He looked around the room, disoriented. Avi had been right there, and now he was gone. Which reality was true? Ted Kohler's words reverberated in his mind: "Every reality seems like the only one when you're in it."

Angelo stood up, ran his hand through his hair in a feeble attempt to organize his appearance, and staggered back into the laboratory.

"You look like yesterday's lunch," Lin joked when she saw him. Angelo started to retort, but gave up. He liked it when she teased him.

"I just had the weirdest dream," he mumbled. "I was applying for this job that I wasn't qualified for. Then Avi showed up and told me not to worry, 'cause I have friends in high places.'"

A blank expression washed over Lin's face. Like Angelo, she could not make any sense out of the dream. Lin walked over to Angelo and, in a motherly way, fixed his hair. "Come on, Mr. Honcho; we have work to do; I'll get you some coffee."

Angelo walked back into the lab and stood for a moment with his hands on his hips as if to ask, "Where do I go from here?" As he was pondering he was jarred by a shriek from the office. "Angelo, I got it!" Lin burst into the lab, took Angelo by the shoulders, and stood before him proudly. Laughing giddily, she declared, "I know what the dream was about!"

"Pray tell."

"'*Friends in high places*'—that's the key! Goldman is your friend in a high place—he was telling you to contact *him*. He'll be an easy test for the communicator. He's already dedicated to this project—maybe even more so since he was cut off in the middle of it. If anybody on the other side will help us, it's *him*!"

Angelo squeezed his brow as he considered Lin's suggestion. After a few seconds his questioning gave way to a sneaky smile. "And if we do make contact," Angelo answered, "he can guide us from wherever he is."

"Exactly. Maybe from his vantage point he's in an even better position to help us."

Angelo picked up the phone, punched the tone buttons frenetically, and tapped his fingers on the table as he waited for an answer. "Carol, it's Angelo. You have to get over here right now. Something amazing has happened. Goldman has contacted us; we're going to call him back."

"My God!" Lin shrieked when she saw Carol's bruised face at the door. "Are you all right?"

"Definitely an E-ticket ride. I swear my angels must be on the job," Carol blurted out, shaking her head.

Father Al helped Carol to the couch and brought her a wet washcloth, dabbing it on her discolored cheek. "Either someone didn't want me to come here tonight, or my karma is catching up with me."

Jerry brought Carol some cold water. She sipped it slowly, savoring it. Her breath was still choppy. "What in God's name happened to you?" he asked.

"I was driving along Route 1 in Big Sur when this guy in the car behind me started blinking his lights on and off to get my attention. When we came to a passing zone, he pulled up next to me and told me that my engine was leaking some kind of fluid. So I pulled over and he pulled up behind me. Then he offered to check my engine just in case it was brake or transmission fluid. He was traveling with another guy who just sat in the car. The first guy played around under the hood for a while, unscrewing and then screwing caps to a bunch of stuff. He got some brake fluid from his car, put it in mine, and told me everything was okay."

"Well, that was nice of him," Jerry suggested.

"Well, now I'm not so sure. . .The two guys took off and then I started to drive again. After a minute, I put my foot on the brake and got no response. I swear, I was scared shitless. I tried the emergency brake, but it didn't help. I was coming up to this huge hairpin curve, so I tried to slow the car down by putting it in low gear. That worked a little, but the car was not about to stop. I was headed directly for a cliff overlooking a two-hundred-foot drop to the ocean."

"So how did you get out?" Jerry asked.

"By the time the car was about thirty feet from the cliff, it had slowed to about twenty-five miles an hour. I opened the door and jumped out."

"Thank goodness you got out alive!" Lin exclaimed.

"Yes, but my car didn't do so well. It just kept going straight over the edge. It bounded over a huge boulder and then hit the beach and burst into flames. Just like in the movies."

"God, Carol, you could have been killed!" said Lin.

"Do you think those guys were trying to hurt you?" asked Father Al.

"I know that my brakes were working before the guy played with the engine, and they weren't working when he finished. You can do the math."

"Could you identify the guy?"

"He was tall, late-thirties, dark hair, slightly balding, a little stocky. The other guy in the car was younger, gaunt face. . .and he wore a small gold earring in the shape of a cross."

"Did you call the police?"

"Not yet. I was afraid to stay there. If somebody was trying to do me in, I didn't want to give them another shot. I stuck my thumb out and got a ride to a few blocks from here. . .Thank goodness I'm a black woman and not a black man, or I'd still be standing there!"

Angelo smiled and shook his head. "Would you like a ride home?" he asked. "Can I do anything for you?"

"I think I'll be okay for now. I want to know why you called."

"Avi came to Angelo in a dream," Father Al explained. "We think he wants us to communicate with him—maybe try the communicator out on him."

"We want you to try to contact Avi," Angelo stated.

"I don't think I could," Carol answered. "I'm too rattled. It should be one of you."

The others looked at each other to see who would volunteer. Before anyone spoke, Carol pointed to Lin and said, "I think it should be you."

Lin's eyes opened wide. "Me? I don't think so—I'm not a scientist—or a psychic or a priest."

"That's exactly why you must be the first communicator. We need an innocent mind."

"Honey, my mind hasn't been innocent since my sophomore year of high school," Lin protested.

"Your brain is not cluttered with facts or hypotheses or dogma," Carol explained. "You are more receptive than the others here, or me in my current state."

Lin looked questioningly at Angelo. He nodded and motioned for her to go ahead. Lin took a deep breath and reluctantly made her way to the chair connected to the communicator, which the team had dubbed "the hot seat." Lin closed her eyes, took a few more breaths, and Carol guided her into a light trance state. After a minute her countenance grew peaceful. The others watched intently.

"Lin, I want you to concentrate on Avi Goldman," Carol suggested. "Remember what he looked like, how he walked, the sound of his voice." Carol paused to give Lin some time to visualize. Angelo, who was anxious to get on with the experiment, got fidgety. Finally Carol asked, "Are you getting any impressions?"

"Not really," answered Lin.

"Then imagine Avi standing in front of you now. Can you picture him?"

"Sort of."

"Is he saying anything to you?"

"No, he's just standing there. . ." Another minute went by. Suddenly Lin opened her eyes and her shoulders wilted. "I'm sorry, guys—this isn't working; maybe somebody else should try."

The team members looked at each other questioningly. Is there anything to this? Are we on some ridiculous poltergeist hunt?

Silence again. Then suddenly Carol blurted, "radio."

"What?"

"I'm getting an impression of a radio. Do we have one?"

"My clock radio is in the lounge," Jerry reported.

"Please get it."

Jerry found the radio and plugged it in. Suddenly annoying static blared; he adjusted the dial. Then, *"Feeeeeelings, nothing more than feeeeeelings. . ."*

"Quick, change it before I barf!" Lin pleaded.

"No!" Carol interrupted. "This is what we're supposed to hear."

"Come on!" Angelo complained. "This is a scientific laboratory—not a torture chamber."

"Yeah," Jerry agreed. "Maybe Avi went to hell, and he is sentenced to listen to dysfunctional love songs for eternity. Quick, pull the plug before he sucks us in with him."

"No, there is a message here," Carol pleaded. "Give me a moment." She closed her eyes and began to concentrate, seemingly oblivious to the music. Abramson rolled his eyes and squeezed two throw-cushions over his ears.

Suddenly Carol opened her eyes, looking a bit stunned. She stood up and walked toward Lin, meanwhile motioning to Jerry to turn off the radio. He issued a sigh of relief and complied. Carol placed her hands on Lin's shoulders and faced her squarely. "Lin, did you like Avi Goldman?"

Lin was startled, then regained her composure. "'Sure, I thought he was a sweet guy. I only met him twice, but we had fun."

Angelo began to feel uneasy. Had Lin slept with Avi? Lin was a player, but she was not promiscuous. The whole notion was preposterous.

"Good. Now I want you to close your eyes and remember the last time you saw him."

Lin followed the instructions. After a few moments she smiled. "Okay, I have it."

"Where were you?"

"Avi, Angelo, and I were sitting in a Chinese restaurant."

"What were you doing?"

"Avi was opening the fortune cookies and translating the fortunes into Hebrew. I started to laugh so hard I almost spewed tea out of my nose." Angelo smiled as he remembered the scene.

"Good," Carol continued. "Now go back there in your mind and recreate the event. See if you can get into the feeling of actually being there." Carol motioned to Angelo to turn on the communicator.

The group was silent for a long time. All eyes were turned to the communicator's LCD screens, ears trained on the audio speakers. Angelo thought he saw a needle jump, but then realized it was his imagination. The energy in the room was pregnant and electric.

After a few minutes Carol said, "Okay, you can stop now." Lin opened her eyes, Angelo turned off the communicator, and the group sat back. All were disappointed.

"What were you going for?" Father Al asked Carol.

"I felt Avi—or someone—suggesting to me to put on the radio. Maybe we were supposed to hear that song to remind us that getting the feeling behind a memory reactivates it and recreates the energy field of those involved. . .It should have worked; I don't know why it didn't. Maybe my instructions weren't clear enough."

"Well, it was a good try."

The group retired to the office and went into a long involved analysis of their failure. For hours they tried to troubleshoot an ailing quest with no guarantee they would ever fulfill it. Angelo looked out the window and saw that it was already starting to get light. All were tense, tired, and frustrated. Finally Angelo suggested, "Look, I think maybe we have gone far enough; this experiment— "

Suddenly Angelo was interrupted by the sound of laughter. The discussion stopped and everyone perked their ears to hear where the laughter was coming from—and who could it be? The voice seemed to be coming from the hallway adjacent to the lab.

"That sounds like Avi!" Lin exclaimed.

"It sure does!" Angelo agreed.

Everyone bolted out of their seats and ran into the laboratory. As they entered they realized the voice was coming from inside the room. Father Al traced the sound to the clock radio. Its cassette player was rolling, the voice of Avi Goldman laughing and intermittently speaking in Hebrew. In the background, the voices of Angelo and Lin could be heard more faintly.

"Where'd that tape come from?" asked Angelo.

"I think I know," Jerry suggested. "I pressed the cassette *record* button when we began the transmission, just as a backup. I shut it off when we gave up, but obviously it had recorded something when we were silent. Last night I set the alarm to wake up with the cassette at five o'clock. So the cassette started to play—it's on a continuous loop—until it reached the point where we recorded during the attempted transmission."

"So the tape recorded our whole session?" Father Al asked.

"Not just us, but Avi," Carol chimed in. "He came through on the tape during our silence."

Jerry rewound the cassette until the group heard Carol softly instruct Lin, "Now go back in your mind and recreate that event." The tape was silent for about fifteen seconds, and then faintly, gradually, the voices of Avi, Angelo, and Lin could be heard. It was an audio recording of their dinner at the Chinese restaurant—recorded not when it occurred, but as Lin remembered it.

"Holy shit!" Lin exclaimed, rubbing the goose bumps on her arms.

"He's come through!" Angelo exclaimed. "Goldman's come

through!" The group ecstatically gave each other loud high-fives.

Carol surmised, "It was the feeling element that put us over the edge. That really *was* Avi telling us to listen to that song."

"But why do you think we heard him on the tape, but not with our ears?" asked Father Al.

"The strength of his communication was too subtle to generate physical sound waves that our ears could hear," Jerry suggested.

"But he could generate electromagnetic vibrations sufficient to rearrange the electrons on the cassette tape," Angelo added. "It makes perfect sense: the purpose of the communicator is to tap into what is happening below the threshold of our awareness and pump up the volume so our physical senses can perceive it."

"Okay," Lin went on. "That proves we can tap into the subtle field and recall past events. But can we communicate with Avi now?"

"Let's find out." Jerry put a fresh tape in the cassette recorder and stayed poised to start recording.

"Angelo, you sit in this time—you knew Avi best."

Angelo took the hot seat as Jerry set up the communicator.

"Now take a few breaths, close your eyes, and think of Avi," Carol instructed.

Angelo complied.

"What was your favorite memory of Avi?"

"I enjoyed our conversations; we would stretch our minds to the edges of the universe and beyond. I remember once, when Avi was here setting up the communicator, everyone else had left and we were here together at midnight. We got into this talk about metaphysics and the nature of reality and how great mystics and visionaries pierce beyond the commonly accepted beliefs that keep most people living small. When we started the conversation I was tired, but I got so excited about the talk that when we were done—it must have been 2 or 3 in the morning—I could hardly fall asleep. It was like we were little kids exploring a mysterious cave, a vast new world."

"Excellent. Now go to your favorite time you had one of those talks, and imagine you are there now."

After a minute Angelo answered, "Okay."

"Where are you?" Carol asked.

"I'm driving Avi to the airport."

"And what is happening?"

"We are stuck in traffic, and we are talking about the fact that time is an illusion, and it flexes like rubber, depending on whether you are liking what you are doing, or resisting it. We get so immersed in our talk that the traffic seems to disappear and I feel utterly happy."

Carol watched Angelo's face as he went into an alpha state. When he seemed relaxed she asked, "Avi, can you hear me?"

Silence.

"Avi, if you can hear me, please speak to us."

Silence.

"Avi, if there is anything we need to know, would you please communicate?"

Silence.

After a few minutes Carol motioned to Jerry to turn off the communicator and the tape.

Jerry hurriedly rewound the cassette and began to replay it. The group gathered around the machine, riveted.

"Avi, can you hear me?" Carol's voice replayed clearly.

Silence. Then static . . .then a faint "Shalom."

"Play that back!"

"Shalom."

"Oh my God, this is too weird!" Lin turned white and reached to turn off the switch. Angelo reached to turn it on again.

Carol's voice came back: "Avi, if you can hear me, please speak to us."

Static. Then, "The real question is, 'Can you hear me?'"

All looked at each other, bug-eyed.

Carol again: "Avi, if there is anything we need to know, would you please tell us?"

The voice, unmistakably that of Avi Goldman, announced, "My friends, it is good to be with you again. As you can hear, I am not very far from you. Rest assured that I am here—you can't get rid of me that easily. Congratulations—we are online."

Chapter 22

It took the Beam Team two weeks to build the system according to Avi's instructions. Quickly they realized that it might have taken them years to develop the same technology by trial and error. Now the new equipment sat before them, ready to be tested.

L.C. sat at the control panel making final adjustments. He had flown out to the west coast to join the team as soon as he heard that Goldman was coming through. Father Al, sitting to L.C.'s right, leaned over to Angelo and asked, "Would you mind giving an ignorant old priest some idea how this thing works?"

Angelo smiled. "The technology is quite complex, but the idea behind it is pretty simple," he explained. "Everything in the universe vibrates according to a unique frequency. You, I, every rock, every frog, every person pulses with a signal that identifies it. As human beings, we generally limit our perceptions to the signals picked up by our sensory organs of sight, sound, touch, smell, and taste.

"But there are all kinds of energies moving in and around us that we are not aware of, simply because our physical sensory receivers don't match the frequencies being transmitted."

"You mean like dogs hearing sounds and smelling scents that we cannot?"

"Precisely. Now here's where this becomes very interesting: Every *soul* has a frequency. The inner being of every person is like a radio station broadcasting at a specific vibrational rate."

"Yes, I read a poet who said that everyone must sing their own song."

"Avi suggested that everyone is *already* singing their own song. So here is the key that makes this apparatus work: *Every soul's frequency is identifiable and quantifiable.* This means that with sufficiently sensitive equipment we could pick up any individual soul's transmission and send them back a signal they could hear."

Father Al nodded, indicating he was following.

"During the last two weeks we've developed a coordinate system that helps us zero in on any soul. We've created a grid, something like the Global Positioning System that pinpoints boats in the middle of the ocean, cars on the highway, hikers in the middle of a desert, anyone anywhere. Our system tells us the precise coordinates of anyone we contact spiritually. We call this number a 'Universal Positioning Registration,' or 'UPR.' Avi helped us to identify his UPR, and that is what we are about to hail."

Father Al looked perplexed. Scratching the back of his neck, he asked, "So can we just go snooping around the universe picking souls out of the ethers? Isn't that a violation of privacy?"

"The answer to that question, Father, is right up your alley."

"Well, thank God I have a purpose in this world!"

"As Avi explained the process, communicating with a spirit is not just a matter of locking in their coordinates. There's another element."

"What's that?"

"Free will. The person has to want to be contacted, and willing to respond."

"So that's how we got through to Avi."

"Exactly."

"And we can't just send out a whole mess of signals and see who shows up."

"We could, but Avi warned us that we would not want to communicate with just anybody. Some souls are, uh. . ."

"Are what?"

". . . are of a dark nature."

"You mean like demonic entities?"

"Something like that."

"Hell, that's not for me," Father Al said, shaking his head. "After I saw *The Exorcist* I couldn't eat split pea soup for a year."

Angelo laughed. "No worries, Father. Avi put a quick halt to the idea of possession. What he meant was that there are souls who are operating at a pretty dense vibration, and we wouldn't want to go into their world with them."

"Okay, so if I understand this correctly, we call in souls with our thoughts, and then the machine helps us by amplifying the transmission and registering their coordinates."

"Avi said that our minds and brains are far more sophisticated than the technology you see before you. He wants us to use our own muscles to attract those we want to talk to. In a way, we have to earn whoever shows up."

Their conversation was interrupted by L.C. "Ready!" he called out. Everyone took their places.

Jerry went to the communicator's keyboard and punched in a string of commands. The red LCD screen over the keyboard immediately displayed:

<u>311.212</u>
97.2

The team sat perfectly still, eyes glued to the communicator and ears straining to hear. After a few seconds static emerged from the speakers and the numbers on the LCD began to fade in and out. L.C. sat at the helm fiddling with the dials, trying to lock in on the signal. After another minute the numbers on the screen remained steady and the static disappeared.

Suddenly the team members heard a terrible eerie sound. "Ooooooooo. . .Ooooooooo," like a tormented soul trapped in a haunted house on Halloween. Lin shrieked and clutched onto Jerry, who was nearly as terrified.

"Oooooooooo!" the voice repeated. Then, "Shalom, my friends," followed by laughter. It was Avi. "Just thought I'd bring you a little entertainment with the spook show."

"Avi, I can't believe you did that!" Angelo called out. Jerry Abramson just shook his head. Carol put her hands on her hips and looked indignant. Father Al looked stunned. Lin made a long raspberry. L.C. kept his eyes on the machinery.

"Sorry if I scared you," Avi said. "I was hoping to get you all to lighten up about death."

"Duuuuuh!" exclaimed Lin.

"Death, my friends, is just a change in perspective," Avi explained. "Once I saw a cartoon of two caterpillars talking. One caterpillar looks up, sees a butterfly, points to it, and says, 'You'll never get *me* up in one of those things.' The point is, you *are* one of those things."

The group laughed. Lin spontaneously called out, "I miss you, Avi—why did you have to die? You were a hoot—you still are!"

"When I arrived in this dimension, Lin, many things became clear. It was like taking a helicopter ride—immediately I could see the road that led me here and how all of our paths intersected. One can read maps from here that one could never perceive from the ground level. Now I understand that the time and manner of my death were an integral part of the plan for my life."

"How is that?" asked Father Al.

"The work we are doing together was one of my soul's purposes for being born. My aptitude for science, my love of metaphysics, my tutelage with Rav Shimon, my meeting Angelo—everything was a link in a grand unseen chain that unites our lives."

"But why would you let yourself be killed if you knew your work on this project was so important?" asked Father Al.

"That is precisely why I had to leave when I did. On a soul level I knew I could assist you far more powerfully from this side."

"God, now I feel guilty," Lin interjected "It's like you died for us."

"No, not at all. First of all, I didn't really die—if I did, I wouldn't be talking to you now. And the choice to leave was my own. Besides, I am having a lot of fun here; I've already visited with many friends and relatives I thought I would never see again. I even got to play with my pet lizard I had as a child! Now I realize that people on earth suffer from discrimination against death; in terms of today's political correctness, you are all mortality-impaired!"

The group laughed again; this had to be Avi.

"Guilt, my friends, is entirely an invention of the fearful mind, and lives only in the minds and hearts of those who pay homage to it. Every person generates his own hell or heaven with the thoughts he dwells on. No one can do anything to you—or for you—without your permission. Each of us is a co-creator with God, continually building and reinforcing the world view we choose."

"But what about victims—of crimes, of disasters, of accidents?"

"'Victim' is a word that holds no reality here. We each magnetize people and experiences according to our beliefs and expectations, most of which we hold below the threshold of our awareness. Everyone who shows up in your life is answering a casting call you have dispatched. You might say that we 'hire' people to show us—sometimes in dramatic ways—what we believe. If you hold self-abusive thoughts, you will attract people who hurt you. If you honor and appreciate who you are, you will draw people who support and nurture you. So instead of cursing those who criticize you, you can thank them for bringing to light the self-defeating beliefs you were harboring before they ever showed up."

"Is that why people stay in oppressive situations?"

"The only thing that can oppress you is your own mind. The outer world has no power to hold you back, unless you allow it to do so. You believe it is the world that causes your thoughts, but it is your thoughts that cause your world. That is why the only effective way to change the outer world is to change your way of thinking. In the end, your inner world is the only world you truly have control over, and it is the one you must master. Such mastery can take place only on the spiritual level. Because we are spiritual beings, it is not material conditions that make our destiny, but the spirit in which we live."

"Like the people in concentration camps who helped everyone they met and gave encouragement and love in the midst of great outer darkness?" asked Jerry.

"Exactly. The delusion of earth is that what is happening on the outside is the reality—but that's only a portion of the picture. It's what's happening on the inside that makes all the difference. When your spirit leaves your body, what you take with you is your inner life. If you keep your inner light burning in the midst of trying circumstances, you have mastered earth."

"But what about accidents?" Lin asked. "All kinds of good people get run over and fall off of buildings when they didn't mean to."

"Accidents, Lin, are wake-up calls. If you examine what was going on in your life at the time of an accident, you will see that something distracted you from being fully present and caused you to be out of touch with your inner guidance, or override it."

"Like people who hear an inner voice that says, 'Don't do this,' and they do it anyway and wreck their car or their marriage, and then afterward they realize that they had that feeling all along?"

"Exactly. And there is another purpose behind what you call 'accidents': They get your attention to make a significant life change. People who are seriously injured in auto accidents, for example, or those diagnosed with a life-threatening illness, are often moved to take stock of how they are living, let go of whatever was distracting them from their true purpose and then they put joy, kindness, or quality time with their family and friends first. Also, someone who is ill or injured may be put in a position where he or she must ask for help and accept love from others. Many people report that their accident or illness was one of the most important turning points in their life.

"All of life, my friends, is woven together with impeccable intelligence. Miracles are occurring around you daily, whether you see them or not. As you open to greater love, you receive striking confirmations that a brilliant Higher Power is running the show. If you can just relax and trust, you will be supported in ways far more powerful than you could ever accomplish through anxious manipulation."

"But Avi, what about this project?" Angelo exhorted. "How are we ever going to accomplish what we want in the little time we have?"

"If you lighten up about it, my friend, you will see exactly how to proceed. Worry is the most counterproductive use of your energy. It keeps your wheels spinning in a little rut that only gets deeper. Just relax and trust, and you will receive help and find the strength to handle whatever is before you.

"As for your road adventure, Carol, that was certainly no accident—you know that."

"Yes, I have to admit that," she answered meekly.

"There are those in your world who are threatened by your work. Be aware that your research has attracted more attention than you know. Some are watching to check your progress. Now that you are coming close to your goal, they believe they must prevent you from succeeding."

A chill of fear washed through the room; half the group paled. Eyes caught other eyes as if to ask, "Are we in danger?" Lin glanced at the laboratory door to make sure it was locked. Angelo wondered if there was a traitor in their midst.

Avi went on as if he had heard their thoughts. "Do not be afraid; fear is the energy that motivates your opponents, and you must not match it. Know that you are protected by the light. Your intentions are pure, and you will receive help from unseen sources. Keep the flame burning."

The UPR readout faded, indicating that Avi had taken his leave. The group sat stunned. Avi had dropped a huge cache of information in their laps, almost too much for them to digest. His warning jarred them. Their project already seemed impossible, not to mention that their funders could pull the plug at any moment; having to contend with some dark force G-men was a major curve ball to reckon with.

Angelo looked at the clock; it was time to pick up Juliana from the airport. Just a short time ago, he would have liked to have dumped this whole ridiculous escapade and got on a plane with her to anywhere but here. Now he had a sense of purpose. Now he knew why he had to see this through. Now Juliana would be at his side, working toward a common goal. Everything was coming together. Everything, that is, except for the news that someone was out to stop them.

As Angelo gathered his jacket and briefcase, he considered Avi's tenets: no accidents, no victims, no death. Nearly every principle Avi had put forth flew in the face of the reality Angelo had been taught was true. Suddenly it appeared that to find the truth, every law of the world had to be reversed. But, Angelo further considered, look at the history of the world—millennia of suffering, fear, pain, and aching human hearts. Perhaps, he surmised, if I am to change the world at all, I am going to have to question the reality I have accepted and use a higher way of seeing. Immediately a wave of peace washed over him. Angelo remembered Ted Kohler telling him that when such a feeling of relief or tingling rippled through his body, it meant that the thought he had just had or the word he had spoken, was true.

That night Angelo lay in bed, coursing with excitement about the staggering possibilities that lay before him. The magnitude of what the group was accomplishing was immense. Imagine, Angelo considered, college classes conversing directly with Galileo or inviting Mozart *himself* to address a music composition seminar. Imagine hearing the Gettysburg address in the voice of Lincoln; entering the King's Chamber of the Great Pyramid as the Pharaoh was laid to rest; gazing upon the hypnotic face of Helen of Troy; unraveling the mystery of Stonehenge; returning to ancient Sumeria and finding out if that civilization's unexplainable knowledge of astronomy was indeed given to them by extraterrestrials. He and the team were opening doors that could easily change the entire course of evolution on the planet.

After an hour of envisioning possibilities, Angelo realized he was just hyperstimulated and there was no way he was going to sleep. He decided to get up and surf the net, just to occupy his restless mind. He sat down at the computer and logged on. The little red mailbox flag was up, indicating he had mail. He clicked on the icon to check it. The message read:

Stop before you go through the portal.
You have no idea what lies on the other side.
The beast masquerades as scientific progress.
The forces of light will not tolerate your arrogance.

Bathed in the eerie glow of the monitor, a chill of fear rolled up Angelo's spine. He remembered Avi's prediction that certain forces would try to thwart him. Now here they were, right on the screen in his bedroom. He recalled the attempt on Carol's life and began to feel quite vulnerable.

Angelo looked at the return address section on the e-mail, but no name was recorded. The writer must have had access to a good hacker who could override the e-mail system program. Angelo decided that when he got to the lab in the morning, he would ask Jerry to try to trace the sender.

Suddenly Angelo realized there was no more time to play around. If he was going to contact Jesse, it would have to be soon. It would have to be tomorrow.

Chapter 23

As Angelo and Juliana entered the lab, Father Al was sitting in the hot seat. Suddenly the two heard a sharp *crack!* followed by the overwhelming roar of a huge crowd. Angelo looked out the window to see what had happened, thinking a branch had broken off a tree, but no such thing had occurred. Then he realized the sound was coming from the communicator's audio speakers.

"That's number 60!" an exuberant static-laden man's voice shouted. *"Babe Ruth, the King of Baseball, has just slammed his 60th home run, breaking his own record. Ladies and gentlemen, today history is being made, and you heard it!"*

Angelo hurried to join the team clustered at the communicator, listening incredulously. "1927," Jerry noted, matter-of-fact; "The Babe just hit the big one."

Father Al, as startled as his onlookers, opened his eyes suddenly. The UPR quickly disappeared and everyone sat back, stunned. Carol turned to Angelo and noted in a droll voice, "Hypnosis works."

"What?"

"Getting the subject into a meditative state really opens up the channel. Also, the more enthusiastic the subject feels about the person or scenario we are trying to engage, the greater our chances of connecting." Carol rubbed the side of her neck, trying to ease some of the tension she had accrued. "When we first put Father Al in the hot seat we tried to contact Abraham Lincoln. No dice. After three feeble attempts he admitted he hated history; his elementary school teacher nun was a shrew. When we asked him, 'What historical figure would you most love to meet?' he smiled and told us, 'Babe Ruth.' You heard the results."

"So motivation plays a big role."

"I'd call it 'heart's desire.' If you love or yearn for something enough, you can generate the power to draw it to you. It happens every day in real life, but hardly anyone recognizes their authority to magnetize events."

"Like people attracting their soulmates in unexplainable ways?" Lin asked.

"Everybody, this is Juliana," Angelo interjected.

"Nice to meet you," Lin smiled, extending her hand.

"Welcome aboard," L.C. greeted her. "We've heard a lot about you."

"Yes," Jerry added. "If you're half as sharp as Angelo says you are, we're lucky to be working with you."

Juliana smiled. "Well, I hope I can live up to my reputation. I'm really glad to be here with you. It's like a dream come true." Juliana turned to Carol and noted, "I liked what you were saying about soulmates."

"You just saw a perfect demonstration of the power of heart's desire," Carol noted. "Father Al had no interest in connecting with Lincoln, but a strong desire to meet the Babe."

Father Al's face flushed beet red.

"The Babe—Ruth, that is," Carol had to add. Everyone laughed.

"That was really phenomenal!" Father Al exuded as he arose from the hot seat. "It was as if I was right there! In my mind I saw the whole crowd rise to its feet and let out a huge cheer! And the smile on the Babe's face as he trotted the bases—I swear I'll never forget it!"

Just then a scruffy man appeared at the lab door. He wore a sweatshirt, hunting vest, dirty jeans, and cowboy boots. He carried some papers in his hands.

"I'm looking for Dr. Mann's office," he announced soberly.

Angelo rose and went to the door. "I'm Dr. Mann." Angelo looked over the man's shoulder and saw two other guys, just as tough-looking as the first.

"We were sent by Mr. Garrison's office. We have orders to remove the scientific equipment on loan to you."

Angelo's heart skipped a beat. His body stiffened and his jaw clenched. "I'd like to call Mr. Garrison, if you don't mind." Angelo asserted.

"I'm sorry, sir. I have orders to remove the equipment immediately. This is a court order right here." He handed the papers to Angelo. He wasn't kidding.

Angelo wanted to just force the goons out and barricade the door, but there was no way that was going to happen. Angelo looked to the others, who looked as bereft as he did. "I don't think we have much choice," L.C. said.

Angelo thought for a few moments, then nodded to the man who had spoken. One of the other men went outside and backed a truck up to the lab door. The other men went into the back of the truck and brought out some large cardboard boxes, crates, and soft packing material. Then they went about the business of removing every piece of equipment that matched the list they were given. Within an hour the lab was bare.

When the last oscillator was out the door, Jerry threw up his hands and exclaimed, "We're totally screwed!"

"The equipment isn't even the most important thing; we could always replicate that," noted L.C. "Avi's programming is irreplaceable."

"So now what do we do?" asked Lin.

"We'll just have to start over," said Father Al.

"You're forgetting two minor points," Angelo said sarcastically. "We need someone who knows more about this kind of technology than we do, and we need money to get new equipment."

A terrible heavy silence hung over the group. Hardly anyone made eye contact. Then Juliana said, "I have an idea." The others looked toward her, fully attentive. "How about Jean-Claude? He's a world-class expert in holographic imaging."

"He also happens to be a world-class jerk," Angelo reported with a pained expression.

"You mean Jean-Claude Michaud?" asked Jerry. "His articles and interviews are in lots of pop-tech magazines. He's the state-of-the-art virtual reality guru. If anybody can help us, he can."

"Oh, man," Angelo complained, "Do you really believe we need that asshole?"

"Even assholes serve a function," Carol declared. "Have you ever tried living without one?"

Angelo winced.

That night as Angelo was opening the door to his apartment, the phone rang. He put down the package under his arm and hustled to the phone on the kitchen counter. It was Carol. "I have some news," she told him.

"Uh-oh."

"I have a client who owns a farm in Sonoma County, just north of Marin. There's a barn on the property; she hasn't used it in years. It's way off the road and nobody ever comes around. I think it would be a good place for us to set up again."

"What do we need to do?"

"I just talked to her. She said we can use the place as long as we want for free."

"Seriously?"

"Yeah, she owes me one. I gave her a reading a few years ago and told her to go on this cruise she was wondering about. She met a guy and six months later they got married. Now she thinks I'm a good witch. She'd do anything for me."

"Yes!" Angelo exclaimed, cranking his arm with clenched fist.

Juliana was taking her jacket off as Angelo hung up. "What's up?" she asked.

"We have a place to rebuild that lab!"

"Excellent!" she responded, then looked at the clock on the wall. "Maybe now would be a good time to call Jean-Claude. It's morning in France."

Angelo made a face.

"If you don't want me to call, I won't," she said. "I'm just trying to help you."

"Oh, all right," he replied, rolling his eyes.

Juliana smiled, gave Angelo a peck on the cheek, and picked through her organizer. She took the remote phone and dialed a long series of numbers. Finally Michaud answered, and the two spoke in German for a few minutes. Then Juliana handed Angelo the phone, cupping her hand over the mouthpiece. She was smiling. "I think he'll do it," she said. "He also has funding he can divert to get us new equipment."

"Excellent!" Angelo started to get excited, then he caught himself. A forlorn expression overtook his face. "Now all we have to do is find Avi Goldman. That may not be so easy."

Chapter 24

Within a week the Beam Team crudely refurbished two thousand square feet of the musty relic of a barn and upgraded the electrical system. It's not Stanford, Angelo considered, but, hey, if we can get the job done here, it works.

Piece by piece, new equipment began to arrive, courtesy of Jean-Claude Michaud's grant diversion. Recreating the hardware for the communicator was easy, since the team had just developed the device. The software operating system was the crucial missing element, and it remained a huge question mark.

As Angelo stood with Lin at the checkout counter in Home Depot, the cashier handed Angelo's Visa card to him and told him, "Sorry, this was declined."

Embarrassed, Angelo gave her a MasterCard. She swiped it through the reader. A few seconds later the little blue letters appeared: *Declined.*

Flustered, Angelo reached for his one remaining hope, an American Express card. "I just opened this account. It should work." Angelo held his breath as the cashier scanned the card. The little blue letters popped up: *APP 569430.* Angelo exhaled.

As they guided two huge shopping baskets full of electrical and carpentry supplies to the new Pathfinder, Lin noted, "You've really leveraged yourself out on this project, Angelo. I've seen you go through half a dozen credit cards."

"I used to throw them out as soon as they showed up in the mailbox," Angelo answered smugly. "Now I just activate them."

As the two loaded the SUV, Lin stopped and asked Angelo seriously, "Are you sure you want to do this, Angelo? You've lost your job, your wife has left, and now you're mortgaging your life in credit cards. What do you owe now? 60, 70, 80? Are you really sure you want to do all this for an experiment?"

Angelo turned and stared at Lin with an intensity she had not seen before. "No, Lin," he answered adamantly, almost angrily, "this is *not* just an experiment. This is my life. This is my son's life. I don't care about my credit card balance. I care about my son."

Angelo discovered a small abandoned cottage in the woods behind the barn, which he and Juliana cleaned up and then brought in some used furniture they found at a yard sale. The cottage was ever so humble, but it sure beat paying rent and it was just a short walk to the lab. Jerry, Carol, and L.C. found a small house for rent a few miles down the road. Lin stayed with her sister, who had a place in San Rafael. Father Al stayed at home in Walnut Creek and came up as often as he could.

Michaud showed up a week later and booked himself into the Executive Suites; he put the bill on Angelo's last credit card. Angelo felt gouged, but at this point he didn't feel like dickering. Michaud proved to be utterly brilliant; he helped the team in ways they could not have helped themselves. At the same time the man was unbelievably obnoxious. He came and went as he pleased, did not keep his agreements, and spoke to his co-workers as if they were his servants. Angelo's mantra became, "But we need him"—and he was right. Michaud's expertise was unsurpassed, and the Beam Team was rapidly advancing toward recreating the communicator.

Within a week after Jean-Claude's arrival the team had gotten the communicator to the point where they could tap into various historical events, as if watching a movie. They had discovered a way to combine Global Positioning System points with chronological time coordinates, creating a time-space matrix they could pinpoint and zoom in on. As for resuming contact with souls, that was quite a more advanced technique which required highly complex programming—such as Avi had imbedded—and the Beam Team was desperately trying to figure that out on their own.

One morning as Angelo was tightening his front door hinge with a screwdriver, he heard a voice from the lab shouting, "Get off my back, would you? I'm sick and tired of you barking at me." Angelo put down his tool and dashed to the barn, where Michaud and Abramson were going at it again. When Jerry saw Angelo enter, he turned to him and pleaded, "Angelo, I can't work with this schmuck. All he does is shout orders at me; you'd think I was some kind of little puppy dog."

"I'll shout if I like," Jean-Claude retorted. "I'm working with a bunch of idiots."

"Okay, okay, what's going on?" Angelo asked.

"This guy has the emotional maturity of a ten-year-old," Abramson fumed. "Every time anything doesn't go exactly how he wants, he throws a tantrum. It's always someone else's fault. Grow up, would you?"

"Look, Jean-Claude. . .," Angelo tried to interject.

"Don't you 'look' me, you imbecile," Michaud fired back. "If it weren't for me, your little experiment would be down the toilet. If you don't like my style, I'll take my funding and equipment, and you can all collect unemployment."

Blood rushed to Angelo's face. "You can't just walk in here and play God. You were invited, remember?"

"Then I'll uninvite myself. Then you can go back to being a child-beater and visiting your vegetable son for the rest of your life."

That did it. Angelo became so furious that he grabbed Jean-Claude by the neck and started to wrestle him to the floor. But Michaud was stronger and threw him off. Angelo was set to charge Michaud when Father Al, who had been standing by the door, caught Angelo and restrained him. "Take it easy, Angelo, take it easy," Father Al told him.

Angelo, breathing rapidly, tried to cool himself down.

"Look, you guys," Father Al went on. "We're all under a lot of stress. We're all doing the best we can. Let's not mess it all up by get-ting on each other's case—we have too much at stake. We're about to test the new equipment, and we need to get along, huh?"

"Father Al's right," Juliana added. "We're so close. Let's focus on our work. We need to decide who's going to sit in for our transmis-sion."

"I'll go first," Jean-Claude volunteered.

"Good," Carol answered. "Let's get to work."

L.C. hooked Jean-Claude up to the GSR and EEG monitors. Carol assumed her usual seat next to the communicator and readied herself for the hypnotic induction. As soon as Michaud was in alpha, she asked, "Who would you like to observe?"

Without hesitation Michaud answered, "Adolph Hitler."

The group flinched; Lin almost let out an audible gasp. Eyes caught eyes and brows furrowed.

"Are you crazy?" asked Jerry.

"I assure you I am quite serious."

"Why would you want to tune in on Hitler?" Father Al asked, dis-traught. "My God, the world's been trying to undo his menace for sixty years!"

"Why not?" retorted Michaud. "Hitler is the most significant his-torical figure of the twentieth century. The Nazis overran my country and killed my grandparents. As true scientists, we should be inter-ested in understanding the mind that wrought such carnage."

Abramson blurted out, "I, too, lost relatives in that war—six mil-lion of them. When I went to the holocaust memorial in Jerusalem, I saw a huge monument with the inscription, 'NEVER AGAIN.' I don't see any purpose in resurrecting that lousy bastard."

"But Jerry," interrupted Carol, "We're not resurrecting Hitler; at this point the communicator doesn't have the ability to make two-way contact—"

"—*at this point*," Angelo underscored.

Carol went on, "Right now all Jean-Claude wants to do is tap into some historical incidents."

"That's right," Michaud threw in cynically; "You got to observe your favorite scientists and statesmen; why cower at the thought of someone from the dark side?"

"Something about this smells rank to me," Jerry retorted "—and I want no part of it." With that, Abramson turned, threw his papers into his briefcase, grabbed his jacket, and stormed out the door. Angelo started to follow him, but L.C. grabbed Angelo before he got very far. "He's gone," said L.C. We need you here." Abramson made his way to his car just outside the barn and sped out of the parking lot. As he turned onto the county road, the communicator's speakers billowed from deep in the barn. A huge crowd of angry voices shouted in unison, "*Sieg Hiel! Sieg Hiel!*"

That night Angelo made his way over the Bay Bridge en route to the apartment complex where he had been staying. He was anxious to collect his security deposit. Just after the bridge Angelo noticed a huge California Lottery billboard. He snickered and shuddered to consider how radically his world had changed in just a few months. Not long ago he would have thought nothing of spending $750 on a nice suit. Now he was hungry to pick up a check in that amount, just to survive. A few months ago he was one of the most prestigious scientists in the world. Now everything he had was gone and he owed big time on plastic. But then a strange yet wonderful feeling washed through Angelo's heart, a feeling he had not experienced since he was very young. He felt free and alive, as if he was sitting in the cockpit of one of those old open-air biplanes, feeling the crisp air blow over his face and through his hair. His life had dramatically shifted from a drudgery to an adventure. None of the things he had abandoned, he realized, were real losses. None of them had ever brought him the kind of aliveness he was feeling now.

Angelo pulled into the apartment complex parking lot and stepped out of the LX470. As he pressed the alarm activator on his key chain he wondered how much he could get for the Lexus. Now everything in his life revolved around building the communicator and making contact with Jesse.

He walked along the broken sidewalk bordering the long red brick complex, and turned right up the steps to the manager's door. Angelo rang the doorbell and was greeted first by the acrid smell of frying pork, then by Joe the manager, who wore heavy jeans and a black Hulk Hogan T-shirt with a tattoo of some kind of Balinese goddess emerging from under his right shirt sleeve. "Dr. Mann—How's it goin'?"

"Taking it day by day, Joe."

"Yeah, aren't we all?"

"I came to pick up my security deposit."

"Sure, come on in. Would you like a beer?"

"Thanks, I'll pass."

Joe went into the kitchen and came back a minute later with a check and a large white thin cardboard envelope. "Your timing is pretty good, Dr. Mann."

"How's that?"

"This express mail came for you yesterday. I didn't have your new address, so I signed for it and figured I'd give it to you when you showed up." Joe handed the check and the envelope to Angelo.

Angelo took it in his hands and saw a six-pointed Jewish star printed in blue on the upper left corner. It was from Israel. "Thanks, Joe. . .Thanks a lot."

"Sure, good luck," Joe answered as Angelo stepped out onto the porch. He closed the door behind him.

Angelo stood at the doorstep bubbling with curiosity. He read the return address: "Shoshana Birnbaum, Department of Physics, Tel Aviv University."

"Holy. . ." Angelo muttered aloud as he ripped open the envelope. He hadn't even bothered to step off Joe's porch.

Inside he found a CD-ROM in a plain little cardboard holder. Attached to it was a note in the same handwriting as the awful fax he had received, the one informing him of Avi's death.

Dear Dr. Mann,

A few days before he was killed, Dr. Goldman gave me this CD-ROM for safekeeping. He told me that if he was ever incapacitated in any way, I should send this to you. I have no idea of its contents, but I hope it will be useful to you. We really miss Avi.
Shoshana Birnbaum

Angelo dashed to his car and peeled out of the parking lot, nearly hitting a motorcyclist entering. He made his way through the city and into Marin, then raced north on 101, doing at least 85, more where he could. He arrived at the lab in just over an hour and a half, then ran into the barn without even bothering to close the car door. Lin and L.C. were puttering with some data printouts at her desk. Carol was tidying the meditation alcove.

Angelo set the CD-ROM down on the desk in front of Lin and told her, "Put this in. . .now."

"Getting bossy, are we?" Lin answered in a sassy voice.

"Lin, this is no time for jokes. . . just run it." Carol saw what was going on and came over to Lin's desk.

"Okay, okay," Lin answered. She placed the shiny plastic disk into the slot and clicked on "run."

The machine made the familiar whirring noise, indicating it was reading the disk, and within seconds the menu showed two files, one called "README" and the other, "HOLYMOSES."

"Click on 'README,'" Angelo urged.

The file came up and, with Angelo and L.C. literally breathing down her neck looking at the screen, she read aloud:

Dear Angelo,
If you are reading this, something has happened to me. I know that with this project we are playing with fire, and anything could happen to any of us. So I decided to make a backup of the programming I imbedded in the communicator, the programming only I knew.

"Yes!" yelled Angelo. "Yes, you brilliant Jewish Dough Boy! You've come through again!" Angelo leaned over and kissed the computer screen repeatedly. Then he kissed Lin on the cheek, then Carol, then L.C., who was not quite as receptive as the women, but accepted the gesture nevertheless.

Lin continued reading:

> *Just copy the HOLYMOSES file to the hard drive of the communicator.*
> *Keep the faith,*
>
> Avi
> *P.S. To maintain security, I coded this CD-ROM like the communicator. If anyone attempts to copy or dissect it, it will self-destruct via virus.*

The four looked at each other, stunned. "Talk about providence!" Angelo shouted. Carol simply shook her head from side to side, grinning.

"Let's get Jean-Claude over here right away," Angelo said as he reached to pick up the phone. But before he could lift the receiver, Carol's hand was pressing down on his.

"Wait," she told him ominously. "I'm not sure that's such a good idea."

Angelo looked at Carol. Then he became serious. "I think I know what you're going to say."

"I have a really bad feeling about Jean-Claude and this Nazi stuff. I don't buy for a minute that it's just for research. I think he has an agenda. I don't know where he plans to go with this, but it isn't good."

"I agree," said L.C. "For a French guy, he spends a lot of time on the phone talking German."

"And most of the new equipment is from German scientific companies," Lin added.

"If we load this program into the communicator, we'll regain UPR capability. And you know who will be the first one Michaud contacts," noted L.C.

All looked at each other anxiously. "We can't tell Jean-Claude that we have this CD," said Carol.

"I agree," echoed Angelo. "But what if he comes up with the technology on his own? Then what will we do?"

"Let's beat him to the punch. We'll wait until he's not around and then we'll plug in this CD and contact someone on the communicator, someone who can help us."

Chapter 25

At 8 a.m. the Beam Team was gathered around the communicator, anxious to send feelers into the past, meet their heroes, and find out the truth about what really happened. The team was especially grateful to Jerry Abramson who, before his departure, had devised a universal translator program which automatically translated the speakers' foreign language words into English; the program wasn't perfect, but it did render the speakers intelligible.

The team agreed to each take a turn tuning in on a particular personage or event. Angelo "dropped in" on Copernicus as he issued his heretical announcement that the earth revolved around the sun. Carol went to study the life of her great-great-great-grandmother who as a young woman had been a slave on a Louisiana plantation. L.C. watched Benjamin Franklin's discovery of electricity (it wasn't exactly as the history books had purported). Lin went to revisit some of the precious moments she had shared with her brother as a young girl in Beijing. Father Al went to Assisi, Italy in the year 1205, to see St. Francis as he won souls to his new order.

After lunch Jean-Claude was up for his next turn. He positioned himself in the hot seat and Carol began his induction. "Where would you like to go?" she asked him.

"Buchenwald, February 17, 1942," Jean-Claude enunciated clearly.

Angelo whispered to L.C., "Wasn't that a concentration camp?"

"One of the worst," he answered.

"I want to observe the incident in which Hitler and his officers put down a Jewish uprising," Jean-Claude ordered. "No translation."

The group flinched; Lin almost let out an audible gasp. Eyes caught eyes and brows furrowed. Angelo felt his gut clench. L.C., monitoring the equipment, squared his jaw.

The audio speakers blared with the sound of machine gunfire, followed by awful screams. Men and women and children were shrieking in agony, yelling in Yiddish and German. The massacre went on for a long time. L.C. and Carol held their ears. Lin felt nauseous and scurried to the bathroom. Father Al walked out the back door of the barn. Angelo and Juliana sat with their eyes closed, faces tight and grimaced.

Suddenly Angelo heard the sound of a vehicle pulling into the driveway. He looked out the window and saw a truck backing up to the front porch. The large yellow letters "HOLT" on the truck's side panel indicated that the shipment of crucial equipment had arrived. This delivery contained video equipment, sophisticated digital imaging paraphernalia, and some highly sensitive electromagnetic resonance devices that would hopefully allow the Beam Team to make video recordings of their contacts.

When he heard the beeping backup signal on the truck, L.C. immediately aborted the transmission. A few moments later, the team heard a knock at the door. Lin answered and briskly signed for the delivery, trying to dismiss the man handily. The others attempted to look nonchalant, but their anxiety was apparent. Angelo wished he had some kind of buffer zone for encounters such as this, but in the hustle to get the lab online, he had overlooked such probabilities.

The nosy delivery man surveyed the room, obviously fascinated by the sophisticated scientific equipment, clearly an anomaly in this bucolic setting. "What is all this stuff—recording equipment?" he asked obtrusively.

"Yeah, that's right," Angelo answered quickly, as the others watched him carefully. "We're trying to develop some better techniques for restoring old documentary footage."

"We have a contract with George Lucas's company, I.L.M., down the road," Lin added. None of them were great liars, but she came close.

"Oh, yeah, I deliver to them, too. Some operation they got! They have megabucks invested in high-tech stuff there."

"I know; we're just scratching the surface."

"When I came in I thought somebody was watching some old German war movie."

The team members searched each other's eyes. Father Al blanched, then quickly excused himself and headed toward the lavatory.

"We're working on upgrading some news footage for a new Spielberg film," Juliana stated authoritatively. "I am the German history consultant," she added in an exaggerated accent.

"I see; maybe I'll see some of your stuff in the movies some time."

"Probably."

"Well, have a nice day, folks."

"Yeah, you too."

The fellow turned and made his way back toward the truck.

As soon as Lin closed the door behind him, Carol blurted, "I know that man."

"From where?" asked L.C.

"Maybe some past life," Lin joked.

"No, it doesn't feel like that," Carol answered, pacing. Her face went livid as she almost shrieked, "Oh my God!—the Big Sur car!"

"What are you talking about?"

"He was the guy in the car. . .Remember I told you there was another man with the one who drained my brake fluid. I remember his earring!" Carol dashed to the window to see if the truck had pulled out of the driveway. As the vehicle completed a three-point turn she got a good look at his profile—it was him. Next to him in the passenger's seat was another man—the one who had tinkered with her motor.

"The other guy is with him!"

"Are you sure? Lots of guys these days have earrings," Lin suggested.

"No, I'm sure. Besides, this trucking company has delivered plenty of stuff to us, and they never have two delivery men. Somebody is spying on us."

"Well, let's get to the bottom of this," Angelo shouted as he grabbed his car keys. Father Al, Lin, and Carol followed Angelo, while the others stayed to watch the lab. The four quickly piled into Angelo's car and shot out of the driveway, kicking up a huge plume of dust as Angelo floored the accelerator. As the car forged through the misty valley, Lin issued a nervous yelp when Angelo screamed around some tricky curves.

Within minutes the team caught sight of the HOLT truck, just about to turn onto the access road to Highway 101. "Hurry up," Lin urged. "We can overtake them if you step on it!"

"No," Angelo cautioned; "let's find out where they're going."

After twenty minutes the truck turned off 101 at the Cotati exit and proceeded west toward the coast. "There's no way this truck has any business out here," Angelo surmised. "This is all farm country." Angelo lightened up on the gas pedal and laid back, staying just out of the truck's sight.

After another ten miles the truck's right blinker flashed and it turned onto a paved driveway with a white trellis on each side. When the Lexus reached the turnoff, Angelo saw a simple wooden arch bridging the trellises, bearing a white sign with black lettering: *Redemption Retreat.* Angelo stopped at the entrance, turned to the others, and flashed a puzzled look. Their faces matched his consternation. With conviction he returned his hands to the steering wheel, put the Lexus in drive, and slowly drove up the tree-lined lane. After a quarter mile the car came into a clearing which revealed a large old stone and wood Colonial house with many gables. The HOLT truck, the only visible vehicle, was parked in the crescent driveway meeting the portico. Angelo scanned the truck carefully, but saw no activity; the two men in the cab had obviously gone inside.

Angelo surveyed the area and found a spot where he worked the car into some woods out of sight of the house. Father Al and Lin volunteered to stay with the car, while Angelo and Carol crept through the brush to get a closer view of the house; no one was in sight. "Any hunches?" Angelo asked Carol.

"Let's try around the back."

The pair found their way to a clearing behind the house where they saw a light in a window. Crouching low, they could make out a plushly decorated room where the van driver and his sidekick were talking to someone else out of view. Carol suggested they try to move within earshot, but they halted when they realized the truck driver, facing the window, would immediately spy any movements.

"I have another idea," Angelo suggested. He retreated into the brush and pulled his mobile phone out of his windbreaker pocket. He pressed the tone buttons slowly, making sure the phone's beeping could not be heard from the house. "L.C., we're onto something and we need your help. Do you have any snooping equipment?"

"Not really."

"Then could you rig something up?"

"What range?"

"Fifty yards."

"Well, I might be able to do something real makeshift . . .I could take the lapel mike we use for the transmissions and some of that wire we got left over. . . and then there's good ol' duct tape. . ."

"Okay, it's worth a try. Here's where we are. . ."

The wait for L.C. was long and cold. Dark had fallen and the four, huddled in the car, could see their breath. Lin, not one to hide her feelings, was getting edgy. "I don't like the way this feels, you guys. I mean, who knows what kind of creeps we are dealing with. CIA? Mafia? Contract hit men?" No one answered. For all they knew, she was right. Shivering, Lin clutched onto Angelo's right arm in the front seat.

Finally L.C. pulled up in his camper, accompanied by Michaud, and everyone piled in with them. The two had concocted some rudimentary surveillance equipment, and surprised the group with a big bag of Dunkin' Donuts and Starbucks coffee. Lin grabbed the treats and quickly scarfed down several doughnuts, commenting, "Carol's not the only psychic in this group—God bless you, L.C."

L.C. slipped back into the woods with Angelo. The two sneaked to the window where, concealed by the dark, L.C. took a few pieces of duct tape and fixed the microphone to the sill. The pair was scurrying back toward the camper when they were surprised by two high-beam headlights. "Down!" Angelo called out, and they took refuge behind a small fenced trash disposal area, which afforded a clear view of the arriving car.

A black stretch Lincoln with dark tinted windows pulled up to the front door. A driver got out to open the rear door. Before he could get to the handle, a tall thin man in a long gray herringbone overcoat let himself out and marched intently toward the house. In his mid-fifties, with short silver hair, he wore a dress hat, dark-rimmed eyeglasses, a crimson necktie, and he bore an air of authority. Three men, including the two they recognized, appeared at the front door and greeted the visitor reverently. The four disappeared into the house.

"Let's get back to the truck and see if we can pick up their conversation," urged L.C.

Back in the camper the others were still huddled and drinking coffee. Angelo imagined that Jean-Claude, if true to style, had probably babbled on incessantly, irritating Lin to no end. L.C. went to his apparatus and switched on the speaker.

"So you got into the lab," they heard an older voice ask.

"Yeah, we saw their whole operation," answered the truck driver.

"How far have they progressed?"

"We heard Hitler's voice," another voice answered.

"Hitler?"

"Yeah, we heard a bunch of Germans shouting, '*Hiel Hitler!*'"

"Why would they be interested in Hitler?" asked the older man.

"Beats me," responded the driver. "One thing is for sure—they have equipment to the hilt."

"They must be close to dialogue. We can't afford to let them get any further."

Angelo turned around and issued a puzzled angry look. The others, listening soberly, matched his consternation.

"We must stop them before they pull in any biblical figures," the fourth voice declared.

"Reverend Ashworth is correct; if the media gets wind of them contacting church founders, we could have a huge mess on our hands."

Some static began to interfere with the transmission. As the noise increased, the voices faded and gradually died off the speakers. "What's the matter?" Angelo asked L.C.

"Shit!" L.C. spouted as he fiddled with the dials. It was the first time anyone had heard Mr. Conservative curse. "It's the microphone battery—I should have changed it before I set it up."

Suddenly Lin screamed, "Ayyyyyyyyyy!" Adrenaline pumping, Angelo turned to see a huge German shepherd jumping against the side window, scratching and barking ferociously. "Let's get out of here!" yelled Angelo.

"And just how do you expect us to get back to your car past Bigfoot here?"

Michaud reached into his fanny pack, pulled out a can of mace and sprayed it in the dog's face, immobilizing the beast instantly. "When one jogs, one must be prepared," he declared smugly.

The troupe made a fast break for the Lexus while L.C. maneuvered a U-turn back toward the highway.

When the car had gained some distance from the retreat, Lin asked, "So what do you make of what we heard?"

"We're a threat to the church," Carol answered.

"But why?"

"The church counts on millions of people showing up every Sunday and feeding their coffers. There are also lots of people who don't attend services, but make large contributions and bequests. Many of those people give because they believe their donation will earn them a place in heaven. Others are afraid they will be punished or go to hell if they don't."

"But that doesn't explain why they're worried about us."

"Imagine that someone came along and brought forth the actual words of Jesus. Better yet—imagine that someone came along and brought forth Jesus himself. Imagine that modern day people could hear his real thoughts and insights, and even converse with him."

"Well, that would be wonderful, wouldn't it?" Lin suggested.

"That's what you and I might think," Carol answered. "But what if Jesus said things today that didn't match what is written in the Bible? What if there are things in the Bible that were written by people who came after Jesus, people who believed in fear and punishment and the wrath of God, people who had an investment in personal interests or controlling others."

"Like King Henry, who couldn't get the Pope to approve of his divorce, so he started his own religion," Father Al said.

"Or King James, who took out everything he didn't like and added what he wanted, and said, 'Here, this is the word of God.'"

"But isn't that-sacrilegious?"

"Call it what you will. It happens."

"It's like when I went to Peru to see Machu Picchu," Carol chimed in. "In an old cathedral I saw a huge famous painting. It shows the last supper with Jesus sitting at the table with the disciples, and on the plate in front of him is a huge roasted guinea pig. . . and the table is full of papayas and mangoes and all kinds of tropical fruit."

"No way! Why would somebody paint that?" asked Lin.

"Because the missionaries wanted to convert the natives, they depicted Jesus in a way that was familiar and attractive to the local culture. Peruvians had feasts with guinea pigs and papayas, and this picture gave people the idea that Jesus was one of them."

"Well, that's kind of nice."

"Yes, it may well be. Such a painting is innocent enough. But it shows you how over the years people have distorted the actual words or deeds of Jesus. Multiply that by 2000 years, and you can imagine how far afield the truth could go."

"So it's like a major game of 'telephone.'"

"A *major* game of 'telephone.'"

"So what would you say to my Aunt Helen, who believes that the

Bible is the absolute word of God, and you don't get to pick and choose what you want to believe and act on?"

"If that's so, Aunt Helen would have a lot of contradictions to explain. In many passages the Bible says that we are all sinners and in other passages Jesus said, 'You are the light of the world,' and 'You are perfect even as your Father in heaven is perfect' and 'Have you not been told you that you are gods?' Yet you never hear fire-and-brimstone preachers quote those passages. So even people who believe utterly in the Bible are picking and choosing what they want to believe and act on. Unfortunately, most of them focus on the parts that tell us how rotten we are. If more people focused on the parts that affirm our positive potential, we might have a lot more happy and productive people walking around."

"Okay, so explain to me one more time why these guys are after us."

"It's actually pretty simple," Father Al suggested. "If Jesus showed up today and told people that we are born not in sin, but in innocence; or that we are forgiven no matter what; or that there is no such thing as eternal hell; or that we do not have to struggle or prove ourselves to get God to love us; or that what Buddha or Mohammed or Chief Joseph said was just as valid as what he said; or that there are lots of people who do not belong to a religion but are really good people; or that people should come to church not because they have to, but for joy and celebration. . ."

"Okay, okay, I get the point . . .So some people in the church are afraid of the real truth coming out."

"Enough to drain my brake fluid," Carol answered, "~and who knows what else they will do now that they know we are close to contact."

"I had no idea we were getting into all of this," Lin stated nervously. "I thought we were doing a science experiment, and here we may be rumbling the underpinnings of Western religion."

Chapter 26

Angelo stumbled his way through the thick dark brush behind the barn, almost tripping several times as he went. He used his feet to feel his way up the cottage stairs and he opened the door as quietly as possible. In the dim moonlight he could see Juliana curled up on the futon, the shape of her body gracefully accented by the soft green comforter. God, she looked beautiful. Angelo felt his gut relax and his heart open just to gaze upon her. He didn't know what he would have done without Juliana being there, what with all the craziness going on around him.

He undressed and slipped into bed beside her. When she felt his presence, she began to stir. Angelo wrapped his arms around her and extended one leg over hers. Juliana responded by giving Angelo a little nuzzle with her back and hugging his arm. She issued a soft purr. Still half-asleep, she asked in a tired drawl, "So how did you guys make out?"

"You remember those old spy movies you used to watch?"

"Sure," she answered faintly, not quite awake yet.

"This has to top them all."

"What do you mean?"

"The church is after us."

"What church?" asked Juliana, fully awake now.

"The Church of People Who Forgot What Jesus Really Said and Meant."

"Who?"

"A bunch of people who are afraid that we're going to blow their whole scene by letting Jesus speak for himself."

"I see. So now what do we do?"

"We need to hurry. These weirdoes could show up at any time
and trash everything. First thing in the morning, before Jean-Claude
shows up, let's get into lab, load Avi's CD-ROM, and contact Jesse.
Carol said she would come and meet us. Then we can get on the
horn with someone who can help us deal with our zealots. Maybe
God will tell us how to protect ourselves from everyone who is protecting Him."

Juliana shifted her position and faced Angelo squarely. "You
know, Angelo, I was thinking about how much I respect what you are
doing. I think you have a lot of courage for hanging in there in spite
of everything that is pushing against you. . .Claudia leaving, Jesse in a
coma, you losing the lab, now these church guys. . .you have a lot of
guts, Angelo Mann."

"Thanks, but sometimes I feel selfish about it. I just want to talk
to Jesse."

"You really do love him a lot, don't you?"

"I had no idea how much I loved him until all this happened."

Juliana leaned over and gently kissed Angelo on the cheek. "And
I had no idea how much I could love a man until I met you."

Chapter 27

At first light Angelo and Juliana made their way to the lab to get a head start on contacting Jesse. As they stepped out of the wooded area they were surprised to see the lights on in the lab. "We shut off the lights last night, didn't we?" asked Angelo.

"I did it myself," Juliana answered. Curiously, cautiously the two approached the barn. As they neared the back window they could see Jean-Claude sitting in the hot seat listening intently. Angelo turned to Juliana and motioned with his hand for her to stay quiet.

Angelo opened the door a few inches to hear the transmission. Through the speakers he could hear the sounds of a man's footsteps pacing heavily on a cement floor. Then the voice of Hitler, rambling in guttural German.

Angelo turned to Juliana, who was also listening intently. "What's he saying?" he asked.

Juliana listened for a while, then answered, "It's *Mein Kampf*. Hitler wrote it while he was in prison in Berchtesgade in the early 1920's. He didn't actually write it himself. He dictated it to Rudolph Hess."

Suddenly the voice of another man speaking German blared over the speaker. Again Angelo looked to Juliana. "It's Hess. . .He's telling Hitler to slow down so he can keep up with him."

Angelo looked toward the road and then whispered to Juliana, "I need you to go up to road and catch Carol before she pulls into the driveway. I want her to see this."

Juliana nodded and doubled back through the path in the woods. Angelo stayed put, watching the fervency on Michaud's face as he was fully absorbed in the conversation he was hearing.

Ten minutes later Juliana returned with Carol, who looked disheveled after trudging through the woods. But she was ready for action. Angelo directed Carol to the window so she could see Michaud.

"What's he doing?" she asked.

"He's listening to Hitler dictate *Mein Kampf.* That was his book that formed the foundation for Nazism."

"Great," Carol answered sarcastically, a troubled look growing over her face. Then she added, "This has gone far enough. We have to stop him before he discovers the formula for two-way communication. You know what that means."

Angelo's face turned to stone. "It means he will have the power to bring Adolph Hitler back to the world."

"Not just back, but with far more power. Without his own body to be in one place or protect, Hitler will become virtually immortal, able to direct his goons all over the world anywhere, anytime."

A cold chill rippled through Angelo's belly; the thought was too grisly to contemplate. Angelo felt terrified. What a horrible ignominy, he considered, to be the individual responsible for opening the door to the return of Adolph Hitler—and potentially every tyrant who has ever cursed humanity.

"My God, Carol, we may not be opening the ark of healing, but Pandora's box! If we make a portal for any despot to walk through, we could engender a mass reincarnation of the most twisted diabolical minds in history. What if Sadam Hussein got hold of this technology and consulted with Hitler and Stalin or Genghis Kahn or Attila the Hun? I don't even want to think about the terror such a pact could wreak. When those warlords were in power, there were no nuclear high-tech weapons, or germ warfare. With today's capabilities for mass destruction, they could ravage entire continents in a flash!"

Carol became pensive, her eyes turning to the side. Angelo had learned that when she looked to her right she was listening for guidance. "What you are saying is quite possible, but we're not powerless."

"What do you mean?"

"We have to contact someone on a higher plane who can counteract the lords of darkness. We have to connect with a being who can guide us to deal with Michaud and Hitler, and God knows who else."

"Like who?"

"Like Jesus himself."

"Sure, why not go right to the top?" Angelo answered sarcastically.

"Angelo, we have to get to Jesus or someone in a high place before Michaud gets to Hitler."

"But how? Michaud is adamant about being in on every transmission."

"We'll have to find a time when he's not here."

"Like when?"

"Later today."

"But who is going to draw him to us? We need someone who believes in Jesus. Father Al would be perfect, but he's gone to see his sister in Redding."

"I grew up in a fire and brimstone family," Carol explained. "Did I ever tell you my father was a preacher? I had so much weird stuff drummed into my head about God and Jesus that—I hate to admit this—I'm afraid of him."

"I'm not afraid of him," Angelo replied. "I just have a lot of doubts about whether or not all the stuff they ascribed to him is true. Sometimes I wonder if he really existed."

"Lin is Buddhist and L.C.'s religion is science. Juliana is agnostic."

"Then who can we get to call him in? If we expect to achieve dialogue, it has to be through someone who is sincerely open to him."

"Do we know anyone with a lot of faith?" Carol asked.

"Yeah, right," Angelo answered cynically.

"Maybe we should just go to a church and grab somebody," Carol kidded.

"Yeah, let me see who, out of all the people I see when I go to church, would be good?" Angelo quipped. Carol knew he hadn't been to church in years.

Except once. "Ho!" Angelo said, opening his eyes wide.

"Ho, what?"

"I do know someone who goes to church. I saw her the last time I was in a church. In fact, she was the *only* person I have seen in church in years."

"Who's that?"

"Sylvia, the cleaning lady at my lab. She not only believes in Jesus—

she loves him. If anybody has a personal relationship with Jesus, it's Sylvia. She's always saying the rosary and praying as she cleans. She'd be perfect."

"So what do we do—just cruise down to Palo Alto and kidnap the cleaning lady?"

Angelo looked Carol dead in the eye. She laughed nervously for an instant and then became very serious. The two stared at each other for a few seconds. Then Angelo announced, "She gets in around five o'clock."

The LX470 pulled into the lab parking lot just after most of the professional staff had left for the evening. Trying to be inconspicuous, Angelo and Carol looked down the hall for the cleaning lady's supply cart, which was parked just outside of Stan Siegel's office two doors away. As Angelo walked past his colleague's doors, doors he had walked past nearly every day for 8 years, he wondered what his compadres were saying about him now. Surely they had decided he was a total fruitcake. Who knows, maybe they were right. But now he really didn't care; what he was onto was so much bigger than anything he had ever imagined.

Angelo and Carol tiptoed to Siegel's door, where they heard the cleaning lady humming and intermittently uttering, "*Gloria al Padre, as Hijo y al Espiritu Santo. Como ere an el principio. . .*" Angelo recognized the Lord's Prayer, similar to the Latin he remembered as a choir boy. "That's our gal," he smiled impishly. Angelo took a deep breath and strode into the office as nonchalantly as possible. "*Hola,* Sylvia."

"*Hola,* Dr. Mann," Sylvia responded with a polite smile. Angelo wondered if she even knew he had been gone.

"Sylvia, could I see you for a minute?"

"*Si,*" Sylvia answered as she wrinkled her face with a puzzled, almost guilty look.

"I need your help with something downstairs," he told her.

Sylvia looked even more perplexed. She leaned her mop against the cart and followed the pair down the back stairs to the parking lot. When they got outside, Angelo led her to his car.

"Sylvia, I need your help with something that is very important." He opened the back door and beckoned her to get in.

"You want me to help you bring something up, doctor?"

"In a way, yes. I am working on a project that could help many people. I need you to translate something. I need you to talk to someone who will understand your language."

Looking even more confused, Sylvia sat down in the back seat. Carol closed the door behind her, then scurried to take her seat next to Angelo.

"Who you want me talk to, Dr. Mann?" Suddenly the car shot out of the parking lot, almost skidding out of control on the wet street. "Hooooah!" Sylvia shouted.

Angelo turned, looked over his shoulder and answered, "God."

"God?"

"We want you to talk to Jesus for us," Carol explained.

"I am sorry; I no understand. I must go back finish clean."

"Sylvia, you love Jesus, don't you?"

"Si, he is my great love." Angelo and Carol glanced at each other, pleased.

"If you could talk to Jesus, would you do it?"

"I talk to Jesus every day."

"But does he talk back?"

"Si, I hear him in my heart."

"Sylvia, what if you could hear his voice with your ears—and even see him with your eyes?"

"Dr. Mann, where we go? I must finish clean!"

"Just down the road a piece."

An hour and a half later, the Lexus rumbled into the gravel driveway, the tires noisily grooving the freshly spread stones. Night had fallen, and poor Sylvia was at her wit's end. As gracefully as possible, Angelo and Carol guided her into the barn and turned on the lights. Carol offered her some coffee. L.C., who had been setting up the communicator with Avi's CD-ROM, was ready.

"Let's get to work," Carol urged. "We don't have time to mess around. Call Lin and tell her to get her butt over here pronto."

Promised that she would be returned as soon as she had answered some questions, Sylvia reluctantly took her place in the hot seat and, looking like a frightened doe, anxiously submitted to the electrodes and monitors. Carol initiated the induction, which, after some initial resistance, went fairly smoothly. With the mind and heart of a child, Sylvia was quite suggestible, and soon sank into a deep hypnotic trance.

"Sylvia, what is your favorite scene in the life of Jesus?" asked Carol.

"When he heal leper," the Mexican woman answered in a sleepy voice, her head hanging forward on her chest.

"Good. I'd like you to imagine that scene now, and tell me what you see."

A long silence followed. Angelo started to get edgy. If this did not work, he would be in a lot more trouble than he was already facing. Defaulting on a contract was one thing; kidnapping was quite another.

Finally Sylvia spoke. "I see square in village. Many people gather around Jesus. Someone bring very sick people to him. Their skin pale, bleeding sores. They bent over, tired, afraid. Some dying. Other peoples stand away from them, cover their face."

"Thank you, Sylvia," Carol encouraged her. "What is happening now?"

"Jesus close his eyes and pray. He lift hands and touch heads. Crowd gasp and pull back, but he no pay attention to them. He speak to lepers."

"Now, Sylvia, I would like you to concentrate very deeply and listen carefully to what he is saying." Carol motioned to Angelo to turn up the volume on the communicator's audio monitor.

"In the name of the Father, be cleansed," a deep voice boomed over the speakers. Sylvia became so startled that she sat up with a mighty jolt, opened her eyes, and dropped her jaw. She looked as if she had been stuck by lightning.

"It's okay, Sylvia, it's okay," Carol quickly comforted her, placing her hand on Sylvia's shoulder. "Just close your eyes and keep listening."

Sylvia reluctantly complied, but remained sitting tall with her back ramrod straight.

"What do you hear now?" asked Carol.

Again the voice reverberated throughout the room. "These people have not sinned," Jesus told the crowd. "But they have forgotten who they really are, as you all have. You do not deserve to be in pain; I tell you this is *not* God's will for you. His will for you is utter joy and freedom. Let go of your fears and self-judgments, and enjoy the life your heart yearns for."

Carol leaned over to Angelo and whispered, "Those lines aren't in the Bible, are they?"

"Not that I remember," Angelo answered.

Jesus continued, "The kingdom of heaven is not far and distant. It is here now, and it lives inside you. You do not have to strive to become perfect; right *now* you are loveable. Love yourself and the universe will rush to bring you the healing you need." Angelo looked at Carol again. Neither of them recognized that as biblical text, either.

Sylvia's face softened. Her tension and fear fell away, and a sweet smile spread across her countenance. Though her eyes were closed, her expression revealed she was beholding the face of her beloved.

"Sylvia," Carol intervened, "imagine that you are in the crowd of people watching Jesus. Walk up to him and look him in the eye. What would you like to ask him?"

Silence. Sylvia was going deeper into her inner world. Then a tiny tear began to trickle down Sylvia's cheek. "Why my son Jorge in so much trouble?" she whispered, anguished. "Why you not answer my prayers?"

Silence.

Then a strong voice, tempered with great gentleness, issued from the uncovered speaker. "I have heard your prayers, Sylvia."

Angelo stood up. Jesus was responding. Angelo felt goose bumps ripple over his entire body; his spine tingled and he felt a shiver roll up his back. This was the moment he had yearned for. Jesus was responding. *They had dialogue.*

"Your prayers have helped Jorge more than you realize," the master continued. "If he had continued on his own path without your attention, he would surely have destroyed himself by now. Your love has protected him in more ways than you know."

Sylvia listened intently, thinking deeply. "But why he still in trouble?"

"Your son came into this life with his own soul's lessons. He took on this difficulty so he can find his own strength." Jesus gave Sylvia a few moments to absorb his words. "Do not be afraid, Sylvia. Jorge will weather the storm and emerge stronger than you imagine. One day, not very long from now, you will be very proud of him."

Sylvia was sobbing. Carol rummaged through her purse for tissues. Even Angelo had to wipe his eyes.

The voice went on, "This is a very difficult time for all of you on earth. Many of you are going through more changes more quickly than ever before. The world you once knew is disintegrating before your eyes, and you do not know where your life is going. But you are not alone and you are not comfortless. Keep your heart open and live what you know is true. I promise you will be cared for in miraculous ways."

"But what about all the evil in the world?" Angelo jumped in. "How can people be so cruel and heartless to one another? Is Satan real, and has he taken over?"

"Satan is a name you ascribe to the fears you project onto your world. The force you call evil has no power except that which you give it with your thoughts and fears. You are stronger than any evil you may encounter, and infinitely more real. Replace fear with love and watch evil crumble. I taught this two thousand years ago, but how many have applied this truth? Only a handful. Now you must put my words into practice. Talk means nothing; love comes to life only through living it."

L.C. spoke: "Is the world really coming to an end? Is all this talk about Armageddon true?"

"The old world is coming to an end. You don't need a prophet to see that so many of the social institutions you have believed in—government, law, education, medicine, economics, marriage, religion—are crumbling before your eyes. Many are living in terror as they behold the undoing of the things they once equated with security. But in the wake of their collapse, you will rediscover the life you lost as you chased illusions. The false must go, to make way for the real. When this transition is complete, the old world will be gone—and you will thank God for this, for in its stead will stand a reality far more rewarding than the one you have known."

"So what are we supposed to do in the meantime?" asked Lin, standing by the door. No one had heard her enter.

"Trust. Trust life. Trust yourself, your intuitions, your visions, your longings. God lives not on some distant cloud, but through you. You hear my voice through these speakers, but I am really calling to you from within your own heart. Find me there, and you will find me everywhere."

The UPR on the display began to flicker. Anxiously, Juliana fired off one more question. "What about Hitler?" she asked. "How can we combat him if Michaud tries to bring him through?"

"Practice fearlessness. To fight against evil is to give it power. Stand for love. It is time. You are ready."

The voice crackled and the readout dropped to zero. L.C. dashed to the communicator to turn the volume up, but the transmission was over. The voice was gone.

The group sat in silent awe. Sylvia emerged from her trance and sat with a half-blissful, half-dazed expression. Angelo wondered if she would ever have come to work today if she knew what she was getting into.

"So what do you think?" asked Angelo. "Was that really him?"

"I had goose bumps the whole time," answered Lin. "I felt like I did when I used to sit on my grandpa's knee. I felt safe and loved. When he talked, I felt that he was speaking just to me."

Eyes turned to L.C., who shook his head in silence. For the first time, the group saw tears in his eyes. "When I hear the truth I feel it in the pit of my stomach, like I knew it all along, and the person who just spoke, reminded me. I had that feeling the whole time he spoke."

After a few moments of quiet, Angelo told Sylvia, "Maybe we should get you back to work."

"I'll give you a ride," L.C. offered. He extended his hand and guided Sylvia to the door. Her eyes were still large and round, and she quivered as she stepped.

Chapter 28

W hat are you all doing here?" a voice boomed from the door. It was Michaud.

"I guess we could ask you the same," said Angelo.

"I had some ideas about how to increase our energy supply to put us over the threshold for dialogue," Michaud answered, studying the group suspiciously.

Without a word the team went through an entire conversation with their eyes. All confronted the same icy fear.

"Who is *she?*" Jean-Claude asked abruptly, pointing to Sylvia, who now looked terrified, as if she were suddenly surrounded by aliens.

"She is Sylvia, from the university," Angelo explained. "I brought her here for. . .an experiment."

"*Si,* I talk to Jesus," Sylvia exclaimed with a huge smile.

The others blanched, then grimaced, then looked at each other with questioning eyes. Lin covered her face with her hands and shook her head.

"You talked to Jesus?" Michaud asked the woman. "And did he talk back?"

"*Si, señor,*" she answered. "He talk back so beautiful!'

Jean-Claude turned to the others, furious. "Why did you not include me in this?"

"We didn't know if it would work," Carol offered. "It was an experiment."

Jean-Claude surveyed the communicator. He looked at the CPU and noticed that the green light was blinking on the CD-ROM drive. He walked to the computer, pressed the release button, and the drive tray whirred open. Michaud removed the CD-ROM and read the label: "*Communicator Core Programming.*" A look of consternation over-took Michaud's face, then gave way to a huge smile.

"This is the missing link, isn't it?" he asked. No one answered. "*It is, isn't it?*" he repeated.

The group remained silent.

"Then we should be over the top for dialogue with anyone," he declared excitedly. Everyone knew who "anyone" was.

"I want a session." Michaud issued a piercing stare.

A long silence followed. Angelo looked to Carol. Her eyes were resolute.

Angelo spoke: "I can't let you do that."

"Excuse me?"

"I can't, I won't, let you use the communicator. I know what you are going to do, and I won't issue my password to let you on."

Michaud's face turned mean, like a cornered bull. His body went taut, his breath quickened, and his jaw clenched. He looked as if he was about to lash out. Everyone braced themselves. Then he seemed to catch himself.

"But Angelo," he said in a controlled voice. "I'm going to do re-search, just like you."

"No, you're not," Juliana burst in. "You're going to contact the führer. You're going to engage him for your own sick purposes. I won't be a party to this either, Jean-Claude. You know how I feel about all of this. My country has been sick with shame for sixty years. You're not going to turn the clock back."

Again Jean-Claude tensed with rage. He slammed his hand on a desktop and leaned forward as if he was going to lay into Juliana. But he caught himself before exploding. Then he seemed to calm down.

"All right, all right," he said, gesturing with his hands, palms flat down toward the floor. "I understand your concern." Jean-Claude paced up and back, thinking and rubbing his cheek and chin with his hand. "What if I agree to not explore any German historical informa-tion, or engage with anyone you do not approve of? Would that be acceptable to you?"

Angelo found Carol's eyes, then scanned the others. They all seemed to be deferring to Angelo. Angelo thought for a while, then answered "All right, but if you break our agreement I will abort the transmission and not issue my password again."

Michaud sighed and said, "That's fine with me. . .Shall we set a session for tomorrow at, let's say, two o'clock?"

"If you like."

"All right," Michaud answered, "we have a date." He turned and left abruptly.

L.C. just shook his head. He turned to Sylvia and said, "Okay, *señora*, I'll take you back now." Carol went to the closet and brought Sylvia a sweater for her ride back; it was late now, and the temperature had fallen into the 40's.

Only ten minutes had passed when L.C. called from his car phone. "Angelo, we've got trouble." Angelo switched on the speaker phone. "What is it?"

"When I turned onto Serron Road I saw the HOLT truck parked just off the road in a little clearing a few hundred yards on the other side of the woods from our lab. No one was in the cab, but I saw lights on in the back."

"Maybe they just broke down or something," Lin suggested.

"They have no business out there at night," L.C. reported. "I'd bet anything that they have surveillance equipment."

"Then you'd better get back here right away," instructed Angelo.

"What about our little cleaning lady?" L.C. asked. But before Angelo could answer, L.C. came back on the line. "Wait a minute. . . she's saying something to me." The team strained to hear what was transpiring in the camper. After a few moments L.C. returned. "She says she doesn't mind coming back. She likes us."

Angelo smiled, then the others. "Ten-four."

Ten minutes later L.C. and Sylvia walked through the door. Angelo marveled at the absurd perfection with which the movie was unfolding.

"So now what do we do?" Lin asked.

"We have to protect ourselves," Angelo said. "They're mounting some kind of campaign. They could just come over like the Klan in the middle of the night, bust up our shop, and lynch us. Maybe we should get some guns."

Lin paled.

"No," Carol stated adamantly. "That's not the answer. We don't need weapons. We need wisdom."

"Carol's right," said L.C. "We can't fight these guys on their own terms. There has to be another way."

"Yes," echoed Juliana. "Let's try to get some help from somebody on the communicator."

"Let's get Jesus back on the horn," suggested L.C.

Eyes turned toward Sylvia. Her eyes grew large, as if to say, "Again?"

"Sylvia, we need you," Angelo said. "Would you . . . ?"

"No," interrupted Carol. "We should do this ourselves. We have established a pipeline to Jesus and we have his UPR. Besides, we don't want to have to go out and kidnap a cleaning lady every time we want to talk to God."

Without further discussion, Carol took her place in the hot seat. L.C. helped her with the induction. Sylvia sat with the group and said her rosary. Soon Jesus was with them.

"Thank you for coming," Angelo offered humbly.

"I come wherever I am welcome," the comforting voice responded.

"Does this mean that our intention is now strong enough to call you in regularly?" asked Carol.

"I am ready whenever you are."

"Then tell us how we can receive your wisdom more clearly," Carol implored.

"Go ahead and connect the video monitor," Jesus instructed.

"But we haven't developed the technology," L.C. politely argued.

"It is not the technology that summons me," Jesus responded, "It is your intention. Do you think my disciples had 'the technology' when I appeared to them after my death? . . .If they had to wait until they had 'the technology,' I would have disappeared into history as an anomaly."

Angelo and L.C. scurried to hook up the video monitor.

"The source of all manifestation is heart's desire; you have that," Jesus explained. Now I will help you with the details."

Angelo pressed the monitor *power on* button and looked at the group nervously. Snow filled the screen and static crackled through the speakers. The team sat for a few minutes watching, listening, waiting, hoping. Angelo wondered if Jesus had been too ambitious in his promise. Then the screen began to clear. Angelo recalled Ted Kohler's photographic imprints, which formed themselves before his eyes in a similar way.

A video image took form—a man sitting on a large rock on the side of a hill. Clearly this was Jesus; his striking face, light beard, and deep eyes were unmistakable. He bore some resemblance to the many portraits painted of him over the millennia, yet he looked more like a real person. If he was a god, he was also a man. Suddenly it struck Angelo why Jesus may have lived and died as he had—precisely to demonstrate that it is possible to walk the earth as a human being, while retaining the presence of the divine.

Jesus's skin was olive, almost leathery, signifying he spent much time in the sun. The lines around his eyes spoke of both deep purpose and laughter. His face held more maturity than many of his popular images; he emanated the wisdom of a sage, tempered with childlike innocence. His hair was long and much darker than the chestnut color often ascribed by painters; the man was obviously of Semitic origin. His eyes were not blue, but deep brown, and his nose was not smooth but long with a ridge in the upper part. As Angelo considered the difference between Jesus's many artistic representations and his real appearance, he realized how apt we are to create God in the image of our fantasies.

Angelo felt comforted in Jesus's presence. He was surprised he was not afraid; not long ago if someone had told him that he would be meeting Jesus Christ face-to-face, he would have shivered in fear of mortal judgment. But in this energy, guilt had no more reality than a crumbled nightmare; Angelo's heart tingled with warmth, excitement, even a sense of ancient kinship.

Angelo asked Jesus directly, "We're really worried about this Nazi and church assault. Can you help us?"

"It's an old story, my friends," the soothing voice returned, this time issuing from the figure on the screen. "Fear drives men to attack, and fear responds. With whom will it end?"

"But we may need to protect the world from a terrible menace. Are we not to respond?"

"Of course you are to respond, but with what? Will you eliminate cruelty by fighting against it?"

Angelo looked around at the others. Their faces reflected his own confusion.

Jesus seemed to sense his listeners' frustration. "I do not mean to put you off. I just want you to think for yourselves. I do not want followers. I want you to walk by my side. I want you to find the same light within yourselves that I found within me. You already have all the wisdom you seek from me. I am not closer to God than you. I just remembered first."

"Well, how about a little hint at least?" pleaded Lin. "Even on *Who Wants to Be a Millionaire?* the contestants get to call someone for help!"

"Then let us trace the problem back to the source. Hitler became a tyrant not because he was strong and courageous, but because he perceived himself as powerless and inferior. Behind his bravado the man was in tremendous pain. Only someone who felt abysmally empty would have to build an empire to prove himself. The gaping hole in Hitler's soul was so huge that he had to conquer nations and murder millions to fill it."

The team leaned in toward the screen, rapt.

"Hitler has been eradicated from the earth, but he remains the führer of terror in the hearts of all who fear him and those like him. When I said, 'resist not evil, but overcome evil with good,' I gave you the formula for the end of Hitler and all like him. When you act from fear, you empower the very thing you resist. If you dismissed your fascination with terror and focused exclusively on peace, the evil in your lives would dissolve in a short time, for it would have nothing to feed on.

"If you succumb to fearing or hating Hitler, you perpetuate the same energy that motivated him to kill so many. Just as you believe you are justified in ridding the world of Hitler, so he felt justified in exterminating the Jewish people. The object of inquisition may change, but its dynamics are the same. If you choose instead to align with your true inner power, you will disarm him utterly."

"But what about the church?" Angelo asked, standing up. "Do we need to defend ourselves against them?"

"The only thing you need to defend against is the belief that you walk alone."

"Why are they so intent on stopping us?"

"The politics of religion are the same as those of nations. Indeed much of religion has become tyranny in the name of God rather than country. You claim to have separated church and state, but they have become practically identical in their means and effects."

Carol nodded. "So what, then, should we do?"

"Carry on with your work. I will help you. Remember your purpose."

Angelo cleared his throat. "Jesus, could I ask you a personal question?"

"My heart is open to you, my brother."

"I need your help with my son. I know that I have not given him all the love he deserves. . ." Angelo's voice began to crack. ". . .but it would destroy me if I lost him. His lingering in a coma is like a long nightmare. Jesus, my heart is breaking. Can you save him?"

As if he was giving Angelo time to feel the depth of his pain, Jesus paused a few moments before responding. Then he spoke firmly with compassion. "The choice is with him—and you. The boy is trying to decide which world he will walk in. His situation reflects his divided intentions. Jesse wants to live, but he does not feel welcome; he believes he is a burden to you. A child needs to feel that he is contributing to his world, beginning with his parents. Because he is not sure where he belongs, now he has one foot in your world and the other in mine."

"Is there any way I can get him to come back?"

"First, Angelo, you must accept yourself. You have never shown your son a model of a man who feels whole, and he is mirroring your inner conflict. The best way you can help your son now is to forgive yourself."

"Forgive myself?"

"Forgive yourself for your anger, your fear, your pain, your loneliness. Angelo, every parent has felt, at some time, the kind of anger you have felt toward your son. You are not bad; you are just human. . .Would it help you to know that I got angry?"

"You got angry? The Prince of Peace?"

"How do you think I learned the value of peace? Believe me, I've had my share of wrestling matches with myself, my feelings, and God. I've shaken my fist at heaven plenty of times."

Angelo rubbed his chin; he was stunned.

"Angelo, we're all in this together. Early in your life, you began to believe that you had to prove yourself, that you had to be perfect at whatever you do. But you've set your standards so high that you could never attain them. So you set yourself up for continual frustration. You don't have to be Superman. You *cannot* be Superman. *I* was not even the Superman you have made me out to be. But I did learn to accept my humanness, and in that moment my divinity shined even brighter."

Jesus paused for a moment. Then he continued, "There are people in your life who love you just as you are. Some of them are sitting right next to you now."

Angelo looked around at his friends. Juliana had tears in her eyes.

"I know what you are a saying is true," Angelo answered. "But I need help to put this into action. When it comes to forgiveness, I feel like a little baby trying to take his first step."

"Then I'll give you a clue: Go back to the well. Your relationship with Jesse hinges on you understanding what happened with you and your father. He is the key. This is as much as I can tell you now."

The picture began to flicker and within moments Jesus's image disappeared. Immediately Angelo rose and stood in front of Carol, who was transiting out of her meditative state.

"Carol, may I take that seat?" Angelo asked sharply, with more command in his voice than request. A bit jarred, Carol gave Angelo her place.

"Who do you want to talk to, Angelo?" Carol asked.

"I want to talk to Lorenzo Mandolucci."

"Your father?"

"Yes."

Angelo saw the surprise on Lin's face. She'd heard the stories of Lorenzo's brutality. She looked pale and concerned.

"Very well," answered Carol.

Angelo stood up and, back erect, walked to the hot seat. As he hooked himself up to the apparatus the group watched silently, respectfully. Lin took L.C.'s hand to assuage her tension.

"Take a few breaths and I'll guide you in." No one else moved. Slowly, methodically, Carol conducted the induction.

Then an image appeared on the screen. Angelo's childhood family was seated around a dinner table. When Lin saw Angelo at the age of six, she started to laugh, but stifled the urge in the face of the gravity of this moment. As young Angelo was stretching his arm across the table for a tray of potatoes, Lorenzo slapped the child's hand sharply with a serving spoon. "How many times have I told you not to reach across the table?" the elder barked. "It's about time you learned some manners."

Anger rushed to little Angelo's face. Just as quickly he swallowed it, attempting to look unmoved. But the child did not banish his pain; he simply submerged his sense of powerlessness in a pool of frustration that, until this moment, he had been terrified to confront. A minute later Lorenzo reached farther across the table for the same tray of potatoes. Angelo said nothing. Instead he made another deposit in his bank of rage.

The scene shifted to the day Lorenzo was thrashing Angelo after he had dropped his father's hammer into the well. The team cringed. As Angelo beheld the scene, big as life, he crunched his face into a grimace. "What is this, some kind of torture?" he shouted.

He looked at his friends, but their faces showed only hopelessness and sadness. They couldn't help him. Then Carol answered quietly,

"No, Angelo, you don't have to go through this again."

Angelo looked at Carol, puzzled.

"Talk to your father, Angelo."

"But I can't; I'm only six years old there."

"No," Carol answered. "Talk to him as you would now; tell him what you've always wanted to say.

Angelo hesitated for a moment, then stood up and shouted, *"Why must you hurt me so much? Why are you so cruel?!"* He stood quivering, face flushed; he did not care what the others thought.

The scene on the screen shifted again. The backdrop looked like the pictures of Sicily that Angelo had seen in his mother's scrapbook. The decor bespoke the early part of the century, the time of Lorenzo's childhood. As the images on the screen began to move, Angelo saw his father at the age of about seven. While sleeping in a small room next to his brother Frederico, Lorenzo was awakened when his father, Phillipe came home late one night, drunk. Lorenzo's mother, Isabella, was chastising his father for staying out late carousing again. The child, frightened by his parents' shouting, wandered into the living room in the midst of the bruja.

"What are you doing up at this hour?" raged the drunk man. "Get the hell back to bed where you belong!"

"Don't talk to the boy like that, you ass," Isabella scolded. "He's up because you woke him!"

"Go ahead and side with the kid, like you always do! Ever since the boys were born I come second around here! I have a good mind to throw these stupid kids out the window so I can have my wife back! Get out of here, you little bastard!" With that, the man swiped at Lorenzo, knocking him onto the floor, hysterical.

"You coward!" Isabella retorted. "Picking on an innocent child. . . Pick on me, then!" Isabella reached into the kitchen drawer behind her, pulled out a huge meat cleaver, and came after Phillipe. He tried to fend her off, but drunk, slipped and fell on the floor. "Get out, you slimy pig!" she shouted, wielding the cleaver over his crotch. "I don't ever want to see you again!"

Phillipe clumsily lifted himself up and staggered out of the house, muttering under his breath, leaving Lorenzo crying fiercely in his mother's arms.

The team looked on.

The scene shifted again; this time it showed Lorenzo as a young teenager, working with Frederico in their uncle's olive grove. Frederico was talking to some girls walking by the road, while Lorenzo worked hard. Soon Phillipe came by to inspect the boys' work.

"What are you boys doing, loafing again? Your uncle and I bust our asses to take care of you, and you can't even give us a solid day's work!"

"Lorenzo took a nap," claimed Frederico.

"No I didn't," Lorenzo defended himself. "Frederico was talking to those girls!" he contended, pointing to the road.

Phillipe looked toward the road, but the girls were gone.

"You little liar!" he roared. Out of nowhere Phillipe produced a heavy switch. Within moments the boy was leaning against the barn door, britches down, absorbing a brutal lashing. Angelo was stunned to see his father in precisely the same position Lorenzo had forced on him. The camera closed in on Lorenzo's face. It bore the same stoic expression Angelo had learned to hide behind.

Angelo sat stunned. "Like father, like son," he whispered.

A voice came: "I could not help myself." It was Lorenzo.

Angelo stared off into space, listening in a kind of stupor. The video flickered and Lorenzo's face appeared on the screen. He looked old and haggard, as he did just before he died. His face was drawn and gaunt, barely reminiscent of the despot who had overpowered his son for most of his life.

"I was angry because I was in pain," Lorenzo pleaded. "I became the only kind of father I ever knew. I became my father, and you have become me."

A single tear rolled down Angelo's cheek. He was speechless.

"Now I ask for your forgiveness. You were not a bad boy, Angelo. I was angry long before you were born. I was angry at my father and myself. My father made me ashamed of myself. Now I have made you hate what you are."

Angelo bolted forward and clutched the monitor with both hands, as if he was trying to shake his father by the shoulders. "But why have you waited until now to tell me, Poppa? Now I am almost as old as you were when I was your boy, and I have become the same ogre to my son. You ruined not just my life, but my son's. He may never live to hear me apologize to him!"

"That is why I have come, Angelo. You must speak to Jesse as I have spoken to you. Do not wait. I swear to you, my hell has been greater than yours. You have no idea of the torture I have gone through, not being able to reach you. I beg of you, don't pronounce the same curse upon yourself."

"But my son is in a coma; he may never hear my voice again."

"Don't wait, Angelo. Speak to him now. This is your only chance to avoid the horror I have endured, and his only chance to live. You must believe me. Speak to him before it is too late."

The picture faded to a blue screen and Angelo was left with his head on the television, sobbing. He knew the others were watching, but it did not matter. The reason for his life's greatest pain had been revealed to him, along with a way out. But was it true, and could he do what he was asked?

Lin approached Angelo from behind him and wrapped her arms around him. Her mascara was a mess.

"Angelo," she spoke in a soft voice, "I know how much you have struggled to be a better father than the one you had, and I know how frustrating it has been for you. Yet all the while I have seen the hurt boy behind the angry man. I have tried to break through your wall but, you thick-skinned coot, you never let me. But today I feel something different in you; maybe you are ready to heal this horrible wound."

Angelo listened quietly, drinking in Lin's words. It was perhaps the first time that he gave her his full attention. It was the first time that she had said all she wanted to say to him.

"I know how much you want Jesse back," Carol said. "Please don't miss this opportunity. Speak to Jesse. Tell him what you want him to know. Tell him how much you love him and want him. You can't go on hiding behind the mask you inherited from your father. You have been your own cruelest enemy, Angelo. No one here has judged you as harshly as you have judged yourself. Look at us."

Angelo raised his head, looked around the group, and made contact with his friends' eyes. He cringed to consider that they had seen him in his naked shame. Again he wanted to turn away, yet again something inside forced him to stay present. He looked into Lin's eyes and felt her tender caring. She had seen his impatient fits of anger, his foolish bravado, his busyness to avoid intimacy, and yet she cared about him. He felt like a little boy whose mother put up with his tantrums because somehow she saw the angel behind the devil. Angelo took Lin's hands and held them tightly to his chest.

Then he turned to Carol, and in her eyes recognized the wisdom of the ages. Her depth was apparent to him now; her psychic gifts, he realized, were not unearned. This woman was an old soul. He felt grateful she had given so much of herself to this project. Angelo took a deep breath and told her, "You weren't fooled by my facade."

"No, Angelo, I wasn't. I see who you are."

Angelo turned to L.C. He put his hands on L.C.'s shoulders and found his eyes. They were blue and very alive. For a long time the two said nothing; then Angelo squeezed L.C.'s shoulders firmly and the two nodded.

Juliana, who was standing beside L.C., came forward. "I can't tell you how happy I am for what you did today, Angelo. It takes a big man to do this."

A voice came over the communicator's audio: "Now, who has judged you?" It was Jesus. Simultaneously the video reactivated the face of Christ.

"Your father has spoken to you from his heart, Angelo. He needed this time with you as much as you did. For your entire life you have been haunted by the voice of an angry father. Long after your father's voice fell silent in the grave, you have replayed his words over and over in your mind, adding fuel to your personal hell. You have become the mob ready to stone you for the slightest error. But today you have heard your father speak new words, words of caring and kindness. And it is time for you to become a new father. As your father has spoken to you, speak to your son."

Chapter 29

Early the next morning Angelo sat in the hot seat, eager to finally speak with Jesse. Carol helped him with the induction while L.C. maneuvered the communicator's control panel. Juliana and Lin watched attentively.

As soon as Angelo was in alpha, Carol told him in a soft voice, "Okay, Angelo, think of a time when you were with Jesse, a time when you were having fun."

Angelo searched his memory bank, rolling his eyes under closed eyelids. "On his last birthday I took him to Raging Waters; it's a water theme park. We went down this huge slide together; it was very steep. He let out this huge squeal and I held him tightly. We landed in the pool at the bottom and laughed for a long time. He liked it so much that we went on the slide at least half a dozen times."

Lin smiled.

"Okay, Angelo," Carol continued. "See if you can visualize Jesse's face before you."

Angelo was silent a few moments, then said, "Okay."

"Do you have the feeling of being with him?" Carol asked.

"Yes."

"Good," Carol responded. "Now speak to him. Say what you would like to Jesse."

The Beam Team sat quietly, utterly attentive.

"Jesse, it's me, your dad. I hope you can hear me. I want to talk to you," said Angelo. Then he stopped and listened. L.C. turned up the audio and watched for the UPR display to register a number. None came up.

Silence.

Angelo spoke again. "Jesse, wherever you are, it is very important that I speak to you. Please let me know if you can hear this."

Silence again. Lin began to get nervous. She made a face and started to fidget.

"Jesse, I love you. Jesse, I want to talk to you. Please, please answer. This is so important to me."

Silence again. No Jesse.

For fifteen minutes, Angelo called out into the universe for his lost son. He received no response. Finally, Angelo disconnected the electronic monitors from his arms and chest and got up from the communicator, a tear gently rolling down his right cheek.

Precisely at 2 p.m. Jean-Claude Michaud arrived with three men in dark suits, men who did not look like scientists. The oldest one was paunchy and bald, mid-fifties, a thick salt-and-pepper moustache, and puffy jowls. A younger man, under forty, was much more fit, wore a navy blue pin-stripe suit, his blonde hair slicked back and his eyes obscured by impenetrable sunglasses. The third, somewhere between the ages of the other two, had sandy hair and sallow skin with some acne scars. None looked friendly.

"These are my friends from Europe," Michaud introduced them, "Dr. Rohrbach, Mr. Mayer, and Mr. Dravitz."

The men extended their hands to Angelo and the others. Their hands were cold, and as they leaned in, Angelo could smell liquor on their breath. Two of them spoke with thick German accents, and the other exhibited more polished English, but it was obvious that German was his mother tongue. Their chins and cheeks were dotted with stubble and they looked tired, as if they had been traveling overnight.

"I thought I would let these gentlemen get acquainted with the communicator," Jean-Claude stated authoritatively.

Angelo was instantly taken aback. He retorted, "With all due respect, gentlemen, I must remind Dr. Michaud that our work is highly confidential."

"And with all due respect, Dr. Mann," Michaud answered sharply, "I remind you that we will need more funding to continue our research. These gentlemen represent an investment capital firm which is very interested in the communicator."

"We never discussed this, Jean-Claude," Angelo objected. "You can't just arrange something like this on your own."

"Well, I did. And now that these men have flown all the way from Europe, I think it would be quite rude if we turned them away."

L.C. stepped in. "This work is quite sensitive, and we are not ready to reveal it to the public," he argued. "Let's arrange a meeting for later, when the communicator is ready to be demonstrated."

"I'm sorry," Jean-Claude responded. "I'm going to have to insist. These investors have to know the nature of the research before they can make an intelligent decision." He paused for a moment and turned to Angelo. "Look, I agreed to follow your silly rules about who I could communicate with and how. I'm keeping my agreement. Don't try to give me a hard time on this now."

Angelo looked to Carol for some kind of cue. She took a breath, closed her eyes, and nodded reluctantly.

"All right," Angelo said. "But if you try anything unusual, we're going to have to ask you to all leave."

"Very well," answered Jean-Claude as he approached the communicator. The three Germans remained standing near the door.

"Oh, yes, one more thing, Angelo," Michaud added. "Would you mind opening up this web site? There's something on it I think you will be interested in seeing." Jean-Claude handed Angelo a small slip of paper with a web address written on it.

"What is this?" Angelo asked.

"Just click on it and you'll see."

Perplexed, Angelo sat down at the computer, logged online, and typed in the web address. After a minute it downloaded. To his astonishment, Angelo saw the face of his wife. It was a video feed with a camera focused on Claudia. She looked horrified.

"Claudia?" What is she doing here?"

"Why don't you ask her?" Michaud suggested. "The web site is set up for two-way communication."

Angelo leaned in toward the microphone and asked anxiously, "Claudia, what are you doing there? Where are you?"

Slowly the camera panned back and Angelo recognized the hotel room that Michaud had been staying in. Next to Claudia were two burly men as ugly as those with Michaud.

"Angelo," Claudia pleaded, "Do what they say. They have Jesse." Tears began to stream down Claudia's cheeks.

"Jesse?"

The camera shifted focus, and Angelo could not believe what he saw. There, to Claudia's left, was Jesse lying in a hotel bed. He was still inert. Angelo's heart began to pound wildly. His breath became choppy and he could feel sweat issuing from his underarms. "What are you doing with my family, you fucking bastards?" he yelled out.

"We thought we could make a little deal with you, Angelo," Jean-Claude said in a businesslike way. He crossed his arms and slowly paced the room. "The password to the communicator for the lives of your family."

The other team members were aghast. L.C. shook his head while Lin let out a whimper. Carol was livid and Father Al closed his eyes in disgust. Juliana watched stoically.

"You've got to be crazy," Angelo bellowed. "You can't just kidnap my family and expect me to turn the project over to your twisted mind."

"No, Angelo, you've got it all wrong. Not only can I do exactly that, but if you do not cooperate I will murder your wife and son right before your eyes."

On the screen one of the henchmen pulled out a knife and pressed it to Claudia's throat. The other took a pillow and began to press it over Jesse's face. The fellow with the knife pricked Claudia's skin slightly and drew blood.

"Stop, Goddamn you!" Angelo yelled. "All right. . .all right. . ." Angelo looked around the room at the frightened faces of his friends. Part of him felt like a coward for giving in; another part realized there was no other choice. "I'll give you the password."

"A wise choice," Michaud responded. He leaned in to the microphone and commanded his goons, "*Halt!*" To Angelo's huge relief, the henchmen pulled back. Then Michaud, still at the mike, added, "But if this password doesn't work, get rid of them." He turned to Angelo. "All right, Dr. Mann, start dictating."

"It's *throughthedoor.*"

Jean-Claude typed the password on the keyboard. The team watched, white-knuckled. After a few moments, the communicator's opening screen appeared.

"Very good, Angelo, very good," Michaud commented. The men on the screen looked to Michaud. Jean-Claude nodded and the monitor went dark, indicating the transmission had been turned off.

"And now, friends," Michaud continued, turning his attention to the cluster of captives. "I am going to have a long-overdue conversation. . .a conversation that has waited for nearly sixty years."

At that moment, a truck pulled into the driveway. Angelo looked out the window to see the letters HOLT emblazoned across the side panel.

The Germans looked at each other in confusion, trying to figure out what to do. After a moment, Michaud turned to L.C. and ordered, "Take the delivery as if it's business as usual. We'll be watching you. With weapons."

The driver with the cross earring emerged from the cab along with his cohort. Their footsteps pounded up the wooden stairs and onto the porch, reverberating through the cavernous barn. L.C. met them at the door. "We have some television monitors for you," said the delivery man.

"Just go ahead and leave them on the porch," instructed L.C., trying to appear nonchalant. His navy training paid off.

In a professional way, the two began to deliver a cache of 17-inch-screen color monitors. In groups of three, the men unloaded the boxed screens on hand trucks. L.C. counted them as they were being stacked. "Eighteen?" L.C. asked the man with the handtruck. "I only ordered three."

"I ordered the rest," Michaud stated. "I have plans for them."

The driver held the electronic signature recorder for L.C. to sign for the shipment. As L.C. finished, the driver asked, "May I use your bathroom?"

"Sorry," L.C. answered. "This is a secured area."

"Just to do movie research?"

"It's none of your business what we are doing here. We'll have to ask you to leave."

"Say, what do you guys have going on here? All of this equipment is a lot more sophisticated than for movies. And all of this German stuff? I have a good mind to report you to the local authorities. . . Let's get out of here, Tony. . ."

"And here is some more German stuff," said Dravitz as he reached under the arm of his suit jacket and pulled out an 8mm Luger. Pointing the gun at the two men, he asked, "Would you gentlemen please step over here?"

"Just one more moment," L.C. intervened. Dravitz kept his gun trained on the two. "May I have a look at your uniform?"

L.C. began to fiddle with the thick company insignia emblem sewn on the upper left breast of the driver's uniform, pressing firmly on each of the letters. When he came to the "O," he mumbled, like a doctor palpating a patient's spine, "What do we have here?"

L.C. took out a little pocket knife and clipped off the emblem. Behind the letter he found a tiny camera about the size of a thumbnail.

"MJ21," noted L.C. "Bulky and archaic. You guys should read some of the new literature; you could have done better than this."

The two men looked at each other anxiously. "And you shouldn't be calling upon dark forces," the driver spouted. "The Lord will chastise all sinners. *'And He shall spew the wicked from His mouth like foul vermin.'*"

"What shall we do with these jokers?" Dravitz asked.

"Lock them in their truck," instructed Michaud.

"Their computer," Carol called out, "—Check it."

"What?" asked Jean-Claude.

"The electronic signature box."

L.C. picked up the box from where the driver had lain it on the steps to the barn. "Now this is a pretty slick technology for a small trucking company. FedEx and UPS use computerized tracking systems, but you guys are local and don't need it. Let's see what we can find out about your system here. . ." L.C. took out his pen knife again and started to fiddle with the back of the box.

The two men became very nervous. "Don't touch that!" the second man called out. L.C. stopped in his tracks. The man added, "We'll all be bird food if you mess with that."

Slowly, methodically, L.C. unscrewed the backing and discovered it was a homemade bomb. "You guys are serious, aren't you?"

"You have no right to summon spirits; it's the work of the devil."

"And who inspired your bomb?" Lin asked. "Mary Poppins?"

Dravitz motioned for the two men to move toward their truck, where he pushed them into the trailer and locked them in.

"How convenient," Jean-Claude said, "We even have a truck for our departure! I guess you'd call that 'synchronicity,' wouldn't you, Angelo? . . .Now I think you folks would probably like some time to meditate. Let me show you to the meditation room, where you can get relaxed."

"You're never going to get away with this," Juliana blurted out. "You're a stupid ass, living in the past."

"But how quickly the past becomes the present–and the future!" he snapped back quickly. "Now we have the technology to manifest the vision. The führer was stopped, but only temporarily. Now he is with us again, and we don't have to worry about protecting him from death. His body is gone, but he lives on–and those of us in bodies will serve him in whatever way we can."

"Don't be ridiculous," Angelo chastised him. "The world would never stand for another Nazi rampage. Look at how quickly Saddam Hussein was cut down. If Hitler made any contribution to the world, it was to generate intolerance for despotism."

"How dare you compare Hussein with the führer!" Michaud retorted. "Hussein is a clumsy fool. Adolph Hitler was–and is–a brilliant mastermind. He was stopped not because of his strategy, but because it was a war of brute force and numbers of troops. Future wars will be won not by the volume of meat and artillery pitted against one another, but by strategy and technology. America has retained world domination because it has set its greatest minds to killing–from the first colonists, to the atomic bomb, to Desert Storm. Hussein's forces were no match for your high-tech killing machines. A mind as brilliant as Hitler's could take atomic power and current technologies and unite the planet in one glorious world government."

"At the expense of everyone without blue eyes and blonde hair!" Lin blurted out.

"The vision of a master Aryan race was Hitler's noblest goal. Look at your world now. The Jews still control all the money and run your economy behind closed doors. Niggers have rotted all of your cities with crime and drug addiction and made a shambles of your society. The Arabs are dumb hotheads; as soon as their oil money runs out they will revert to being bedouin pigs. The Asians are stewing in ignorance, overpopulation, and poverty. Third world Hispanics live under the thumb of the church, which by disapproving birth control has kept them poor, hungry, and easy to manipulate. Even before Hitler, Marx rightfully named religion the opiate of the masses. Religion has become a mega-business with more corruption behind the scenes than the worst dictatorship; even your most ruthless corporate executives have a lot to learn from the church hierarchy, which has succeeded for two thousand years to keep itself rich and its constituents downtrodden. Is this an ideal world?"

Michaud stopped for a moment and surveyed the group at gunpoint. "On the other hand, consider the power that the small country of Germany has gained over just the last century. Twice its military prowess nearly brought the entire world to its knees. It has consistently developed technology that has set the standard for the rest of the world, and no matter how many times the nation has been leveled, its economy has bounced back to become the strongest. My friends, the possibility of an Aryan master race is more real and exciting to me than any other hope for the planet. I am fully dedicated to its manifestation. Now, thanks to you, we have the technology to do so, and it is only a matter of time until the Swastika flies triumphant over every national capital."

The team stood stone cold. This lunatic was serious.

L.C. spoke up. "That's a very nice little speech there, young feller, but besides the fact that you are pitifully sick, there is one point you are forgetting—you don't know how to recreate this machine. Avi Goldman's programming died with him. The communicator will self-destruct if anyone messes with it. If this machine ever went haywire or got destroyed, you would immediately lose it all."

"That is why we are taking the communicator back to Berlin," Michaud answered smugly. "Even as we speak, the most brilliant computer wizards on the planet are setting up the programming to crack those codes and replicate this device. Then we'll have simultaneous guidance from the führer all over the world."

"We have taken Dr. Goldman's family into custody," added Mayer. Angelo paled. "If we have any difficulty breaking the code, we expect we can influence Goldman to give it to us from the other side. He may be immortal, but they are not. Unfortunately, his mentor Rav Shimon was not so cooperative; we had to exterminate the old fool."

Angelo's blood began to boil "You're pure scum," he retaliated, and spat into Michaud's face.

Michaud cocked his shoulders and reared back to slug Angelo, but restrained himself at the last moment. "Get them out of my sight," he barked. Rohrbach pulled out a gun of his own, and Michaud's accomplices began to force the team into the meditation room. "Leave them out," he told Rohrbach, pointing to Angelo and Juliana. Then he turned to Angelo and said, "I think we'll keep you and *fraeulein* here. You can run the equipment."

Dravitz joined the other German in barricading the door with a heavy desk. Michaud took his seat at the communicator. Angelo moved into the engineering position, while Juliana monitored the audio. The three Germans stood aloof, one with his gun trained on Juliana and Angelo, the other two with arms crossed. Michaud quieted himself and put himself into his alpha state. Angelo and Juliana watched with trepidation. They knew what was to come.

Sure enough, within a few seconds the face of Adolph Hitler appeared on the screen. Angelo wanted to throw up. Juliana grimaced. The führer looked exactly as he did in the old German newsreels, with his small black moustache, fiery eyes, and Nazi uniform with large black encircled swastikas.

The moment Hitler appeared, Michaud stood erect, thrust his

right arm forward and shouted, "*Hiel Hitler!*" Immediately the other Germans followed suit. They clicked their heels and snapped to attention. Hitler, on the monitor, nodded and extended his arm in kind.

Angelo could not believe this was happening. The devil himself was being reincarnated before his very eyes—and Angelo Mann was the source of the technology that allowed this to happen.

Jean-Claude began to engage in an animated discussion with Hitler. Angelo turned to Juliana and asked, "What are they talking about?"

Juliana shook her head and answered, "Plans for replicating the communicator. They have people stationed around the globe, ready to use it. They have been planning this for a long time."

"They just said that?" Angelo asked.

"No, I know it."

"How do you know that?"

Juliana's face turned stiff. She hesitated to speak. It was the first time Angelo had seen such trepidation in her eyes.

"I have been following Michaud for a long time."

"I know, you told me you used to date him."

"No, Angelo, it's more than that." Juliana turned her head slightly to the side, so Angelo could not see her eyes.

Angelo's gut began to clench. He took his hands and lifted them to Juliana's cheeks, turning her head to face him again.

"What is it, then?"

"I have been following Jean-Claude because I was assigned to."

"Assigned by who?"

"By my government."

"The German government?"

"Yes."

Angelo's eyes bulged. He was incredulous.

"You work for the German government?"

"I've been a German agent for twelve years."

Angelo's jaw dropped. "You weren't kidding when you said you wanted to grow up to be a spy."

"Michaud is the leader of a growing underground Neo-Nazi movement. I was assigned to conduct surveillance on the movement and make recommendations on how to liquidate it."

"And that's why you dated him?"

"That's right."

Suddenly Angelo's stomach felt like it was falling off a cliff at seventy miles an hour. "And how about me? Is that why you were with me?"

Juliana took a long deep breath. Again she tried to avoid his glance. Again he reached for her chin and forced her to look at him.

"I never expected to fall in love with you, dammit," she said. "Yes, at first you were an assignment. I admit it. We recognized the potential military importance of the work you were presenting, so I was assigned to listen to your lecture at Tel Aviv and make a report."

. "I can't believe this!" Angelo exclaimed, "I really can't believe this!"

"But then when we connected, I wished I wasn't on assignment. The afternoon at Mishnayat, our night in Tel Aviv, our rendezvous in San Francisco. Angelo, each time we got together I fell more and more in love with you. I asked my supervisor to take me off the case, but he insisted that this was our big chance to flush Jean-Claude out and get rid of him."

"You're making this up, right?"

"Oh, Angelo, I wish I was. I wish I had met you in another way. But when we met I saw something in you, something I have always been looking for. You're strong and intelligent. You're a visionary. And since you've been going through this ordeal with Jesse, I can feel your vulnerability. I've never known a man like you, and I probably will never meet one again."

Angelo rolled his eyes and shook his head. He was speechless.

Juliana continued, "I know what a shock this is to you. I wish I could have told you earlier. But I couldn't. Look, Angelo, I won't blame you if you never want to see me again. But whether or not you do, I want you to know that my love for you is real."

Chapter 30

As Jean-Claude Michaud became immersed in his dialogue with Adolph Hitler, Dravitz and Rohrbach began to unpack the television monitors. Mayer kept a pistol trained on Angelo and Juliana, who watched in horror as the two Germans cleared desks and workstations and formed a formed a large "U" with the tables, with the communicator at the top. Then they took the monitors and set them on the tables so they could all be viewed from one point. They opened a box they had brought separately and removed a complex interface device that would allow all of the screens to operate simultaneously. The men worked feverishly to get the apparatus ready.

While the Germans were setting up, Angelo tried to wrap his mind around what had just happened with Juliana. It wasn't easy. Juliana was a spy. While she claimed she loved him, she had used him. He looked at her and saw the tears on her pale cheeks. Yes, he believed that she loved him; he could feel that. But now he wondered if he could really trust her. After all, he and Juliana had spent so much intimate time together, and she had withheld a secret of immense proportion. Who knows what else she hadn't told him? Even more important, he doubted he could ever build a life with her. Over the years he had gone through so much with Claudia, and until recently she had always been there for him. Claudia loved Angelo and she loved Jesse. She was a good mother. Yes, Juliana was beautiful and passionate and intelligent, but she was definitely not a family kind of woman. Being involved with her would mean starting all over again to build a relationship, and who knew what kind of problems her lifestyle and past associations would bring them? Angelo thought about Claudia and Jesse trapped in that hotel room with those butchers.

He suddenly longed for his family in a way he had never imagined, longed for all of them to be together once again. Was it too late?

"Ready," Dravitz called to Michaud. Jean-Claude withdrew from his conversation with Hitler, picked up the phone, dialed, and spoke in German.

"What's he saying?" Angelo asked Juliana.

"He told someone to get over here now. . . .and bring her."

Michaud barked some orders to his cronies, who went to the barricaded meditation room, moved the desk, and let the others out. As soon as the team emerged, Jean-Claude told them snidely, "I just thought you might like to attend a sneak preview, friends. We want to show you what a simultaneous broadcast looks like. We couldn't have done it without you."

As the team stood at the mouth of the U, Michaud took his place at the hot seat. "Silence!" Jean-Claude demanded as he began his self-guided induction. The team members stood dazed, anxious about what they were about to see.

After a minute a desert scene appeared on one of the monitors. A band of prehistoric tribesmen, armed with rocks and thick tree branches and sharpened bones, was attacking the encampment of another tribe. Taken by surprise, the victims were quickly crushed by the marauders. As the scene became a brutal bloodfest, Carol and Lin looked away; the men, too, were horrified. This was no dramatization; it was an Akashic recording of a mass murder at the dawn of human civilization.

As the victorious tribesmen rummaged through the carnage for valuables, another scene appeared on the screen to its right. It was another tribal battle, this time thousands of years later. The movie showed a Semitic culture waging war with rudimentary weapons forged of iron and other metals. While the technology was more advanced, the principle was the same: domination by power and aggression.

Another video flashed on, portraying a mid-nineteenth-century train passing through a prairie filled with grazing bison on the United States' western frontier. A man on the train shouted, "Buffalo!" and a dozen men reached under their seats and pulled out shotguns. One of the men bribed the engineer to slow the train down, and the gunmen positioned themselves at various windows, where they began a shooting spree. Within seconds almost 30 black and brown bison had dropped. As the other buffalo began to scatter, terrified, the men began shooting wildly. "Like fish in a barrel!" one of them called out, laughing. The herd, trapped on one side by a ravine and on the other by the long train, found no sanctuary; as the pack frantically hurtled westward, the train followed them, keeping pace. By the time the train resumed its normal speed, over 200 majestic buffalo lay ravaged. Not one was taken for food or honored; all were annihilated for sport and left on the plain to rot.

As if lit by a fire out of control, the next monitor flashed on, depicting a group of Spaniards corralling African natives. The Africans were whipped, bound in heavy chains and shackles, separated from their families, and packed like animals into the hull of a huge clipper ship. Angelo grimaced to see the men and women mercilessly stuffed together on their sides. With little food and no means for sanitation, many were sick and dying. The scene shifted to the boat docking in St. Thomas, where corpses were being thrown overboard as shark food. The weak survivors were prodded off the ship like cattle, met on the shore by men who were exchanging money. The next scene showed the Africans sweating and toiling over huge grimy pots of boiling sugar on a hot and humid Caribbean day. Angelo's heart ached to see the faces of little children about Jesse's age, working beside the adults, struggling to keep up with the pace. The children had lost all light in their eyes, and they looked tired and bitter.

Finally, after seeing enough of these repulsive scenes, Angelo called out, "Why must you torture us like this? What value do you find in this?"

Michaud was quick to answer, "These are true historical events in which superior men emerged victorious through the intelligent use of strategy and technology; it is not the meek, you see, who will inherit the earth, but the shrewd. Every one of these scenes proves that the humble are not rewarded, but butchered. Thousands of years of evolution have honed the strongest warriors; each generation of victors stands on the shoulders of the last. Now, after millennia of evolution, the last century has produced the greatest genius of all."

A fifth video screen flashed on, showing Adolph Hitler standing on a Berlin balcony reviewing the passage of thousands of Nazis marching the Goose Step. Proudly the führer lifted his arm in approval.

Another monitor chronicled the Nazis invading Poland; another, the bombing of Britain; another, the German siege of Leningrad where Russians were starving so desperately that they were tearing wallpaper off the walls and eating it to try to get some nutrition from the paste. Another monitor depicted a group of bony Jews laying listlessly in their crude wooden bunks in the Dachau concentration camp, wincing in their final moments of waning life as they heard their families screaming under showerheads spewing poison fumes in the gas chambers. Lin, watching aghast, began to vomit. Within minutes every screen was filled with scenes of Nazi murder and mayhem and the most base expressions of fear, degradation, perversion, and destruction.

"Behold the power of the technology you have created, Angelo Mann!" laughed Michaud. "Once a frequency is established, the communicator is now able to access the entire Akashic memory bank of all persons, incidents, and events related to that theme. We have here a living library of all human history!"

The screens continued to display an endless series of sordid images—more wars, brutal crimes, animals preying on weaker creatures, horrific mushroom clouds exploding over Hiroshima and Nagasaki, drunken men beating their wives and hurting their children, gang rapes, American warplanes spraying fiery Napalm over Vietnamese villages, the oil refineries of Kuwait spewing massive plumes of turbid smoke against a murky sky, bodies of fish and birds floating lifeless in the Persian Gulf, suffocated by an oil slick hundreds of miles long. Some segments lasted but a few seconds, others drew particular events to their depraved conclusions, always annihilation and despair.

Horrified, the watchers were trapped in a macabre museum of heinous crimes, resurrected all at once from the collective graveyard of the human psyche. Eventually all looked away, unable to stomach the disgusting presentations. Carol and Lin hid their heads on the men's chests, while Juliana simply looked down at the floor. Angelo was racked by the deepest embarrassment for the entire human race which, unlike any other species in nature, has inflicted such sorrowful suffering upon itself.

A car pulled into the driveway. Angelo looked through the open door to see in the front seat the two creeps who had appeared on the video screen with Claudia. Terror gripped his heart as he feared they may have done away with her—and Jesse. One of the men opened the back door of the car. Claudia stepped out, her hands tied together behind her back.

Thank God she's all right, Angelo thought. He exhaled a deep sigh of relief. But what about Jesse? As soon as the men and Claudia stepped inside, Angelo cried out, "Where is my son? What have you done with him?"

"He is in the hotel room," Michaud answered. "He isn't going anywhere."

"But the boy is ill," Angelo pleaded. "He can't be left alone!"

"Oh, quit bellyaching," Michaud snapped as he began to confer with his cronies.

"If anything happens to my son, I swear I'll kill you with my bare hands!" Angelo shouted.

Michaud snickered. "I don't think you're in much of a position to threaten me."

One of the Germans pushed Claudia to join the others. As she and Angelo locked eyes, he could hardly believe how happy he was to see her. The thought of anything happening to her was unbearable. Angelo reached over and untied the cords around her wrists. "Are you all right?" he asked her.

Claudia fell onto Angelo's shoulders and she began to sob. "My God, Angelo, it was horrible! They showed up at the house in the middle of the night and broke through the door. They had Jesse in the back of a van. It was full of junk. It was so disgusting."

Angelo held Claudia tightly and stroked her head.

"Then they dragged me out of the house and into the van. I had no idea who they were or where they were taking me or what was going on. They spoke German, no English, and they kept pushing and poking me around. I was so afraid they would hurt Jesse. They took us to this hotel room and I thought they were going to rape me. But they just tied me up and waited. When I finally saw your face on the monitor I was so relieved. Are you all right?"

"Yeah, I'm okay."

Claudia reached up and kissed Angelo. "Thank God you're alive. I was so worried." Claudia rested her head on Angelo's shoulder, closing her eyes for a few moments. When she opened them, Juliana was directly in her line of vision. Juliana looked right at Claudia. Her lips turned up slightly, then a single tear flowed down her left cheek. She and Claudia held eye contact for a few moments. Claudia stiffened, then looked up at Angelo. "So this is her?"

Angelo and Juliana looked at each other for a brief intense moment. He said nothing.

Chapter 31

*A*chtung! Schnell, wir sind in Gefahr!" shouted Mayer, motioning to the window.

Angelo stood up from the control panel and looked out the window, where he saw two white panel vans pulling into the driveway. *Redemption Retreat* was painted in black letters on their sides. Inside the vehicles Angelo saw about eight men of all ages wearing khaki camouflage uniforms and toting rifles. The vans pulled to an abrupt stop, the men streamed out and with military precision took protected positions behind their vehicles. Within a few moments, they had their pieces trained on the barn windows and doors.

A fair-skinned man with a crew cut, the one Angelo had seen through the window at the retreat, held up a bullhorn and barked, "In the name of Jesus Christ, we order you to come out and surrender. Satan, get thee hence!"

The Nazis searched each other's eyes frantically. Dravitz and Mayer scurried back and forth to the windows, looking out, then shouting to Michaud, all raising their voices louder with each interchange. Michaud rose from the hot seat and looked out the window himself. Finally he issued some kind of order, and Dravitz and Rohrbach went to a suitcase, where they pulled out two submachine guns. "What's going on?" Angelo asked Juliana nervously.

"He told them to sneak around the back and find a place to ambush the intruders."

While Michaud stalled, the two Germans made a hasty exit out the back door with their weapons. As soon as they were out of sight,

Jean-Claude went to the door and called out, "We know we're outnumbered—we surrender." Slowly Michaud and the two remaining Germans stepped toward the door with their hands raised high in the air. The team members watched in relief as the Germans marched onto the porch. But Angelo knew that he and the team were still far from safe. What could these fanatics have in mind?

The Christians emerged from behind their vehicles and slowly walked toward the barn, keeping their rifles trained on the three Germans standing at the door. "We know what you are doing in there," the leader shouted. "We have been sent to destroy the beast. We are the Protectors of the Word!"

"Nazis in another uniform," L.C. whispered to Lin in the rear of the lab.

"We ready, Billy?" a stocky man asked the leader. The leader nodded.

Three of the Protectors hustled to the back of one of the vans and emerged with large red plastic cans of gasoline. Angelo could smell the gas even from where he was standing.

"By the authority of God, we have come to destroy these evil works!" shouted Billy.

Meanwhile the monitors were still rolling through thousands of images of conflict and annihilation, each more grisly than the last.

Out of the corner of his eye Angelo saw Lin start to inch her way toward the back door. She was shorter than the others, and some large equipment blocked the Protectors' view of her. While the gunmen's attention was focused on the front door, she slipped out.

Billy and two of his men forced the Germans back into the barn. Billy came all the way in while the other two Protectors stood at the door, keeping their rifles pointed at the Germans and the team. The remainder of the Protectors advanced to the porch, rifles pointed. Billy took a position in the center of the cluster of monitors and watched a few moments of the many war scenes still rolling. "This is truly of the devil," he spouted, shaking his head. He reached into his breast pocket and pulled out a small Bible. Then he held up the Bible with one hand and raised his rifle in the other. Looking directly at the group of captives, he shouted, "He who lives by the sword shall die by the sword!"

Suddenly all the screens went blank. Angelo looked around the room to see if someone had turned off the communicator. L.C. turned to Angelo, confused, then surveyed the snake of wires on the floor to see if an electrical plug had been disconnected. The entire system seemed to be intact.

Angelo, standing near one of the side walls, was in a good position to see the bank of monitors across the room from him. One of the monitors began to crackle and soon an image appeared. It showed a town square in what appeared to be medieval Spain. In front of a huge church door stood a platform with three guillotines. An ornately dressed priest with a high hat and many crosses on his gown sat in a tall chair next to another well-dressed man. The priest was motioning to an executioner to escort two men and a woman up the steps to the guillotine. When the prisoners were secured in the guillotines, the priest signaled with his hand and the shiny blades fell, sundering the prisoners' heads, which fell into large baskets in front of the blade. Blood was gushing everywhere. Angelo thought he was going to throw up. The camera's viewpoint shifted to show a long line of people, dressed in the clothing of commoners, hands tied behind their backs. A large crowd was gathered to watch the mass executions.

Claudia, standing next to Angelo, averted her eyes from the screens. She put her head on Angelo's chest and began to weep. Angelo put his arm around her to comfort her. Suddenly he realized that now he and his wife were in the same position he found himself with Juliana at the Mishnayat school. His mind started to go tilt as he considered the events that led to this moment, and the turnabout of his relationship with Claudia and Juliana.

Another screen flashed on, showing Israeli guerrillas blowing up a Palestinian Arab school in 1947. Like the Mishnayat massacre, tons of rubble crushed many children to death. Screams and cries tried to make their way through the wreckage. As the guerillas left the demolished school, they planted a flag with a Jewish star.

A third monitor showed a group of small African children

with bloated stomachs, their ravenous eyes crying for sustenance from mothers who could give them none. The camera cut to a scene showing warring religious factions blocking roads, turning away trucks that were attempting to deliver food. The camera cut once again to show a docked steamship containing thousands of sacks of rice and good-will supplies, with fat rats feasting on them.

Yet another monitor showed a young mother in Belfast, Ireland, kneeling on the steps of a Catholic church screaming at the top of her lungs as she held the lifeless body of her baby daughter. "May you rot in hell, Protestant bastards!" she cried into the night.

Eventually all the screens became illuminated again, this time depicting bloodbaths of many different religious wars. While the earlier display portrayed a collage of horrors inflicted in the name of nation, these showed equally grotesque atrocities in the name of God.

"My God," Carol uttered in awe, "It's all the same, isn't it?"

Suddenly the jagged riveting of automatic weapons pierced the air. Dravitz and Rohrbach had sneaked around to the front of the barn and opened fire on the Protectors. Instantly the five Protectors who were standing on the porch, fell to the ground, with multiple bullet holes oozing scarlet blood from their backs. Lin and Claudia screamed as the team members dropped to take cover behind the machinery. Angelo wrapped his body around Claudia's to protect her. She was terrified, breathing rapidly, and held onto Angelo's arm tightly.

The two Protectors inside the barn ran to the door and returned fire, while Billy kept his gun trained on the Germans and the team. One of the Protectors, a sandy-haired man about 25, got a bead on Dravitz and shot him in the chest. Dravitz keeled over in a small patch of grass and let his weapon drop onto the graveled driveway. The other Protector, a paunchy black-haired man in his forties, wearing wire-rimmed eyeglasses, engaged Rohrbach, who was better protected behind one of the *Redemption* vans.

Inside the lab the monitors kept rolling images of war. Some of the holy war scenes were replaced by political war scenes, many from World Wars I, II, China, Bangladesh, Vietnam, Iraq, and Kosovo. Within seconds all eighteen monitors were showing intermixed scenes of national and religious conflicts.

Angelo looked over Billy's shoulder into the parking area and saw Lin, crouched low, scurrying along the cattle fence that bounded the property. Methodically she sneaked past Rohrbach to the other side of the van that was shielding him. Angelo, with his heart in his throat, watched Lin open the passenger's door out of Rohrbach's sight and climb in. Angelo knew that if Rohrbach saw her, he would surely kill her. Moments later the van engine suddenly started and it surged out of its place, leaving Rohrbach suddenly exposed. Immediately the Protectors fired a volley of shots and Rohrbach was gone.

The Protectors on the porch seemed satisfied that they eliminated their ambushers, and turned to join Billy inside the lab. "Your guns," Billy demanded of the Germans. "On that table." He pointed with his rifle to an empty workstation.

The Germans reached under their jackets to remove pistols from their shoulder holsters. Angelo tensed, wondering if they would try to seize the moment for a rebuttal. To his relief, they set their Lugers down peacefully. Billy spied the open door to the meditation room and ordered the Germans, "In there!" motioning with his rifle. The men raised their arms and started to walk. "Not you!" Billy called out, pointing to Michaud. Surprised, Michaud turned around. "I figure you're the leader. You are to behold the work of the Lord." The two Protectors barricaded the Germans in the meditation room as Jean-Claude stood next to the team watching and waiting to see what the Protectors' next move would be.

Billy took one of the gasoline cans and doused the communicator. Then his two cronies soaked the rest of equipment. Triumphantly Billy shouted, "Now you shall look upon the destruction of Satan's works!"

Gesturing with his gun, Billy indicated for Michaud and the team to step outside. Under the watchful eye of the Protectors, the group moved toward the door, then down the stairs into the parking area, where they had a vantage point to see the lab and most of the equipment. Angelo shuddered to consider that the Germans in the meditation room were about to meet a fiery death. One of the protectors went back to a van and returned with a large sheet, which he twisted into a bulky rope as he walked. He handed it to Billy, who doused it with the remaining gasoline. Then he set one end at the foot of the communicator and the other end on the floor near him. He took out a box of large wooden matches and struck one. "So long, Adolph Hitler!" he shouted. "So long, demons! Back to hell where you belong!" He tossed the match onto the end of the sheet, which burst into flame. Then he scurried out the door in the direction of the assembled group.

"*Nooooooo!*" cried Carol as she started to run to save the communicator before the flame on the makeshift fuse reached the equipment. Angelo caught her and held her. "It's no use," he told her.

Suddenly Jean-Claude pulled out a gun he had picked up from one of the dead men and grabbed Billy. Holding the gun to his head, he dragged Billy into the lab and called out to the team, "Get in here and help me!" The other Protectors, still toting rifles, looked confused and immobilized. They tried to take aim at Michaud, but could not get a clear shot with Billy blocking him. Angelo stood outside with the team, churning with mixed emotions. He certainly did not want to help Michaud, but this was his chance to try to save the equipment.

Angelo dashed into the barn, grabbed the burning sheet, and cast it out the door. But by that time the fire had spread to the gasoline doused on the floor, and was quickly leaping to the many wires strewn about the floor. Some of the CPUs and speakers touching the floor were already getting singed. The barn was becoming intensely hot, smoking, and the smell of burning wood and plastic assaulted Angelo's nostrils. With Billy still hostage and the Protectors immobilized, L.C., Carol, and Juliana tried to get to the communicator, but the flames were already ominous. In a heroic effort, L.C. dashed past several pieces of flaming equipment and reached the CPU containing Avi Goldman's precious disk. He pressed the CD-ROM release button, but the CPU had already been immobilized and would not open. The flames and smoke began to overtake L.C. and, convinced there was no more use trying, he made his way back outside.

In the midst of the fray, Juliana found her way to the table where the Germans had been forced to leave their guns. Angelo watched her pick up a Luger and try to get a bead on Jean-Claude, who was still holding Billy hostage. The scene was utter chaos, and she could hardly get a view through the flames and the frantic movements of the others. Juliana did her best to thread her way around the back of the lab, where she could get a better line on Michaud. Then, as soon as she could see him clearly, she took aim.

"This one's for the führer," she called out, and pulled the trigger. Her bullet struck Jean-Claude in the upper right side of his back. He gasped and immediately let go his hold on Billy, who ran outside. Michaud fell to the floor.

Angelo was utterly relieved to see the demise of Michaud. At the same time he was aghast to see Juliana kill him. He was frightened by her deftness the way she postured herself, held the gun with two hands, and took aim like a marksman; this woman, Angelo realized, had been well trained to kill. He wondered if she had killed anyone before Jean-Claude, and how many. Suddenly she didn't seem so appealing as a romantic partner.

L.C., Carol, and Claudia dashed into the lab to try to salvage the equipment, but it was too late; with each moment the flames grew higher and the room was becoming filled with smoke. L.C. found Carol's hand and guided her to the door. She emerged coughing heavily; L.C.'s face was discolored with smoke. Juliana began to make her way to the door, but she tripped over some wires and fell. Angelo watched her try to get up, but she appeared to be hurt or trapped. Angelo started to move toward the lab to help her, but before he could get to her he saw Claudia, who was finding her way out of the inferno, turn and go to Juliana. She helped Juliana dislodge her foot, and the two ran out together. Angelo was proud of his wife's courage.

The team stood in the parking area near the remaining Protectors, who seemed disinterested in the team as they watched the fire engulf the lab. Billy, looking disheveled after his escape from Michaud, silently nodded as if he was pleased to see the lab disintegrate. He scanned the bodies of his troupe on the porch just ten yards away from him. "Martyrs for Christ," he declared aloud.

Suddenly Jean-Claude, who had been lying motionless, began to stir. Angelo watched him try to get up to make his way toward the door, but couldn't. Too weak to move, he struggled to wriggle away from the burning communicator. Angelo realized that it would be but a minute before the open gasoline can closest to Jean-Claude would be sparked and he would be annihilated.

Angelo began to move toward the lab. Claudia grabbed at his shirt. "Angelo, where are you going?"

"I'm going to get Jean-Claude."

"But you'll be killed!" shouted Carol. "It's going to all blow at any moment."

Angelo disregarded the warning and made his way into the lab, trying to keep his distance from the gasoline can. He picked up Jean-Claude in his arms and began to carry him out.

Suddenly one of the videos went on again.

"That's impossible!" uttered L.C., watching from the parking area. "Those videos have no source of power!"

Carol smiled. "Wanna bet?" she asked.

For no obvious reason, the fire began to abate. The team and the Protectors looked on, incredulous. Behind Angelo one of the screens showed a scene from Calcutta in the latter twentieth century. Mother Teresa, on a crowded street, was holding a dying man in her arms. She looked deeply into his eyes and told him tenderly, "My dear, dear brother, I love you." The man, though obviously in the last minutes of his life, recaptured a spark in his eyes and offered the slightest smile. "May your soul be blessed, and may you go to be at peace with God," Mother Teresa told him. With that, the man expired with an expression of utter serenity on his face.

"What's happening?" Juliana asked L.C.

"Looks like we're getting a transmission from Central Broadcasting," he answered.

"Angelo!" Claudia called, "Turn around!"

Angelo turned and saw the image. Stunned, he realized that he was holding Jean-Claude in the same position that Mother Teresa held the dying pauper.

Angelo looked toward the communicator to see how it could possibly be drawing a transmission. It couldn't—the entire machine was fried. All of its wires from the power supply were destroyed along with every one of its cables to the monitors. Some of the plastic casings had melted. The screens were being illuminated by some kind of energy from beyond this world.

On the adjacent screen, another image appeared, showing Jesus trudging through the streets of Jerusalem, bearing a heavy wooden cross on his shoulders. As he labored, both Jews and Romans laughed and spat upon him. As he passed a woman in the crowd, she took a cloth and wiped the perspiration off his brow, cleansing some of the blood and dirt from his cheeks. For a moment, comfort and appreciation exuded from the condemned man's eyes. Another woman offered Jesus a cup of water. As the soothing liquid touched his parched, torn lips, a tiny smile of thanks exuded from the lips of Christ. Then a man with dark skin broke through the barricade erected by the Roman soldiers and took the cross from Jesus. Jesus, though in great pain, stood upright and walked some of his last steps in dignity. After a minute, the guards subdued the man; as the man was about to be dragged back into the crowd, Jesus kissed his hands.

One by one, the team slowly entered the lab. The communicator was still burning and gasoline was spread around the lab, but they were not afraid. Obviously the same supernatural force that was illuminating the monitors, was protecting them.

The video screens continued to flash on, each showing scenes of kindness, service, and courage. Each was a testimonial to the power of human beings to move beyond fear and give love in the most trying situations. A young woman wearing second-hand clothing went to a bank, withdrew her savings, and went to the city jail to bail out her brother. An elderly German woman hid two Jews in her basement and put off Nazis searching for them. White people entered the ranks of blacks as they marched for civil rights in Birmingham in the 1960's. A young man brought a meal to another young man who was lying in bed, covered with sores, and very weak. The first man tenderly fed the other, then pulled the covers up to his neck and kissed him on the forehead. A shopkeeper forgave a boy for stealing some candy. A veterinarian stayed up through a cold night to deliver a calf whose mother was in danger. A little boy ran into a man on the street, and instead of rebuking the child, the elder gave him a kindly pat on the head. On the western prairie a group of Native Americans prayed over the carcass of a buffalo they had just hunted, thanking the Great Spirit for bounty and blessing the buffalo's journey to the next life. A nurse in a hospital patiently helped an elderly man out of bed so he could go to the bathroom. In a concentration camp a young man passed some of his meager rations to an old man on the other side of a fence. Russian and American navies converged to save a whale stranded off the coast of Alaska. An old man, making out his will, included a large donation to a shelter for the homeless. The young wife of a medical student massaged her husband's tight shoulders as he studied late into the night. As a child in ancient China was about to be beaten by a bigger boy, his friend distracted the bully so the little one could escape. A cowboy made a grave for his fallen partner and fashioned a cross to mark his resting place in a stark and lifeless desert.

On and on rolled the images of compassion and caring. Angelo watched with awe and reverence, feeling he had been lifted from hell to heaven.

Suddenly Angelo felt that it was time to leave the building. He carried the limp body of Jean-Claude, and the group followed. As soon as they reached a safe distance, the flames began surging again, and the lab was consumed. The group moved to a little flower garden thirty yards from the porch near a small weather-beaten statue of the Virgin Mary. In the distance they heard the monitors sputter and burn. Angelo laid Jean-Claude down on a soft grassy area at the feet of the Madonna.

The three remaining Protectors, watching the supernatural event, looked frightened. When they saw the flames magnify after being quelled for the video transmission, they fled to the cab of the HOLT truck, still containing their trapped cohorts. The men piled into the cab and sped out of the parking area as fast as they could.

Angelo turned to Jean-Claude, who was very weak. He kneeled, took off his sweater, and made a little pillow for Jean-Claude's head. Mother Mary's hands were extended in a blessing, and it looked as if she was pouring grace to the nearly lifeless Jean-Claude Michaud. Angelo cradled Michaud's head in his arms.

Jean-Claude looked up at Angelo through bloodied eyes and a ravaged face. He was gruesome to behold, but Angelo looked at him with tremendous compassion. The group gathered around the two.

"Why?" gasped Michaud painfully. "Why would you help me?"

Angelo was silent for a few moments. "Because behind all your bravado, you are me. Given slightly different circumstances, I might have ended up doing what you did."

"But I would have destroyed you if I lived," Jean-Claude whispered.

"Your ambition destroyed you first, just as mine almost annihilated me."

"And I'm on my way to hell."

"You've been there for a long time," Carol interjected. "Maybe this is your chance to get out."

Michaud formed the slightest smile and nodded his head a bit. His eyes opened just enough for Angelo to see the same tiny glimmer he had seen in the eyes of the pauper Mother Teresa had held. Jean-Claude took his last breath and let his head fall back.

The group was silent. Angelo closed his eyes and appreciated that he and the others had escaped alive.

"And the gentle *shall* inherit the earth," a deep voice spoke.

Everyone looked around to see who had spoken; it was no one on the team. The voice sounded like that of Jesus when he had spoken through the communicator.

"I told you that you would be cared for," the voice added.

The voice was definitely that of Jesus. The group looked into the barn to see if somehow the communicator or the monitors had been activated. But they saw only charred rubble.

Carol called out, "It's coming from the truck!"

The team turned toward the remaining *Redemption* van and, sure enough, over the radio the voice spoke again. "Do you think I am limited to the apparatus in the barn?" the voice asked laughingly.

The group piled into the van, Angelo and Claudia in the front seat and the others in the rear. The ignition key had been left on accessory. Angelo reached to turn up the volume on the radio. "If I had to wait until you invented the communicator so I could communicate with my people, my work would have been severely hampered over the last two thousand years," said Jesus.

"But you did come through the communicator, didn't you?" asked Carol.

"Of course I did—because that was your way of reaching out. The communicator was your form of prayer, and I am happy to answer prayers however they come."

"So we could have set up a string and a paper cup and, if we believed in that, you would have spoken?" Angelo inquired.

"Even through this Motorola."

"Does that mean that you don't even need any device? You could just transmit directly to us without a machine?" asked L.C.

"Turn the radio off," Jesus instructed.

Angelo turned the key, and all simultaneously heard the voice of Christ in their own minds. He continued, "Your brain is a highly sophisticated receiving device. It makes the technology you have created seem like a paper cup by comparison. If you learn to listen on the right frequency, you can talk to me anytime you like. I am as close to you as your willingness to hear me."

"Will we be able to re-create the communicator?" asked Angelo.

"You will be able to create anything you wish – you always have, and always will."

"What about Hitler and those like him?" Carol asked. "Will they ever be stopped?"

"First you must come to terms with the Hitler within you. The man is but a symbol of your own sense of powerlessness and uncontrolled rage. As you learn to live from love rather than fear, there will be no energy in your world for a Hitler to feed on.

"My friends," Jesus went on, "your enemy is not anyone or anything outside you. Your enemy is fear. Most of you have settled for but a tiny trickle of aliveness. Your only question now is how much more pain you are willing to put up with before you turn inward for your answers. You have tolerated an earth unlike heaven because you do not believe you deserve love. But here is the truth that will guide you all the way home: *Your true purpose is to give and receive love.* Nothing else is important, nothing else works, and nothing else exists."

"But what about my son?" Angelo asked adamantly. "What about Jesse?"

"He hears you, Angelo," Jesus replied. "He hears you."

Angelo put his arm around Claudia and held her close. She closed her eyes and drank in his touch.

"I will be leaving now. But I won't be very far at all. Remember that the real communicator is within you."

Chapter 32

Angelo and Claudia dashed to his car and sped out of the parking lot. It would take at least half an hour to get to the Executive Suites in San Rafael, and Angelo prayed that Jesse was all right. He reached into the glove box for his mobile phone and called the hotel manager. "My son is in room 312," he told the manager in a heated voice. "He was kidnapped and left there. He is very sick. . .No, this is not a crank call. I swear to you that I am telling you the truth. Please, just go up and open the room and you will see. . .I am on my way to the hotel now."

Angelo pressed the *end* button and immediately dialed 911. "This is Dr. Angelo Mann. I need an Aeromedical Transport Helicopter at the Executive Suites on Route 101 in San Rafael. My son is in a coma and his life may be critical. I need immediate transport to Packard Children's Hospital at Stanford. . .Yes, here's my cell phone number. . ."

Angelo drove as fast as he could, weaving in and out of traffic. Several drivers honked and cursed at him. Claudia held onto his arm and looked very concerned. The car just wouldn't seem to go fast enough.

When they arrived at the Executive Suites, an ambulance and two police cars were already waiting at the front door. The Lexus screeched to a stop and Angelo and Claudia ran out without even closing their doors. One policeman and an EMT squad member accompanied Angelo and Claudia to the third floor, where the door to room 312 was wide open. A man in a brown suit, probably the manager, stood outside the door having an animated conversation with a policeman. Another policeman was on his walkie-talkie, the loud screeches and static reverberating through the hall. Angelo passed them all and entered the room to find little Jesse lying in the bed, unconscious. The child did not look good; his face had lost color and his breathing was shallow. Two paramedics and another policeman were moving about the room, readying their equipment. Claudia rushed to Jesse's bed, took his hand, and began to stroke his forehead.

The EMT crew rushed into action. They checked Jesse's vital signs, placed an oxygen mask over his little face, and set up a glucose I.V. Within minutes they had wrapped up the sleeping child, strapped him in a stretcher, and wheeled him down the corridor to the elevator. Angelo and Claudia followed them to the lobby, where a crowd had gathered. "Oh, my, I hope the little boy is all right," an elderly woman exclaimed as the stretcher passed her.

As they reached the parking lot, the emergency transport helicopter was landing, the wind from its propellers kicking up huge gusts and blowing papers all over the place. As soon as the chopper was stabilized on the blacktop, two paramedics swiftly lifted Jesse's limp body into the helicopter and secured him in the mobile treatment area. Claudia approached one of the helicopter's paramedics, a young woman with short black hair and pointed chin. "I want to go with him," she yelled, trying to raise her voice over the wall of sound.

"Are you the boy's mother?" the paramedic asked, also straining to compete with the loud whirring of the propellers.

"That's right," Claudia answered.

"This way," the paramedic instructed Claudia, motioning toward the chopper door. Claudia turned to Angelo and yelled, "I'll meet you at the hospital." She moved toward the helicopter, then turned around and trotted to Angelo. She stood facing him, looked him in the eyes, and told him, "I love you." Claudia kissed Angelo on the lips and then ran to the open door of the helicopter. Soon the machine lifted off the ground and made a southerly ascent.

Angelo felt a hand on his shoulder. He turned to find a San Rafael lieutenant with a thick metal binder in his hand. "You're the boy's father?"

"That's right," Angelo answered.

"I'll need to get a statement from you, sir. . .What is this about a kidnapping?"

Suddenly Angelo felt like he had just stepped into a bog of sludge. He knew that if he told the officer anything, he would be detained for hours. All Angelo wanted to do was get to Jesse.

"Look, Lieutenant," Angelo answered. "It's a long story, and I'll tell it all to you, but, you see, my son is on a fine line between life and death, and I have to get to him."

"I understand, Mr. Mann. But kidnapping is a very serious charge."

Angelo caught the man's eyes. "Lieutenant. . ." Angelo looked down at the officer's name badge. ". . .Haas," Angelo said. "Do you have any children?"

"Yes, sir, I have two."

"Do you have a son?"

"Yes, my youngest is a boy."

"And if your son was possibly going to die, and you had one last chance to talk to him, would you want to be answering a bunch of questions 90 miles away from your son?"

Lieutenant Haas looked down at the ground for a moment, then up at Angelo. He reached into his binder and pulled out a card. "Call me at this number first chance you get." The men locked eyes for a moment and the officer issued a small smile. Angelo patted the man briefly on the shoulder and got into his car.

Angelo hurried through the revolving door at Packard, the door he had passed through hundreds of times over the last six months. But today was different. Today everything else was a blur. Today only Jesse mattered.

He found Claudia with Dr. Kravitz by Jesse's bed in the I.C.U. Angelo gave Claudia a quick but strong hug, then turned to the doctor. "Hello, Angelo, —" the doctor started to greet him. When he saw

Angelo's disheveled garb and fresh wounds on his face, he stopped in his tracks. "What happened to you?"

"You don't really want to know. What's going on with Jesse?"

"This movement has been very traumatic for Jesse. It has stirred his system up. His EEG is showing signs of brainwave activity he was not showing before."

Claudia lit up. "Does that mean he's waking up?" she asked hopefully.

"In a way," the doctor answered. "But it doesn't necessarily mean he's recovering. The shock of moving him around has stimulated his system to defend against the stress he's undergone. What this means is that the stakes just got raised. He will either wake up or we will lose him."

Claudia gasped and squeezed Angelo's arm. Angelo took her hand and held it.

"How long do we have before we know?" asked Angelo.

"Overnight," the doctor answered. "Jesse should go either way by the morning."

Angelo and Claudia looked at each other anxiously.

"This will be a crucial night for your son." Kravitz read the fear in their eyes. "—and you." Then he added, "I'll be on call; I've given the nurse instructions to page me immediately if we have any significant change."

Dr. Kravitz placed his hand on Claudia's back in a comforting way, forced a small smile, and exited the room, his white tennis shoes squeaking on the green tiled floor. Angelo and Claudia looked at each other as if to say, "Okay—this is it."

Claudia pulled herself together and soberly told her husband, "I'd better go call my sister and tell her what's going on. I'd like her to be here in the morning." Angelo nodded and watched Claudia leave the room; as she disappeared into the corridor he realized how much he had missed her.

Angelo pulled a chair to the side of the bed, sat as close as possible to his son, and took a deep breath. Suddenly he sensed that everything that had ever happened in his life had led to this moment. In a flash Angelo watched a fast-forward movie of his entire relationship with Lorenzo, and then his relationship with his son. Now it all seemed so clear. All the pain and terror was a disguised call for love—so simple, yet so hard to master.

Angelo wanted to take advantage of this time alone with Jesse. He held the boy's hand firmly and looked into his closed eyes, imagining they were open. Jesse's complexion was so pale that Angelo was momentarily distracted, but he forced himself to stay present.

"Jesse. My son. My beloved son. This is your dad." A tiny tear welled up in the corner of Angelo's eye. He knew it was just the beginning.

"I don't know if you can hear me, but I am going to talk to you as if you can." Angelo leaned toward Jesse's face, just inches from the boy.

"Jesse, I love you. I love you very much. I love you more than anyone or anything else in the world. Jesse, I want you to stay. I want you to live and be my son. I want to be the father to you that I never was. I know that I have not always been here for you, but maybe you can understand that I was just afraid. Please don't be fooled by my harsh words and anger and raving; they were not your fault. Jesse, it is not you that I didn't love; it was myself. I have never loved myself, but now I am just getting a tiny inkling of how I can. Jesse, I never meant to take out my heartache on you. I was hurting so badly and I didn't know what to do with my pain. You didn't deserve for me to pass it on to you. I became a dad to you like the dad I had—I didn't know any other way; I had never seen a father love. But the whole terrible pattern has to stop here now.

"Jesse, I want you to come home. If you can hear me, and if you are making a choice, then you must hear that I want you to come home. Your mother can't even talk about how much she misses you. Jesse, if you leave us, it will destroy her, and I don't know if she will ever love again. I would gladly trade places with you if I could, if that would bring you back to your mom."

Angelo's tears were copious now. He reached for a tissue to wipe his nose, now running profusely.

"Jesse, all I can say is that I love you with all my heart and soul, and I promise you that if you wake up I will be the father that you always wanted." A stunned look washed over Angelo's face: "—and the father *I* always wanted."

Angelo looked at the boy's cherubic face for another moment and then sat back in the chair. He was in God's hands now.

Chapter 33

Rav Shimon, as Avi Goldman had told Angelo, once said that hospitals during the early morning hours are like portals between the worlds. Some souls exit the revolving door between earth and the next world, while others enter. He said that death and life are simply different sides of the same coin; when a soul leaves the earth, the worldly family mourns. Yet when a being departs heaven to enter earthly life, loved ones in that dimension grieve.

As much as he had mentally and emotionally girded himself for it, Angelo was not prepared for the death of his only son. It is said that there is no greater loss than that of a child, and Angelo felt every fear that had ever plagued him melt away to insignificance as he envisioned life without Jesse. Perhaps God had created the entire ordeal as a lesson for Angelo to appreciate his son, who was now in a far distant place.

As the first rays of dawn quietly touched the sill of the old wood-framed window, two bodies lay in Jesse Mann's bed: the inert child, and that of his father embracing the boy tightly from behind, spooning him as he used to do when he read him *The Cat in the Hat* before he went to sleep. Angelo spoke to him still, but not of a child's story. As he had all through the night, Angelo whispered into his son's ear.

"Jesse, you are a beautiful, precious child of God. You are a gift to me and your mother, and everyone who knows you. You are good and wondrous and innocent. You deserve only love, and I give you all that my heart has to give. Jesse, wake up and I will show you a new life." Nearly hoarse from speaking through the night, Angelo was exhausted but resolute. He whispered to his son, "I am not the father you knew. Please do not fear living with me. I will not hurt you again.

I will honor you and protect you and give you all the tenderness you deserve. I will show you a world of color and beauty and magic. Jesse, there is so much to live for, and I want to live it with you. Jesse, you are my beloved son. Jesse, please come home."

Angelo was amazed at how many ways he could say, "I love you" over the seven hours he had lain with his son. He had not even thought to eat or go to the bathroom; all he could think about was finding even the tiniest finger to latch onto and snatch his son back from the brink of the abyss.

The heart of Angelo Mann, long suffocated under cold stone, had broken open. He could not seal it again, and he did not want to. He had found his way out of a cold and lonely dungeon, and he was not about to go back. He had escaped the terrible tyranny of his judgmental mind and learned to trust his spirit. He had been asleep for nearly all his life, and now he was awake. Now, if only Jesse would do the same.

Angelo looked across Jesse's bed at Claudia, who, after battling to stay awake, had finally fallen asleep in that uncomfortable chair, the one she and Angelo had spent countless hours in. He was glad she was getting some rest; God knows she had been through hell.

Angelo placed his right hand on Jesse's heart and felt the tiniest pulsation. "Thank you, God," Angelo whispered aloud. "Dear God, and Jesus, and angels, and anyone else who is out there by any name," he entreated, "please be with me now in my hour of deepest need. Place your hands over mine and touch my little boy. Bring him back to me that I may know my son and love him as you know and love him. Give him the life he deserves, and I will do the same."

Angelo imagined two strong arms extending into his own and touching Jesse's smooth milk white chest. Then he envisioned invisible hands reaching deep into the boy and spreading a golden substance into Jesse's being, energizing all his cells and organs, down to his very atoms. He saw the brilliant light rousing Jesse's body and his spirit. He imagined that though the boy was physically inert, he lived intact in an unseen realm.

Then Angelo pictured many angels surrounding the bed, holding their hands over the child and himself in blessing. He felt as if he was basking in a sunshine more glorious than any he had ever known in the physical world, so bright that he could almost not bear it. As he thought of the light healing Jesse, he accepted it for himself, too. Over the bed he could make out some faces, lovely cherubic images. He saw Rav Shimon, Avi Goldman, friends and relatives who had passed on, and some he did not know.

Then he saw another face, one which startled him. It was the face of an older man with thick white hair, strong chiseled features, and leathery skin. It was Lorenzo.

Angelo began to recoil, feeling violated by his father's intrusion into the miracle he hoped for. But then he realized there was something different about his father's face. Lorenzo's customary gruffness was gone and he looked soft. His eyes were not scowling, but clear and kindly. His demeanor was not punishing, but blessing. He was here not to admonish, but to help.

Lorenzo placed his hands on the hearts of the boy and his father, and Angelo heard him say, "You are both my beloved sons." Angelo's tears streamed steadily now, and his breathing became heavier. With his own chest pressed tightly to Jesse's back, he felt as if a force greater than himself was breathing life into him and he was passing it into his son.

Angelo did not know how long he was being breathed; it could have been seconds or minutes or hours. He entered a timeless domain where nothing existed but the power that moved through him. He surrendered fully, feeling that whatever was happening had to be good. It was perhaps the first time in his life that he fully gave up control and felt at peace.

After a few minutes Angelo thought he could feel Jesse's chest begin to move with his own. A beautiful rhythm was transpiring. As Angelo kept breathing deeply, he felt Jesse's lungs expanding and contracting with his own. When he realized what was happening, Angelo continued consciously, as if he was giving mouth-to-mouth resuscitation through his heart. At one point he felt heady, and it seemed as if there were not two who were breathing, but one.

Suddenly Jesse began to stir. The child's legs twitched slightly, and Angelo could feel the boy's hand stretch to touch his father's.

"Claudia," Angelo called softly. "Wake up." Claudia, looking jarred, began to open her eyes. She seemed quite disoriented. When she looked at Angelo, he pointed to Jesse's hand as it began to explore the sheet in front of his chest.

"Angelo, he's moving!" she called out. Claudia stood up quickly and came to the bed.

Angelo smiled and nodded.

Then Jesse began to stretch, just like as he used to when he woke up in the morning.

Angelo began to kiss his son on the side of his cheek as Claudia got down on her knees at the side of the bed to look into Jesse's face in hope that she might see his eyes. Then it happened; the boy's tiny eyelids began to quiver, and Claudia could make out the faintest crack of white below his long dark eyelashes.

"Angelo, he's waking up!"

"I know, I know," Angelo responded, immersed in tears.

Slowly Jesse began to wriggle and stir; he looked pained, as if he was trying to throw off a hot and heavy blanket. Angelo slid away and gave the boy some room, watching him as if he was being born.

Suddenly Jesse's eyes opened and he looked directly at his mother. "Jesse," she cried, "You're awake! Hello, baby." She held his head in her hands and began to kiss his forehead copiously.

Jesse, though physically about, was still not yet quite present in this world; he was disoriented and seemed to be looking right through his mother. His parents watched him gradually come into his body as if he was slipping into a pair of stiff shoes he had not worn for a long time. Suddenly Angelo felt Jesse click into the room and the moment.

"Did I wreck my bike?" he asked innocently.

Claudia, her eyes brimming with tears of joy, answered, "You sure did, honey, but it's all right; we'll get you a new one. The important thing is that you're okay."

She bit her lip and hugged her baby with all her strength. "You're okay, you're okay," she said over and over again.

Jesse turned and faced his dad, who was watching him and his mother proudly. When Jesse caught his fathers' eyes, he simply said,

"Hi, Dad."

Angelo looked deeply into Jesse's eyes and answered, "Hello, son. I missed you."

As if disregarding Angelo's words, Jesse told his parents, "I had the weirdest dream. I dreamt that I was standing on the diving board over the pool. But it was real high, like a hundred feet. I was jumping into the water, and just as I was gonna hit, I felt this huge bungie cord attached to me. Just when I was going to go under, this big old rubber band type thing pulled me up. It was so weird!"

Angelo and Claudia looked at each other for a few moments; Angelo reached out and put his a hand on the side of his wife's tear-wet face.

Jesse surveyed Angelo's deranged attire. "How come you're so grungy, Dad?"

"Oh, I've just been saving the world from Nazis and religious fanatics—you know, the usual."

Jesse looked at his dad, puzzled.

Angelo smiled. "I did some traveling, Jesse. I went to Israel."

"You did?"

"I met a very wise man there. I wrote down this blessing that he gave me. I want to say it to you." Angelo, trembling, reached into his pocket and took out his wallet. As he picked through a battered compartment, a piece of folded paper fell out onto Jesse's blanket. Angelo, still fumbling through his wallet, did not notice it, but Jesse picked it up, unfolded it, and began to stare at it.

"I didn't know you had a Polaroid, Dad."

"I don't; what's that paper you're looking at?"

Jesse turned the photo he had been looking at, so his dad could see it. It was the last photo that Ted Kohler had given to Angelo. Claudia studied the picture and wrinkled her brow. "Where did you get this?" she asked, perplexed.

All three studied the picture. It showed Angelo, Claudia, and Jesse in the hospital room, Angelo spooning his son, and Claudia hugging him as he opened his eyes. It was an exact picture of the moment of Jesse's awakening.

"Cool!" Jesse exclaimed. "How did you get this taken?"

"It's a little trick I have to show you." He paused and looked at Claudia for a moment. She looked utterly amazed. Then he turned back to Jesse. "There's a lot I want to tell you about."

Chapter 34

Angelo screwed the white plastic cap on the Crest tube and dried his mouth with the baby blue hand towel that matched the large fuzzy one wrapped around his waist. His back still glistened from the hot water he had savored on a foggy Bay Area morning. The oldies station blared, *"I can see clearly now"* from the black boom box on the window sill. Angelo hummed along with the song as he opened the bathroom door on his way to get dressed.

As Angelo's foot stepped into the upstairs hallway, it did not touch the carpet as he expected; instead he felt plastic, which gave out from under him, sending him staggering against the banister. Clumsily he caught himself and then took a few seconds to regain his balance. Looking down, he saw the red and yellow dump truck.

Angelo marched into Jesse's room and found the child in bed, eyes open, staring up at the phosphorescent stars in constellations on his ceiling.

"Jesse Joseph," he began in a strong voice, his hands placed firmly on his hips, "When are you ever going to learn. . ."

Jesse looked at his dad, startled, worried that he was about to be chastised again.

". . .that you have the coolest dump truck collection in San Jose!" When he saw the silly grin on his dad's face, Jesse broke into a giggle. Angelo made a running leap into Jesse's bed and began to tickle him mercilessly. When Angelo finally had Jesse pinned down by his arms, Angelo looked his son squarely in his eyes, ". . .and I love you more than anything in the whole world."

Jesse looked up through his big brown saucer eyes and replied, "and you are the greatest dad." Angelo closed his eyes and drank the words in.

The child became pensive and asked, "Dad, did you really save the world from the Nazis and those other guys?"

Angelo thought for a moment. "I don't know, son— but at least I faced the Nazi in me, and let my heart be bigger than he was; maybe that's all any of us ever has to do. Angelo smiled. "C'mon, breakfast is on the table. Last one down has to clean up this room."

Claudia was watching the television as she scrambled eggs. Father and son took their places around the table in the red and blue nook, and Claudia delivered the steaming eggs to them. Jesse immediately dowsed his eggs with a mountain of ketchup. Angelo began to stop him, "Jes—" but then caught himself.

"Yeah, dad?"

"Nothing, son; I was just hoping you might like some eggs with your ketchup."

Jesse giggled and squirted a tease of ketchup on his dad's eggs.

Claudia set Angelo's plate in front of him, then hugged him from behind his back. As she leaned over she whispered in his ear, just soft enough so Jesse could not hear. "Do you think I could book a return engagement with the guy who showed up in my bed last night? He left me dreamin' in Technicolor."

Angelo raised an eyebrow. "Are you kidding? That was just the overture; get a good seat for tonight—the next act is sure to bring the house down."

Claudia purred, kissed Angelo on the cheek, and went back to the stove with a little more color in her cheeks. She looked at the clock and called out, "C'mon, Jesse, we have to hit the road; no more late notes from me. I'll help you pack your bag."

Jesse and Claudia disappeared into the den while Angelo finished his eggs. When he heard the word "Israel" on television, he looked up to see a news reporter standing in front of a circle of Semitic people dancing in front of a huge bonfire.

"Residents of the *B'nai Shlaimat* kibbutz here in the Galilee are happy indeed tonight," the reporter announced. "They are celebrating the release of three of their children who had been taken hostage by the *Al Sharmat* Arab terrorist group. *Al Sharmat* released the children amidst rumors of a possible cease-fire in the wake of negotiations between Arab and Israeli leaders. Behind me, the nearly one hundred members of this community have been dancing for hours in the circle dances that have surrounded bonfires like this for thousands of years."

The camera shifted focus from the reporter to the circles. A men's troupe formed an outer ring around a group of women closer to the fire. All were chanting, *"Lo yisa goi el goi cherev, lo yilma du od milchama,"* over and over again.

The reporter cut in, "—and nation shall not lift up sword against nation" is the chant these people are singing. And I have to say, this is as joyful a gathering as I have seen in Israel since the bombing of Tel Aviv."

Angelo, watching intently, rejoiced in the celebration at first, but then his heart sank as his thoughts turned to Avi Goldman and Rav Shimon. Their loss still felt like a huge cavernous wound in his gut, and he wished they could have been with him now to appreciate the communicator's success and his reunion with Jesse.

As the group of men circled, some of them turned and waved jubilantly to the camera. Angelo thought he recognized several of the men, but quickly dismissed the notion as coincidence. When he looked again he saw, to his utter astonishment, the faces of Avi Goldman and Rav Shimon passing by in the circle. As they danced through his field of vision they looked right into the camera and waved, it seemed, to Angelo. When he studied their faces, he saw that it was indeed them, but they both looked young, trim, and healthy. Instead of 80 years of age, Rav Shimon appeared about 30, with an upright back, full head of hair, and thick dark beard. Avi looked jolly as ever, his eyes shining with his unique impish twinkle. Both faces were glowing with a light that did not seem present on the others. Their garb was pure white, in contrast to the others' shades of gray and brown. As he peered more intently, Angelo saw that the two men were almost transparent; he could see the fire burning not just behind them, but through them. Perhaps, he thought, this was the burning bush that Moses had discovered—not a shrub on a mountain, but a flame of love that burns eternally in the hearts of those who have discovered the light within themselves. Avi and Rav Shimon waved once more to Angelo and slipped into the crowd with the others, luminous.

"He always did have to have the last word," Angelo laughed aloud.

Angelo looked out the kitchen window as Jesse hopped into the maroon mini-van and closed the heavy door behind him. The brightness of Jesse's yellow day pack caught his eye against the gray seat as Claudia leaned over to help the boy strap on his seat belt. He never thought he would see this day.

As Angelo watched the mini-van pull out of the driveway and head down the street, he took a long deep breath. His mind reeled as he considered what he had been through. He reached to gather the breakfast dishes and noticed the letter he had received from Stanford. He read it one more time, amazed that the department chairman was offering him the directorship for the project to develop the communicator. He took another moment to savor the salutation to Dr. Angelo Mandolucci, the name he had gone back to using. Angelo was proud of it now. He was proud of a lot of things.

Acknowledgements

I am deeply grateful to those who have contributed to My Father's Voice, by way of skill and service and love and support. To them I offer deepest thanks from my heart, and I take delight in knowing that they have assisted you to receive this book.

I have been inspired and educated by the editorial input of Pat MacEnulty, whose creative vision, skill, and dedication have been a magnificent asset to this work.

Michael Ebeling and Mary Traynor at ACP Inc. have gone 110% to support this project, create space for me to write, get the book into form, and make the process a joyful dance.

Daya Ceglia has created beautiful cover art, magnified by her patience and willingness to be a masterful co-creator.

I thank Sherry Baker for her loving and attentive proofreading service.

I am very grateful to a number of my friends and colleagues who looked at the manuscript in various stages and gave me their insights and feedback: Steve Sisgold, Kalei Sheehy, Brian O'leary, Kathy Kemper, Carla Gordan, Mary Guide, Mick Carnett, Jade Sherer, Frank Levinson, and Jill Mangione.

Above all, behind all, through all, I am grateful to Great Spirit for the blessing and honor to participate in healing and awakening through great words and noble ideas.

About the Author

Alan Cohen is the author of 15 popular inspirational books, including the classic *The Dragon Doesn't Live Here Anymore* and the award-winning *A Deep Breath of Life.* He is a contributing writer for the *New York Times* best-selling series *Chicken Soup for the Soul.* His books have been translated into 10 foreign languages. His column *From the Heart* appears in magazines internationally. James Redfield, author of *The Celestine Prophecy,* calls Alan "the most eloquent spokesman of the heart."

Alan resides in Maui, Hawaii, where he enjoys the beauty of nature, writes books from his heart, and conducts retreats on spiritual awakening and maximizing personal potential. He is regularly sighted with his trusty dog and guru, Munchie.

For a free packet of information about Alan Cohen's programs throughout the world and a current schedule of his upcoming events, visit Alan Cohen's website:

www.alancohen.com

or contact:

Hay House
P.O. Box 5100, Carlsbad, CA 92018-5100
(800) 462-3013

To book a presentation, contact:

Alan Cohen Programs
455A Kukuna Road
Haiku, HI 96708
(800) 568-3079   (808) 572-0001   fax (808) 572-1023
email: admin@alancohen.com

By Alan Cohen

Books
Are You as Happy as Your Dog?
Dare to Be Yourself
A Deep Breath of Life
The Dragon Doesn't Live Here Anymore*
Handle With Prayer*
Happily Even After
Have You Hugged a Monster Today?
I Had It All The Time*
Joy Is My Compass
Lifestyles of the Rich in Spirit
The Peace That You Seek
Rising in Love
Setting the Seen

*Also available as Book on Tape

Cassette Tapes
Deep Relaxation
Eden Morning
I Believe in You
Journey to the Center of the Heart (also CD)
Living From The Heart
Peace

Video
Wisdom Of The Spirit